TRAVELS IN THE LAND OF THE GODS

VI VOLUME.
of the
Ill spelled diaries,
of
R Gordon Smith.
commencing
JAN 1st 1905

TRAVELS IN THE LAND OF THE GODS

(1898-1907)

The Japan Diaries of
RICHARD GORDON SMITH

Edited by
VICTORIA MANTHORPE

PRENTICE HALL PRESS • NEW YORK

Published in 1986 by Prentice Hall Press
A division of Simon & Schuster, Inc.
Gulf + Western Building
One Gulf + Western Plaza
New York, NY 10023

Originally published in Great Britain in 1986 as
THE JAPAN DIARIES OF
RICHARD GORDON SMITH
by Viking/Rainbird

PRENTICE HALL PRESS
is a trademark of Simon & Schuster, Inc.

This book was designed and produced by
The Rainbird Publishing Group Ltd
27 Wrights Lane, Kensington,
London W8 5TZ

Art Director: Karen Osborne
Designers: Gerry Beegan,
Bernard Higton, Jenny Wigston

Library of Congress Cataloging-in-Publication Data

Smith, Richard Gordon, b. 1858.
  Travels in the land of the gods.
    1. Japan—Description and travel—1901–1945.
    2. Smith, Richard Gordon,
       b. 1858—Journeys—Japan.
    3. Smith, Richard Gordon, b. 1858—Diaries.
    4. Travelers—England—Diaries.   I. Manthorpe,
       Victoria.   II. Title.
    DS810.S65 1986   915.2'043   86–12361
    ISBN 0-13-930512-2

Printed in Spain
D.L.B. 16425 – 1986

10 9 8 7 6 5 4 3 2 1

First Prentice Hall Press Edition

ACKNOWLEDGMENTS

From the beginning Anne Manthorpe has given
meticulous help with the genealogy of the Smith
family and their kin; I should like to thank her for
her constant encouragement and companionship –
from Urswick to the Riviera. I am also grateful to
Walter Manthorpe for his sensible caution and
always generous support.

Peter Coxhead and Karen Osborne worked in
difficult circumstances to provide, respectively, the
fine copy editing and art direction. Stephen Dodd
MA (Oxon) has laboured long and hard to help
unravel Gordon Smith's singular interpretation of
the Japanese language. Dorothy Castle, formerly
of the Royal Geographical Society, has done
essential work in tracing obscure Japanese place
names.

John Bowles of the Cheltonian Society has
provided fulsome information about the old boys
of Cheltenham College. Alwyne Wheeler of the
Department of Zoology at the British Museum
(Natural History) has lent his knowledge of fishes
and of Gordon Smith's collections. Vickers
Shipbuilding and Engineering Ltd, the current
owners of Bankfield Hall, have been most
cooperative and kindly provided the early
photograph of the hall.

In addition, I count the good company of
Gordon Smith's grandson as one of the benefits of
this project.

Lastly, to Peter Beard, who first saw the
potential of the Diaries and who, over many years,
contributed practical and financial support to their
development, and personal support to me – thank
you.

Contents

Introduction

When Richard Gordon Smith died in November 1918, The Japanese *Weekly Chronicle* published an obituary which included these lines:

> We regret to learn of the death early on the 6th inst. of Mr R. Gordon Smith, after a long and painful illness, at the age of 60. The deceased . . . came out to the Far East more than twenty years ago to collect natural history specimens for the British Museum and travelled extensively through Japan, Korea and Formosa . . . Having seen a great deal of the world he was an entertaining companion, and if he has kept a diary it should be most interesting.

He had indeed kept a diary. In fact, he had kept eight diaries. Eight large leather-bound volumes emblazoned with exotic illustrations and filled with mementoes from all over the world.

The following year, 1919, probate of his estate was granted in London to Alfred Hardy Bentley, Solicitor. The inheritance, which was divided between his three daughters, included a wealth of antiques, curios, carvings, prints and paintings collected throughout Asia and the Orient. Two generations and the Depression have seen that legacy dispersed – yet what has survived is unique.

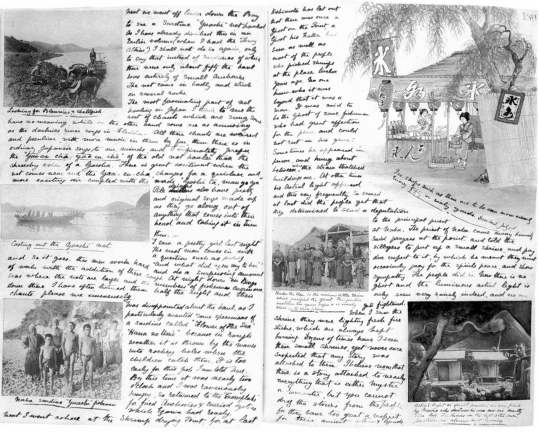

A typical spread from one of Gordon Smith's Japan Diaries

His journals have lain neatly strapped and buckled against the decades in the Cotswold home of his grandson. Because Gordon Smith was more notable for his absence than his presence, his descendents knew little about him. His grandson, inheriting perhaps some of his grandfather's character, had been busy blazing his own trail through Australia. So these splendid volumes might well have stayed unread had it not been for a chance encounter between the grandson and a television director, Peter Beard. I was working with him at the time and because he knew that I had an appetite for the historically curious, he asked me to look into the content of the books and the background of their author.

It was several years before the Diaries were placed with a literary agent and during that time I pieced together a family tree and a map of Gordon Smith's life. So verbose on some subjects, he was extremely reticent about private matters. Where he did give clues, it was often an odd line buried in a mountain of description of Canada or Burma. Added to this, the name Smith is not conducive to detective work. Fortunately, he called himself Gordon Smith (sometimes other people hyphenated it) although strictly speaking his surname was simply Smith. Fortunately also, his family had money and that always leaves a trail – wills, houses, business papers and so on. One of my greatest disappointments was to find that his solicitors' offices had been bombed during the last war.

However, there were many pleasures and triumphs – finding the villa in which his family lived in Biarritz, discovering his sister's grave in the south of France and, after drawing many blanks, finally discovering the date of his marriage through a notice in the *Montreal Gazette*. As I gradually put his story together, Richard Gordon Smith became a companion as well as an over-riding interest. Weekends and holidays were spent on happy pilgrimages to graveyards and archives, and to houses and hotels through which he passed.

So what is this last legacy of Richard Gordon Smith? He called them his 'Ill-Spelled Diaries' and in them he invested the same energy and diversity with which he lived his life. They witness over forty years of travel from the days when an English gentleman might roam the world at will. He began the first volume as a shooting book – a record of his bags. It quickly became an account of expeditions abroad enhanced by maps and

photographs and some of his own sketches. The following volumes grew into daily journals of his travels filled with observations and an increasing number of illustrations. Packed with incident and anecdote, the Diaries form a panorama of Victorian colonial life, and, as we are about to see, of life in Japan at the turn of the century. They also reveal a very singular character.

Richard Gordon Smith was born in 1858 in a house called Bankfield in Urswick, not far from Barrow-in-Furness. His grandfather, Richard Smith, owned the

Bankfield Hall – Gordon Smith's birthplace

manor of Poulton-cum-Seacombe (now part of Birkenhead) but mining interests in Ulverstone had brought him to the northern side of Morecombe Bay. Richard Smith had nine children, the youngest of whom, John Bridson Smith, was Richard Gordon's father.

His mother, Annie, was the daughter of George Lawrence of Moreton-on-Lugg, Herefordshire and later of Cheltenham. Her uncle John Lawrence of Caerleon House, Caerleon, was a renowned sportsman and Master of the Llangibby Hunt. It was from the Lawrences that Richard Gordon Smith inherited his sporting instincts.

From Urswick, Gordon Smith's parents moved across the hills to Ambleside in the Lake District. The impact of that dramatic scenery must have shaped his taste for he always loved mountainous landscapes. The Smith family also spent a considerable amount of time in France – in Biarritz and on the Riviera. It was fashionable to winter in French resorts – the climate was thought beneficial, it was often cheaper than staying in England, and there were plenty of social amusements amongst the civilized society of well-connected and aristocratic families. The Smiths were not parochial people.

While he was apparently fluent in speaking French, the rest of Gordon Smith's education is something of a mystery. He spent a few terms at Cheltenham College in the hope that he might enter the Army. Lacking sufficient academic drive, he failed to pass the exams for Sandhurst. His real interests were already established – fishing and shooting. Deriving a pleasant income from his family's business investments, meant that, though never actually rich, he never had to work for a living.

In 1877 he recorded his first expedition to hunt chamois in the Pyrénnées. The following year he made his first trip to Canada with Colin Campbell and their adventures read like a *Boy's Own Paper*. Young, healthy and avid for sport, they roared through the winter landscape of Quebec. To this day Canada is a paradise of wildlife

Ethel Newcombe

– in the nineteenth century it fairly teemed with mammals, fish and birds. Gordon Smith cut a swathe through as much of it as he could. Killing anything and everything was considered good sport. There is no doubt that Canada suited him.

On 20 August 1879, he married Ethel Constance Ida, youngest daughter of the late William Newcombe in St James's Church, Montreal. He was twenty-one, she probably several years younger. There are indications that she didn't live up to his expectations of a sportsman's wife. Bear hunting is not to everyone's taste. Be that as it may, they settled in the Gaspé Peninsula amongst a small settlement of French Canadians and started a family. The first two children died soon after birth, then in 1883 a son survived: Arthur Gordon Smith. A baby girl, Edith May, followed in 1886, and in 1888 Lillian Valentine was born.

Hunting with the Indians and trappers in the winter, fishing and cruising on the lakes in summer, travelling to the United States and France for months at a time – their lives might well have continued quite satisfactorily, but in the winter of 1888 tragedy struck.

Little Arthur contracted diphtheria and died within days. Instead of sympathizing, the villagers of the Gaspé backed away in fear of the disease and refused to help the bereaved family. Gordon Smith gathered up his wife and daughters and took them down to Montreal. Then he ordered a tombstone and made the long lonely journey back to the

The Smith family in 1897

Gaspé to place it on his son's grave. Immediately on his return they sailed for England. By 8 January 1889 they were in Cannes. The love affair with Canada was over: they never returned.

There is only a scanty record of the next few years. Gordon Smith leased houses near Portsmouth and probably continued to spend time in France. He entered pigeon-shooting competitions at Hurlingham and Monte Carlo, and shot and fished on the estates of his relatives and friends. He made a few trips to Spitzbergen and Madeira. A third daughter, Constance Augusta, was born in 1892.

The turning point arrived in 1897. It seems likely that Gordon Smith's income increased – perhaps an inheritance – and he bought a 51-acre estate in Sussex. With a 15-bedroomed house and a trout stream it was an impressive purchase but within months he had sold it, leaving only these words as a clue to the domestic upheaval which precipitated it:

> 'In May I bought Westbrook Hall, and settled down to country life. It was a lovely place and little did I then dream how soon it was to be broken up as a home. But it was in October through nothing but the villainous temper of a certain person.'

Was that person Ethel? From his later remarks, I would assume so.

Divorce was neither desirable nor respectable in the 1890s. However, it was quite usual for rejected suitors and unwanted husbands to travel abroad for long periods. This was Gordon Smith's solution. At the age of forty he began a new life.

Travelling, of course, was a major undertaking. Transport was slow, there were few conveniences and an enormous number of personal items had to be carried with you to ease discomforts. Steamships stopped at coaling stations to take on fuel; food was often bad or tinned; medical treatment for all the tropical illnesses that flesh is heir to was limited and ineffective; insects got into everything. There were dreary periods of waiting – for officials, medical certificates, loading and unloading, for connecting boats and trains – and so on. It was, however, a relatively inexpensive, full-time occupation and it was often convivial.

First-class passengers (Gordon Smith always travelled first-class) were likely to have overlapping social circles and, in any case, the close society of the ship nurtured friendships. Gordon Smith met a large number of interesting people and, on his earlier journeys, evidently had a good deal of fun with shipboard games and fancy-dress parties. Then, at various ports of call

Westbrook Hall in 1897

there were people to be visited – a friend stationed in an outpost, an army officer, a government or company official, a consul perhaps. These were the great days of the Empire and the British were running things everywhere.

Glad that he was that much of the world map was shaded pink, Gordon Smith was not about to limit his sightseeing to the imperial hotels and the English clubs. Not only did he want to hunt big game, he also wanted to find out about the native peoples and their cultures. In Ceylon and Burma particularly he made a point of travelling up country and camping out amongst the villagers.

By the time he reached Japan in the winter of 1898, Gordon Smith was a seasoned traveller but nothing had quite prepared him for the exquisitely exotic and alien country which unfolded before him. Until 1858, Japan had been closed to foreigners for centuries and only a few Dutch merchants had been allowed to trade with her. The culture had been kept quite separate from outside influences and had grown rarefied, complex and mysterious. When the Emperor Meiji ascended to the Chrysanthemum Throne in 1868, he began the long task of pulling his country into the Industrial Age. The 'westernizing' process was thirty years underway when Gordon Smith arrived, but what he called 'the real Japan' was still there for the finding.

In Europe and America, Japan had already been popularized. A.B. Mitford (Lord Redesdale) had sprung his *Tales of Old Japan* (London 1871) on an avid audience. Sir Ernest Satow had written a dictionary of Japanese in romanized spelling, while Basil Hall Chamberlain had compiled *The Classical Poetry of the Japanese* (London 1880) and produced the very successful catalogue of *Things Japanese* (London 1890). Accounts of Japanese customs by diplomats and their wives inspired the public imagination and a host of lesser travellers chattered in print about their experiences. A title such as 'The Japs at Home' is far from uncommon.

Europeans felt that the Japanese, unlike the other Oriental races, were 'civilized' in a western sense but there was already a reaction to the romanticizing of the culture. Pierre Loti deflated the image of the perfect Japanese woman in his novel *Mme Chrysanthème* (Paris 1888) although, this in turn, gave rise to the romantic opera 'Madame Butterfly'. On the lighter side, Gilbert and Sullivan had given a less serious twist to the customs of Old Japan in 'The Mikado' (1885).

The art historians were eager to examine the cultural artefacts. Louis Gonse published his *L'Art Japonais* (Paris) in 1883. Antique and curio dealers were early on the scene, buying and shipping out the military paraphernalia which the eclipse of the Shogunate had made useless to an impoverished military aristocracy (the Samurai). Japanese prints, courtesy of a Dutch syndicate, had been exhibited at the Paris Exposition Universelle as early as 1855 and, as more pictures seeped out of the East, they influenced European styles – particularly some of the Impressionists. Japan and all things Japanese became very fashionable.

As a result there was a well-trodden tourist path. Sir Ernest Satow and A.G.S. Hawes, and later Basil Hall Chamberlain, produced detailed guidebooks. Descriptions of the sights, food, currency, rules of behaviour, modes of travel, and potted histories and mythologies were all available in the West. Most tourists probably saw Tokyo and Yokohama, the tombs at Nikko, the old capital at Kyoto and one or two other well-documented sites such as the spas at Hakone. If they were intrepid, the guidebooks gave itineraries of trips that could be undertaken in reasonable comfort. There were good railways on Honshu and plenty of *jinrikishas* for hiring (an innovation of the early Meiji period, by the way).

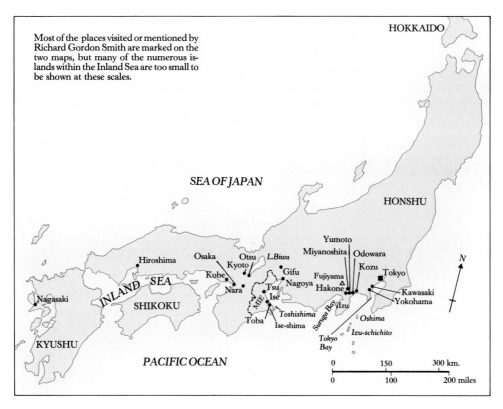

Most of the places visited or mentioned by Richard Gordon Smith are marked on the two maps, but many of the numerous islands within the Inland Sea are too small to be shown at these scales.

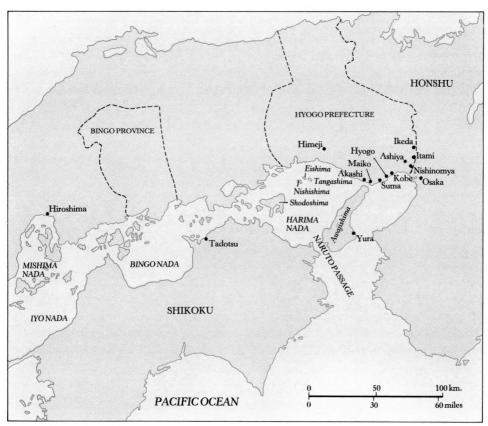

11

For most tourists the cherry blossoms, Mount Fuji, the temples, shrines, and the picturesqueness of the people were what they had come to see. After all, the food was difficult if not downright unpalatable. One needed an interpreter or a guide, or both. The winter and summer climates were extreme. Though there were European-style hotels in the big cities, if you ventured into backwaters you would find yourself staying in teahouses with paper walls, no heating, no furniture, and no privacy. If you went too far off the beaten track, as Isabella Bird did in 1878 when she trekked through the northern island of Hokkaido, you were likely to find conditions very rough indeed and the people extremely primitive and poverty stricken.

Gordon Smith avoided many of these problems. Certainly his first trip was that of a sightseer but afterwards he always rented his own houses so that he could organize his comforts and supervise his servants. Usually he didn't travel more than three or four days' journey from Kobe unless it was on a hired steam yacht – where once again he could, to some extent, control conditions. Added to this, he was an outdoor man – used to the wilds of Canada and to long cold damp days out shooting.

The very fact that he settled in Kobe indicates that he had no intention of abandoning western life. Kobe, which had been only a fishing village, became one of the six Treaty Ports opened up to world trade. Its position at the eastern end of the Inland Sea and close to industrial Osaka was ideal. In 1875 an area of land by the quay, or Bund, was designated a Foreign Settlement. This area housed the foreign traders and their warehouses (hongs), the diplomats and their consular offices, shopkeepers and shippers – and the clubs. It looked rather like a frontier town – wide unpaved streets lined with impressive Victorian buildings – many with two-storeyed verandas. The English came to Kobe from the very earliest days and soon made their mark upon it. Douglas Sladen in his *Queer Things about Japan* (London 1903) called it 'the lotus land of a contented little colony of English traders'.

In 1890 the population of Kobe was 135,000 which rose rapidly to some 215,000 by 1904. In 1900, of the 728 foreign residents only 183 were women. This inequality was, no doubt, alleviated by some local alliances; marriages to Japanese women were as easy to arrange as they were to dissolve – an attractive custom to Europeans. Japanese women were known to have been trained from birth to please their menfolk before all else; thus there were consolations for a lack of intellectual rapport. The writer Lafcadio Hearn, for one, made a very happy (and legitimate) marriage in Japan.

Gordon Smith chose not to live in the Settlement on the Bund. He was not in any case enamoured of club life which harboured remittance men and other socially undesirable expatriates. Instead he rooted his English way of life into the Japanese community. As a sporting gentleman he continued to shoot and fish even though he had to import hunting dogs and train local peasants in the arts of beating and trawling. For a man of his skills there was scarcely enough game to keep him fully occupied so he turned his attentions to collecting fauna, including fish, for natural history museums in England, Germany and Japan, and he made a considerable contribution.

A great collector of curios, his knowledge of the arts was, at first, limited. It soon became apparent to him that any appreciation of Japanese art – and Japanese life – required some study of her religion and mythology. The ancestor worship of Shinto with all its nature spirits had, from AD 552, been blended with Buddhism and its pantheon of Bodhisattvas. Learned men had already made translations and collections of many of the stories. Gordon Smith came fresh on the scene and enthusiastically began collecting folktales from every possible source, but largely from the oral tradition of the ordinary people. Some are reconstructed in his journals but he also filled a further five volumes and had each tale illustrated.

The text of the Diaires is filled with obstacles. Gordon Smith's method was to jot down events in notebooks and write them up in longhand when he had time – evenings, rainy days and on ocean voyages. His writing is legible but he could not spell and had a hazy appreciation of sentence structure and punctuation. On the plus side his style is immediate, colloquial and characterful. For this edition his spelling has been corrected and a good deal of punctuation added. Sometimes it has also been necessary to change the order of words to make a passage readily comprehensible. In places, too, I have added words in square brackets to clarify the text. Some careful interpretation has been necessary.

Japanese words and place names he wrote as he heard them – usually rather differently each time. They have been regularized and modernized with much advice from a Japanese scholar and a geographer, but there are still one or two which are open to argument. Where he has used both forenames and family names they are given in that order although the Japanese do the reverse.

Items in square brackets in the text and notes at the back of the book give information about as many of the people he mentions as it has been possible to find. Where there is no clue to their identity they simply remain a name. If some reader recognizes an ancestor, I should be delighted to hear about it.

The selection itself has been made from Gordon Smith's years in Japan – his other travels must wait their turn. I have tried to maintain the flavour and continuity of his life and only added linking passages where it seemed helpful. Because he made entries for nearly every day, space has excluded the possibility of reproducing complete sections of any great length. Where a few days are missing in this edition it means that little of interest happened or that I have chosen a day which is more interesting or furthers the story. Similarly I have edited the individual entries to avoid repetition of his views and activities.

The illustrations have been reproduced entirely from his Diaries and photograph albums – only the maps are modern. Although usually on a smaller scale than the originals, the pictures have been arranged very much in his style – but no one page is a replica of one of his. Many of the earlier photographs he bought in shops, later he took them himself and hand-tinted them or had them tinted. The paintings he commissioned from provincial Japanese artists and in this edition the work of Baiho is most prominent. What should be underlined is that Gordon Smith devised the pictures and dictated their content so that the results are western compositions in a Japanese style.

Finally, some readers will find his views chauvinistic. He was a man of his time, proud to be British and not afraid to have opinions. Yet he found in himself an unexpected sympathy with the Japanese people. He admired their delicacy and refinement which contrasted with his bluff ways, but he also admired their discipline which was akin to his own. His Diaries are a record of the extraordinary life he created for himself and though in his interests and pursuits he was typical of his Age in his curiosity, his vigour and his opinions, he was always distinctly himself.

VICTORIA MANTHORPE
London 1986

CHAPTER 1

Japan at Last

1898

Nagasaki: first impressions – invitation from Mitsui – Kobe: temples, raincoats and lack of modesty – smoking with geishas on the boat to Yokohama – rigorous customs officers – first view of Fuji – crafts and craftsmen – curry for Nicholais – on to Tokyo: the Mikado's Palace, vegetables, teahouse luncheon – street scenes and festive preparations

SATURDAY DECEMBER 24TH At daybreak I found myself in Nagasaki Harbour, *Japan at last*. One of the ambitions of my life had been to see it and here I was. Hills loomed around, a heavy mist was on the water, but as the sun came up above the horizon, everything became clear. The coal boats came alongside and then the Japan of my imagination came suddenly to life. The coalers were girls and women – all, of course, of the lower labouring classes but it was at once visible in their faces that this was a land of good humour, a land where even the low-class labouring women looked up at you, smiling. I went ashore, of course, though we had only a few hours. On shore I was struck – at Nagasaki at all events – with the similarity of the Japanese houses to those of Norway and Canada. But what a difference inside, and the cleanliness of them! They are really marvels of neatness.

Port of Nagasaki

The curio shops one hardly likes to go into. Whitest of washed straw mats to walk upon, and the shops are stocked so full that you hardly like to turn around for fear of knocking down some of the many expensive objects. None are really the least in my line but I can imagine the ordinary curio hunter, or a lady, remaining in one for days. Carved ivories, ancient and modern, old armour, china, bric-à-brac and lacquer, pipes, swords, and ornaments of every description. Toys, most of them, I thought, presents to be given to *geishas*[1]

Street vendors

and *musumes*[2], and anything new or original would be sure to amuse them infinitely, for they are essentially children.

In the market, what interested me more, were real European woodcocks, pheasants of several varieties, salmon, a kind of half salmon and half mackerel, sardines and some curious vegetables. Ugly and yet pretty little maids were visible nearly everywhere, some unwashed and dirty, but mostly clean. The men are not so interesting, but they are mostly in a good humour also, and that is something. Tattooing is still common amongst them and the picture shows the perfection to which this art can be brought.

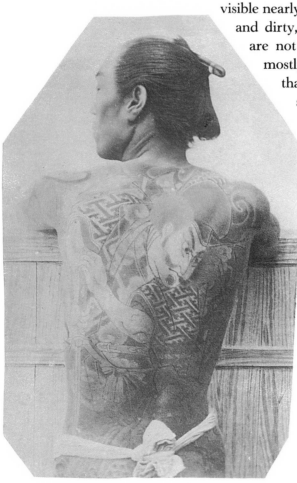

I called on the English Consul for an inland passport but was told that from January 1st this would be unnecessary, especially as I had an English one already, and a letter to our Minister as well. I bought a pair of native sandals, which are made of straw, as well as some stockings for my servant [Nicholais, whom he brought with him from Ceylon (Sri Lanka)] who appreciated them very much and said, 'Master, these very good, must take, to Ceylon, like much; Japanese people they come and laugh, not a bit like Chinese.' He is evidently appreciating things quietly, is Nicholais.

I saw and spoke to several American soldiers invalided from the Philippines[3] (they looked pretty bad and too young). Their opinion was that the U.S. had got more than they bargained for in retaining these islands and they hoped England would buy them. They mostly 'guessed' that *they* would not go back anyway for they all considered themselves damaged for life, and certainly they looked it. I was also told that 'America and England could lick the world', which pleased me, for I should like to see them do it, and it showed that America is beginning to realise that there is a world outside itself and that that world wants 'licking', and that if it has to be done it must be done by united Anglo-Saxon races.

At 2.30 p.m. we sailed off into the Inland Sea and before dark passed lovely islands and rocks far too numerous to mention. My own diary must be my own impression of things that interest me individually. Photographs I shall cease to take for I can buy better ones – all coloured and very cheap. The Inland Sea reminds me of the Lower St Lawrence River with the one exception that wherever possible the surrounding land is terraced for wheat or other crops. Everywhere there are fishing boats of curious construction and wonderfully dry boats for rough weather.

Mitsui[4], the great Japanese banking people, have asked me to dine in Tokyo and I have promised to do so provided the meal is true Japanese. M. Mitsui has been a passenger all the way, a quiet, unobtrusive but thoroughly Japanese gentleman (*of importance* I observed). He has had regular deputations to meet him at Singapore, Hong Kong, Shanghai and here. I have had little to say to him until last night when, in his shy manner, he asked me when I was in Tokyo if I should like to try a Japanese dinner. When I said I should, he seemed pleased (but very serious) and said 'Would you dine with me?' in such a manner as to mean: would you *mind* dining with me. When I accepted he seemed delighted. I noted all this, for it gave me an insight to the pleasant humour and character of the Japanese since their war[5]. Bumptiousness and rudeness I had been told I should find prominent everywhere. On the contrary – so far at all events. Mitsui, a man of real consequence in Japan, approaches me, an ordinary European, with such care and delicacy in offering hospitality that he showed distinctly that my acceptance would be an honour to him and my refusal a snub. I only hope I shall be able to go for I am sure to find many novelties in such a dinner.

16

SUNDAY DECEMBER 25TH XMAS DAY Slept pretty well last night in spite of the cold. Early morning found us steaming at 18 knots and in the Hiuchi Nada which is south of Oshima Island and noted for whale fishing. We passed many small islands. They remind me much of the lower fjords in Norway but they are more civilised looking; wild and fantastic rocks are everywhere. Thousands and thousands of fishing boats are visible, fish of every imaginable kind from tropical ones to semi-Arctic ones abound – the same with trees. At Kobe I saw quite tall palms and orange trees, while the most prominent wild trees are fir and pine. We passed the northern end of Awaji Island [Awajishima, at the eastern end of the Inland Sea] at 1.30 p.m., an island said to contain the largest population in the world for its area [230 square miles with a population in 1900 of 189,769].

We reached Kobe at 2.30 p.m. and, after establishing myself in the Oriental Hotel, I proceeded to the Waterfall Teahouse for tea. This was served in ridiculous little cups without handles, and with toy cakes, by a couple of very pretty girls curtsying and giggling in the apparent custom of the country. From here I went to the Nanko Shinto Shrine, which I thought a poor affair. The bazaar outside and around the shrine interested me far more and one might have spent a profitable few hours there in picking up old carved ivory which had fallen into the hands of the lowest of dealers.

The rickshaw boys here are clothed in what looks like the top half of a sailor's suit but there are curious devices in white upon them.

Two celebrated geishas

They go at a tremendous pace, and many were the collisions which I expected but with marvellous accuracy they avoided.

The whole of Kobe is lit up with coloured lanterns, thousands of them of every colour and shape; all are hung in the most artistic way and at night the streets are a veritable fairyland, compared to which Earl's Court is as nothing. All the houses are of wood and paper and a fire would be an extensive disaster but so dextrously is everything managed that such an occurrence is of rare occasion. The curio shops are without number, as are the charming and fascinating girls – one sees them everywhere. The men, on the other hand, are correspondingly plain though they are particularly well-set, strong little chaps with the sturdiest looking legs I have ever seen, and their knees look different from any others. Their legs being thick and strong, are made for running. There must be a good deal of picking for the navy for I noticed all the blue jackets were *giants* of their race.

I thought the cold was intense, but few, including my boy, seemed to feel it.

MONDAY DECEMBER 26TH Up very early and went up first to the Shinkyoji Temple and from there to the Ikuta, a Shinto shrine. It is not worth seeing so far as the building is concerned but the view from it is lovely over the town and

Gateway to the Fox Shrine

Inland Sea. It is situated well up on the hill in a grove of camphor trees. What interested me most was the fact that it is called the Fox Shrine. My guide went up to the altar and shook an enormous thing suspended from the roof, made of many offerings such as shells, rags, strings etc; this was 'to call God,' he said. He then took off his hat and made a bow to the altar. Had he completed the ceremony he should have shaken a receptacle made of bamboo containing a quantity of smaller numbered sticks, also of bamboo, drawn one out, taken its number and replaced it; then, made a small offering to the Fox God, taken the number to a house adjoining and asked for his fortune, which is given him according to the number he has drawn. If the fortune denoted on a slip of paper is good his prayer has been answered satisfactorily, and he generally takes it home to show his friends and relations. If it is bad he is very sad and sorrowful, and either throws it away or twines it around some adjacent twig of a tree. The trees are covered with these unsatisfactory answers. Generally, when one goes up to this shrine to pray, one leaves, stuck in the ground, a little bamboo stick, 4 inches long, attached to a bit of paper half its size with one's name and the date on it. This is to show that you have done your duty, and there are many hundreds about, though, of course, they get trodden into the ground and rot away. There are several real fox earths in the side of the hill around the shrine and many of these little flags are placed around them. In fact, never before did I ever hear of such homage done to a fox. What, I wonder, would an old Shire fox in England think of it? Foxes are, of course, never killed, the greatest veneration being paid to them. At this particular shrine the deity worshipped is 'Waka Hirume-no-Mikado' who, according to Murray's Guide [*A Handbook for Travellers in Japan.* John Murray. 3rd Edn., London 1891], may be styled the Japanese Minerva.

From 12 a.m. it began to rain, and I saw many short rainproof overcoats brought out and worn by coolies; they cost, I am told, 4 sen (2d.) and are quite rainproof. They looked excellent for stalking deer or driving partridges because you would be practically invisible.

I have come to the conclusion that there is absolutely no modesty amongst

18

either sex in the Japanese. Today I saw sights which, in a street, I never thought possible but everything seemed to be taken in a matter-of-fact way, which may not be altogether so discreditable as I thought.

The coiffure of the women is remarkable and I cannot possibly believe it is done up every day but rather must be a kind of helmet arrangement, in the older ones, that is taken off and put on at will. Married women do their hair one way, and unmarried ones another, but which it is, at present, I have been unable to

Coolies' straw coats

discover. The dresses are all charming and one soon gets to like the look of the huge *obi* or bow worn at the back and by far the most important part of the dress. [Strictly, the *obi* is the broad sash; the bow itself is called *otaiko*.] The children are also most quaint.

I went to the fish and fruit market and there saw many new fish. These in themselves would be quite a study. I noticed amongst them the large prawn of Ceylon and a smaller kind, grey mullet and red; sea perch and snappers of many varieties, diminutive fish no larger than whitebait, a kind of small sea crayfish and a curious blue crab. In the fruit there were some fantastic specimens made to grow so, and an orange no larger than a big cherry. In the game line there were quail resembling Egyptian quail, woodcock, and ducks. Of delicacies, in fact, there is no lack and I had a most excellent luncheon.

Advertising is pursued in a manner almost rivalling America. On my luncheon table was a little Japanese doll and when I picked her up to see what it was, out fell some tooth-picks with DRINK TANSAN [mineral water] on them; in my bedroom it was the same with the matches. Wherever I look I see DRINK TANSAN and, I must say, I do, for it is good.

The ship sailed again in the evening with four geishas who are being taken to Yokohama by a European of somewhat lower caste, probably to sing and play for sailors.

TUESDAY DECEMBER 27TH Since writing last night I find myself entirely mistaken about the four *geishas* and the low European. The latter is a Japanese in European disguise, one of the ladies owns an hotel at Nagoya and the other three are *geishas*. I had, on the whole, a merry morning with the whole five. They were travelling simply for pleasure (1st Class Passengers). I had them in my cabin to coffee and cigarettes, showed them my diary and they were delighted at being asked to write their names in it. One of the *geishas* supplemented this by giving me her card, as diminutive as her little self. I don't

Theatre Street, Yokohama

think any of them were over 4 feet 4 inches tall, and, though they are singularly fascinating, they remind me of sleepy cats from the way in which they nod and turn their heads, or of ducks which push them forward.

The weather during the day was abominable, a cold drenching rain, and nothing whatever to be seen of Fuji, the great mountain of Japan.

On reaching Yokohama we were first run broadside on to the pier which severely bulged one of the ship's plates. Subsequently we went through an absurd ordeal with the Japanese doctors. Finally, I landed at the customs soaked through, as were my seventeen packages of luggage, and then had to undergo a rigorous examination of everything in spite of an order, or rather a letter of request, from H.M.'s Imperial Consul at Colombo to treat me as leniently as possible. There is just one thing the Japanese will have to be taught, sooner or later, and that is the *absurdity of officialdom* if carried to excess. Eight days ago this was exhibited by the captain of some English ship being worried beyond his endurance by an idiotic medical authority. The skipper gave him one straight in the nose. It was reported to the Consul. The Consul said 'served him right'. Subsequently it was reported to the Minister, and the latter said the same. This was told me on board a French boat at Nagasaki by the purser, and he added with envy, 'Yours are the only officials who dare use their own discretion'.

I found the Grand Hotel very comfortable. An excellent band discoursed music, and I had the assistant-purser to dine, a particularly nice young fellow and a captain in the French Army Reserve.

Bright morning. Saw Fuji Mountain for first time. The haze here is really rather pleasing even to myself who likes everything clear and prominent in scenery. I called on Mr Walter, to whom I had a letter of introduction and subsequently lunched with him at a very pretty bungalow. In the afternoon I took a guide called Tagima Kobe and

went first to see the best of the lacquer work made. It was interesting but I dislike the things when finished.

From there I went to the woodcarving establishments. Some of the European ideas are creeping into the Japanese even in this craft so, sooner or later, real pure and simple unadulterated Japanese art will be a thing of the past. Their own carvings and devices are of course *perfect*. Next, I went to see the enamelled pottery and this interested me more. Over a year can be spent in making one thing. It is no wonder when one sees what has to be done and how it is done. All these artefacts are made in little paper houses – there is no factory,

Winter costume

so to speak. Even the baking of immense jars takes place in a small shed of half paper and half leaves and canes. I bought two exquisitely made little enamel incense boxes here and got them for about half the price I should have paid at a shop. Also I was presented with a plate by the sister of one of the joint owners who preferred, she said, 'to give rather than to bargain for a damaged thing' for the plate had one or two little faults. It made me feel rather cheap, however, because I had previously asked her to let me take her photograph and she may have thought that that was so great a compliment that she must do something in return.

I don't think I have ever suffered from cold more than I have here and yet the natives don't seem to care. The winter costume of the women is very pleasing but most of them go about without the arrangement they wear round their heads and which is pronounced 'zerkine' but how it is spelt I do not know; I have never seen one that is not either a delicate mauve or a peculiar grey. Of course, the inevitable umbrella is always carried except in the summer, when it is a fan and more probably both.

My boy Nicholais is quite daft with cold – the first time in fact that I have seen him not quite as smart as it is possible to make a Singhalese.

THURSDAY DECEMBER 29TH Awoke early. Cold, in fact, kept me awake most of the night, and Nicholais only turned up at 8.30 a.m. (an unheard-of crime when in sound mind). I hunted up some Singhalese jewellers and, after some trouble, found them. Knowing the true hospitality of their race to each other I told them, 'Come and see my Singhalese boy, take him to your house and give him curry' – and so they did. Called upon Mr Dodds, and then went and walked about the streets, looking at this, that, and the other though in truth Yokohama affords little to study. I kept to the native streets and noticed many little peculiarities, amongst them the small and curious restaurants and other shops made to be carried by one man, whose sole worldly belongings are probably included in his little stall, and which he no doubt carries from village to village.

I saw several solitary snipe in the market as well as many ordinary snipe, a few woodcock, hares, and a deer of a kind I have never seen with rough woolly hair.

I never saw a single good-looking native man; it is quite astonishing what a contrast they are to the women. I am no longer surprised at the awful masks

they make and how such faces ever came into their imagination. They are all exaggerated likenesses of themselves. One does not often come across features that are taking: they have immense heads, enough brains to mature anything, either good or evil, and be it said to their credit they employ it mostly for good and for the advance of themselves and their country; and everyone knows what they have attained.

Not so many years ago an execution like the one shown in my photograph was more or less common. You might be crucified or you might be stood between the bars, supported by your chin and only the very tips of your toes touching the ground. When your toes gave out your head was hacked off and 'there you were, you know, in Japan but minus your head'. This sort of thing has probably gone for good, though the photo was taken by a Japanese and it is not so long ago they learned photography.

Nicholais returned at 8.30 p.m. from the dinner with his newly made Singhalese friends, delighted at their hospitality. 'Two curries,' he said, 'a fish one and a beef one and good hot rice; very good, master, nearly so good as Colombo.' Well, I am glad I pleased him for it may put a little life into him.

FRIDAY DECEMBER 30TH Left Yokohama by the 11.30 a.m., a crowded little train that took us (after stopping at six stations) to Tokyo. We got really perfect views of Fuji Mountain all the way and, clad in snow, it towered above all the others. There was cultivation – rice fields and gardens – the whole way. A curious way they have of stacking rice straw reminded me of Sweden, for they tie it up around the trees in sheaves to a height of perhaps 20 feet with a diameter of 3 feet. This gives the trees the appearance of being thickly clothed against the cold, and so thought Nicholais. At Omori and Shinagawa [both northeast of Yokohama], tea gardens showed that we were really more in Japan than at Yokohama. There was no sign of the European, other than in what he had taught the Japanese to make. We saw the five forts which were built by the Shogunate to protect Tokyo – five good-looking island forts now dismantled, I am told, as obsolete.

We reached Shinbashi Station half an hour late and here I am sorry to say that Nicholais required reprimanding somewhat severely for his impoliteness to a Japanese porter. We reached the Imperial Hotel, a splendid building, at 1 p.m. in time for luncheon. After this I called on Larrain Zarivarral (the Chilean Chargé d'Affaires). I found him in ecstasies over Japan, but his wife extremely ill, and I took it upon myself to advise his immediately removing her from the hotel and getting a doctor to see her. He had done absolutely nothing, and knew of no doctor, and as he knew I had a letter to the British Minister, he asked me to make use of it at once for advice as to doctors, which I did.

The cold in Tokyo is even worse than in Yokohama. I wandered about the truly Japanese streets, with their stalls, bazaars, shops. *Everything* is essentially Japanese excepting the Government Building which latter, Law Courts and Admiralty remind me more of French buildings; they are all very large and fine anyway, but an eyesore to me. The Mikado's Palace is invisible, surrounded by an enormous trench some 150 to 200 yards wide and 100 feet deep, the bottom of which is filled with water to make a large lake surrounding the entire palace. At the top is a wall constructed of extraordinarily large stones and the whole is overhung with sombre fir trees. It is the most impressively fine boundary to a palace that can be imagined, but not pretty.

The soldiers interested me. Smart little men they were, especially the artillery and cavalry, the latter rather simulating French uniforms. All have their own peculiarities. However, cavalry, artillery, infantry and all look *sound, tough, clean,* and *intelligent,* so what more can one want than cash to furnish them and generals to command them? The former is perhaps Japan's most severe stumbling block, and the capability of their generals has pretty well been displayed to their credit [in the Sino-Japanese War]. But it is in the shops and the streets among the people that I find most interest, especially if they be among the lower grades and

Lamp painters

untouched by European ideas. Lamp makers are essentially Japanese, and these interested me very much; so did the umbrella makers; so did the food shops, the little places where you could buy all kinds of curious (and often savoury in smell) bits of food. Raw fish stalls, toyshop stalls where only battledore and shuttlecock games were for sale. Paper flower stalls for the hair, comb shops, chopstick stalls, and a stall I found for only ornamental pins for the hair, the like of which I had never seen before. Another street contained only vegetables, carrots of 2 feet in length, *radishes* that length and over, enormous sweet potatoes, leeks ten times their ordinary size. There were other things reduced to absurdities – monstrosities such as ancient trees up to thirty and forty years of age, cherry and plum, grown and kept in pots, pruned, and grafted with many different things, and all for the sake of having blooms in December, for the opening of the New Year. And thus I find myself in Tokyo for one of its greatest festivals. There were many other odd things such as the white rice cakes (which are eaten on the entry of the New Year) and the very smallest orange I ever saw. It contained three large pips in seven compartments, about three drops of juice, and a most delicious flavour.

SATURDAY DECEMBER 31ST Earthquake last night but in spite of bad night I never felt it. Had a shocking night and thought I should have been suffocated with bronchitis. Up early feeling wretched.

At breakfast I got an invitation to dine at our Legation from Sir Ernest Satow[6]. I thought it so particularly kind that I went to thank him in person and

White plum   *Pine tree*   *Peach*

he entertained me for some time about things in Japan, especially the pruned trees [*bonsai*], which strike me as so curious. The Legation grounds themselves are quite charming.

At 12.30 p.m. I drove about seven miles down the big river (Sumida) over the Azumabashi (*bashi* is bridge) and on through the celebrated cherry tree avenues (which were not now, of course, in flower) to a teahouse known as Weijham. Here I ordered an extra-special Japanese luncheon. And while this was in preparation I took photographs of the gardens and little houses, all works of art and good taste in themselves. Of course, I took some of the girls to help, and a merry little party we made. They simply delight in being photographed, and after each one I took they wished to see the view through the lens to see if I had made a pretty picture of it. Simple *musumes* was all they were but they were little ladies for all that, and their manners were charming.

When luncheon was ready it was necessary to take off my European boots and put on soft slippers. For to enter a real Japanese house and trample on the mats would be to ruin them for ever. These little paper and wood houses are scattered about in the garden on islands, on rockeries or anywhere where they are likely to look well – and pulled down if they don't. They vary in size and when I asked my guide (whose guest I practically was for the day so that I might get as true a Japanese lunch as possible) how much they cost to build, he said that a good Japanese house of this kind is valued according to the number of mats on its floor. These never vary in size and are always 6 feet by 3 feet. I have forgotten the figure he gave by mat and only mention it as a curious way of measuring or rather of valuing.

The rooms are generally square, and all the walls are of thin white paper glued onto small thin frames of wood. There is always one raised little corner 4

or 5 inches higher than the floor and on this no one may go. It is for Shinto emblems and gifts and is kept, as it were, for the gods. There is another corner for books, and a few shelves over which paper slides are drawn. You feel as if you were in a bandbox. There is nothing to sit upon except a cushion, and you hardly dare move about for fear everything will give way, but it does not for it is really the most beautifully built and fitted woodwork I have ever seen.

Well, you sit on your cushion with your legs tucked as much under you as you possibly can – but ruining the knees of your trousers for ever by the undue and unnatural strain brought on them – and patiently wait to be fed. First to come in is your particular *musume*, who attends to you exclusively after bowing low and telling you your food is coming. She goes out and returns with a small

Japanese tea ceremony

lacquer tray containing chopsticks and a bowl of soup, so called, but in reality warm light-green water with raw parsley, raw fish and raw mushrooms artistically arranged at the bottom and looking very pretty. I nobly tackled the parsley first, being the only thing which I could negotiate with the chopsticks, much to the amusement of my little *musume*. However, I sent for a knife and, with it, made an implement out of one chopstick resembling a crochet hook, the ingeniousness of which gained for me much credit from the *musumes* and my guide, and from then on I felt at home and capable of facing anything that was likely to come.

The raw fish in the soup were quite good and so were the raw mushrooms. After this came the second course: raw fish called *hirame* (sole). This was served with *seaweed* (which was quite delicious), but the fish itself was difficult to swallow as it was cut from the practically living fish in long thin strips, and rather stuck in your throat in the absence of either bread or rice to drive it down. However, I managed four pieces. With this dish were served several other things: a sauce called soya, horse radish and shellfish.

Next came a small cup of hot *sake* or native wine made from rice and for which I thanked God as I felt that it might keep the raw fish quiet.

Course No. 3 rather flabbergasted me as it was yet more raw fish – swordfish cut in thin strips – prawns, raw turnip and vinegar sauce. (No *sake* followed this so I sent for my flask, which a merciful Providence had warned me to bring.)

Course No. 4 was cold baked fish (not at all bad) with ginger, also fried lobster with white plums stewed. And after this I began to wish that I were sitting on a high chair instead of cross-legged on the floor.

Course No. 5 was a broiled fish called *tai* rather like a perch and with every detail of fin and tail sticking out as if he were alive (beautiful to look at but difficult to negotiate even with my chopstick contrivance which, by the way, was now beginning to wear out. Nonetheless, I persevered, got all his best parts off him, and ate two more raw mushrooms on top.)

Course No. 6 was a curious kind of fish cake which looked like cream cheese, cut in thick slices, with a brown sheen. I managed one mouthful of this, but would much rather have gone back to the raw fish.

Course No. 7 I was really pleased to see, for it was pure and simple rice and I consumed my entire portion, calculating that it had put several inches of obstruction between myself and the other things. With more *sake* after this I began to look upon the whole process of Japanese feeding as a kind of lacquering. Dessert followed and consisted of salted radish and spongecake, then two kinds of tea. I topped the lot with neat whiskey and then lit a cigar.

I was glad to stand up after all this, and took the two *musumes* for more photographs but not, however, until they had packed the remainder of our luncheon into two new wooden boxes, for in Japan you take away what you do not eat even in the highest society, and with the best of dinners. A large number of Europeans go to tea gardens and go half through the above menu, I am told, but only very few can manage the entire meal.

Street seller of vegetables

On my way back I went to the Asakusa Temple [in Ueno Park, Tokyo], a large, interesting Buddhist temple with a bazaar leading up to it. Many people were praying there in curious manners and at curious images, pulling bells to call the particular god they wished to listen to their prayers, and altogether leading one into confusion concerning their religion.

I forgot to mention an incident of refinement in Japanese girls or *musumes*. You are supposed to give a small tip to the *musume* who waits upon you individually, and as they do not like the vulgar idea of money being paid directly to them as *payment* for the attention shown, they only accept *presents*. Money must always be enclosed in small envelopes of which you yourself carry a supply. Thirty cents [sen] is the usual 'tip' and fifty is extremely handsome.

After the Asakusa Temple I walked about in the squares and streets surrounding it. The most interesting was the 'Street of Shows'. Boxing, wrestling, dancing, curiosities, monstrosities – everything, in fact, that the best of English racecourse penny peepshows could show – and one stall interested me very much. It was a large tank enclosed in a shop over which an old man presided. The tank was full of fish (principally of the carp species) varying in weight from a quarter to one and a half pounds. They all flocked about in 6 inches of water practically jostling each other. For 5 cents you were given a rod, 2 feet long, string and a tripod of hooks. Your object was to hook a fish and deposit him without handling into a small zinc basin in front of which you stood. If you succeeded the fish was yours. Many did not succeed, and the

Country people

result was that there was much gore and suffering. I think it was about the most absolutely cruel sport or game I have ever seen.

The preparations for the New Year are elaborate. Street vendors and pedlars of every description abound, country people are buying toys and things with which to make the New Year merry, and the interest displayed in this event is intense. The streets are gaily decorated with straw, trees and bamboos, but those which interest me most consist of two small fir trees, until today tied up like a cauliflower with strings. This evening they are cutting the strings loose for the New Year. A lobster (or crayfish) and an orange are hung at nearly every door, which means 'luck to you in growth on land, and strength at sea' or something to that effect. (What a waste of lobsters this is, I think I hear some Londoner say.)

After dinner an extraordinary performance took place: windows were

New Year ceremony

opened in the hotel, fires scraped out and cleaned, and much dusting went on everywhere. I drew the line at all this being done in my room with the thermometer down at freezing point, but I had to retire to bed to safeguard my own fire, and thus, no doubt, rendered myself rather unpopular as a 'foreign devil'. However, I was quite determined to retain the little warmth I could get near, and fight over it if necessary.

CHAPTER 2

Native Customs Observed

1899

*New Year celebrations in Tokyo – dinner with Sir Ernest Satow –
visit to the Temple of the Forty-seven Ronins – the Maple Club –
Shiba Park – geishas at a tea house – return to Yokohama – first
meeting with Yukari: learning Japanese – the rage for kite flying – the
attractions of Japanese women – a trip to the theatre – packing up and
farewell to Yukari*

SUNDAY JANUARY 1ST A good deal of tom-toming went on throughout the town during the night, but that was nothing to what took place in the hotel. While I was having my bath a diabolical noise was being made by a procession of tom-toms and devil dancers. They were engaged by the hotel manager to walk up and down the passages and drive out the last of the Old Year's devils and, I suppose, call in the New Angels. I met them all in my dressing gown with my hair on end, having just washed and dried it in my bath, and the tom-toms were beaten with renewed vigour, for I am sure they thought they had met 'His Majesty' at least, in myself.

I hurried and dressed for I had been told that the rest of this extraordinary performance was to take place in the hall of the hotel and that the principal dancer with a long-haired mask would do 'some funny things'. He did, for his acting was *perfect*. At one moment he was representing agony on the floor, writhing and biting his legs and arms as if in pain, recovering himself and biting a flea out of his toe and a hundred and one other barbaric performances. When tired he was replaced by two inferior masked dancers of a comical type, and when he returned the enacting of pain

Devil dancers

and agony commenced again. Excepting myself, Nicholais, the servants and a few children there were no spectators. Nicholais was very much impressed and said the acting was away ahead of any Singhalese devil dancers he had

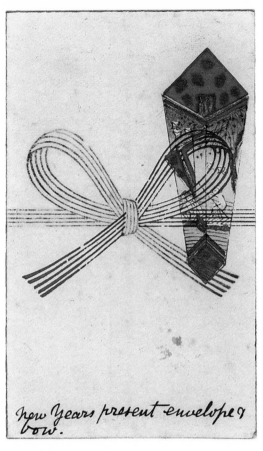

New Years present envelope & bow.

ever seen. But what impressed him most was that the moat opposite the hotel was frozen. I had told him of it and in spite of his belief in me he had to go out and see in order to verify my statement. I let him without any remonstrance, and when he came back he said, 'Oh master, what people say in Colombo? There must pay money for ice' (and how the poor devil loathed it all the while!!).

After breakfast I took a walk in the streets, which were crowded with everyone paying their New Year calls. There was any amount of bowing and ceremony even amongst the lowest orders. I had to do a certain amount of it myself in shops. They are decidedly gene-rous, these people, at this time of year: wherever you buy you get a present and it is always enclosed in an envelope or, if too large, tied with double coloured strings and affixed to a small envelope which always represents a present, and the loops of the bow must be turned upwards like those on the *obi* or bad luck will be sure to follow. In a native chemist's shop, where I bought some hairwash, I was presented with a pink gargle for my throat, which latter, as a matter of fact, is about the only sound part of me. I received two other presents both in envelopes with bows – one containing a small case of ivory toothpicks and the other a cotton handkerchief.

It was really very pretty to see all the calling, bowing and ceremony going on all around one. *Geishas* dashed about in their rickshaws intent upon keeping up their reputation for good looks, and the only thing that really marred things to my mind was the horrible way in which small children were painted white with red lips, but their dresses, as far as colour was concerned, were gorgeous.

The tinkling of the *shamisen* [or *samisen* – a three-stringed lute played with a plectrum] was heard continuously, and here and there tom-toming.

Later in the morning boys flew kites, and girls and women played battledore and shuttlecock all over the street. From January 1st to 7th they play this game with its hard little shuttles incessantly. They hit them with a solid wooden bat high up into the air, and generally three play in a cocked-hat fashion. Every game you lose you have to put either black or white paint on your face and a girl covered with this looks very sad and unhappy, taking it, probably, as a bad omen for the New Year. There is also a great deal of sweet making and selling of the same on New Year's day and they mostly resemble our own old-fashioned 'bullseyes', 'peardrops' and 'pine drops'. The small boy of Japan is, like his brother in the West, a large consumer.

I lunched alone at the hotel and watched with interest a party of ten serious Japanese men who had come to open the year by having a European meal. They were very sullen and hardly ever spoke, looking at each other and smiling occasionally at the awkwardness with which they used forks and knives, and there seemed to be more difficulty in using a spoon. Four or five tried curry. Their faces were a study, and a fit of coughing followed. (My native luncheon yesterday was revenged.)

I paid a formal call on Mitsui; he was out but I left two cards, though I believe the real Japanese custom is not to leave one on the wife. I was grovelled to at the door by the butler, and it was really rather interesting. On my return I met half the naval officers in the Japanese Navy going, I should think, to attend some New Year's party.

At 10.30 p.m. a large fire broke out and all the watchtower bells tolled out the alarm. They have, I am told, 1,500 firemen here, and I should think they need them.

MONDAY JANUARY 2ND A fine day, the morning of which I spent shopping, buying silk handkerchiefs of artistic design, and various other curiosities. The smells in some of the streets were perfectly appalling and with my cold and general state of fever I felt more like typhoid than I have ever felt before. However, time was not to be lost and I went here, there, and everywhere – amongst other places to the Fox Shrine of Inari and the Buddhist temple of Shiba; both were of interest though they are much the same, one and all. Outside, at the entrance of the Buddhist temple, were two Gods of some size enclosed in wire fencing and representing life from beginning to end, the God representing the commencement of life having his mouth open, and the one representing the end, shut. It is the custom to write what you wish to pray for on a small piece of paper which you then proceed to chew into a pulp and when it is quite soft you blow it out at the God. If it passes through the wire netting – the mesh is, perhaps, half an inch square – and sticks to the image your prayer will be heard, and if it doesn't it will not.

Dined at the British Legation with the Minister, Sir Ernest Satow, and had I felt well should have spent a very pleasant evening for there were some very nice and interesting people there. The Military Attaché, Capt. Churchill[1], and Paget[2] the Secretary; also the American Naval Attaché and his wife. The latter rather amused me by speaking of the Indian Mutiny as the English Mutiny. Churchill gave a very good account of the Japanese Army.

*Nakamura and his family
with Sano, my guide*

TUESDAY JANUARY 3RD Up rather late feeling no better and am really rather afraid of typhoid.

Went first to K. Nakamura to buy a couple of tables for which I paid 100 yen (£10). His shop was most fascinating and some of the 'cloisonné' quite too lovely but very expensive. One small vase five inches high was worth £12 but it was really the most lovely delicate piece of work and colouring I have ever seen. It represented a scene under water, of the most delicate aquamarine blue which faded away towards the top of the vase into pink reflections from cherry blossom, blue and silvery white. As I do not much care for art it may be imagined that it was a very beautiful thing or I should not have taken the trouble to note it down.

I then drove off with two men to my rickshaw to the Forty-seven Ronins Temple some distance away in the direction of Shinagawa. The temple is really called Sengakuji and a most dramatic story is attached to the Ronins[3] who are buried there and have been for 200 years, and since which time incense sticks have ever been alight at each grave. The Forty-seven Ronins were heroes and martyrs of some kind (a long story my guide unfurled to me but I felt so seedy that I did not hear half of it, and the smell of drains merely made me sick). The chief of the Forty-seven (all nobles) was named Kuranosuke Oishi and especial reverence is shown to the spot which covers his remains. After his death I believe the rest of his party 'disembowelled themselves', an operation which I sincerely envied them in being able to do.

I next went to the Maple Club, a place in itself which defies description. The place is a club but such is its beauty that visitors are allowed the privilege of going over it by taking off their boots and paying 10 cents. The house is very large for a Japanese one but no doubt there are many members. All the rooms are for tea or dinners or other entertainments of Japanese order. You are received by about twenty little *musumes* all perfectly dressed; they bow in a manner which makes you feel positively ridiculous. Your boots are taken off and then you are escorted round the different rooms by one of the *musumes*. There is nothing to see and yet there is everything to see. So clean and so absolutely artistic in every detail that you are left in wonder and to wonder to yourself, are *you* the *civilised* Briton, really civilised at all? What is your house or your club in comparison to this? The whole looks as if it ought to go under a glass case. Not a speck of dust or dirt could you find if you hunted until Doomsday. The mats which cover the floors give under your feet and they look absolutely new. The paper sides are spotless, the sliding sides are all in perfect order and move without sound or jar. Of ornaments there are hardly any, and those there are, are as simple as they are artistic. Either a dwarfed cherry or plum tree, 2 feet high, with a wild aesthetic appearance, or a single twig of the same put into a vase and placed by itself. How much better this than what we call a bouquet – I shall always laugh when I see a bouquet now.

After we had seen the whole club our little *musume* escorted us to a room where we were to have tea, and this she brought on a pair of the most exquisite lacquer trays. Rice biscuits, thin and delicate, the shape of maple leaves, one white and the other rose pink, were on a light-green lacquer tray and covered with a piece of paper on which was written a verse to the maple tree. This was

all I could bring away with me, beyond my idea that I was no longer a refined and civilised being but a vulgar enormous and uncouth beast, who had no more business in a Japanese house of any standing than a hippopotamus would have in a crockery shop in Regent Street. I was quite as much out of place with my heavy Irish coat and ordinary homespun clothes which I very much doubt if a Japanese would deign to walk upon as a carpet or scrape his feet as a dust mat. Even the little attendant *musumes* were dressed with a care and a taste quite out of our sphere. No jewellery, no ornaments beyond the simple flowers in the hair. Dull grey, pink or blue, whatever they wore it all blended even with the extraordinary vivid colours some of them wore in the bow at the back of their *obis*. Even their names are full of art – that is to say as far as they are allowed names, for in Japan no woman has a name – she is called after some particular thing such as snow (*yuki*) and you address her by putting *O* before it and *san* after, which means Miss; thus she would be addressed O-Yuki-san.

After leaving the Maple Club, which in reality is a kind of Tokyo Hurlingham[4], we went to the Shiba Park and walked all over it and very beautiful it was, utterly different from any other. I got home late to luncheon, after 3 p.m., and felt so seedy that I made up my mind to stay in for the rest of the day and write.

WEDNESDAY JANUARY 4TH Decidedly better this morning and consequently ordered a carriage to be ready at 10 a.m. to convey me to the Crematory (a most unusual place for a foreigner to go to) but I was interested therein and besides it was on the road to the Ogiya tea garden.

A funeral in Japan .

Ueno Park through which we passed is by far the best in Tokyo, and is also of considerable size, as are the trees themselves. The Zoological Gardens are there, several temples, many tea gardens and a variety of other attractive things. And the large lake of Shinobazu is there also, with its island temples and collection of artistic arrangements – for that is all I can attempt to call a quarter of all I saw. We drove through many streets until at last we arrived at the Crematory. Here, between forty and fifty people are burned every night. The rich ones are burned full length, the poor are doubled-up, shoved into a palanquin, run down to the place at once, and pushed into a perfectly square box. The burning takes three hours; 8 yen and 11½ yen respectively are the prices; fifteen quarter-split logs of pine, 2 feet long, do the business. I went all over it, got covered with ashes of the departed, and saw some rather revolting sights – one a coffin which had only just burned the outside off and a poor little child fizzled as the fire was out and could not be relit until nightfall by law. My guide was quite upset, but I am generally interested in cremation and wished to see all and complete comparisons between Milan, Woking, Burma and here. On leaving the Crematory my guide was very quiet. 'It make me want to cry,' he said.

Ogiya teahouse

We reached the Ogiya teahouse at 12.30 p.m., a lovely spot. To this one I took bread, soda water, or rather Tansan, and cold chicken, and of the rest I ate their food, much like the lunch the other day and served in exactly the same way. I sent for two *geishas* to amuse us, wait upon us, and play the *shamisen*, all of which they did to my entire satisfaction, though I cannot say that I cared much for the songs or the *shamisen* – it may sound well in the open but two of them in a Japanese room was too much.

Our geishas at Ogiya

To both my own and my guide's surprise our coachman came up and asked if the 'Honourable Sir' would like him to sing a sailor's song and show his body, which was covered with tattoos. His intrusion I thought a confounded impertinence, but it was evident that *sake* wine had caused him thus to forget himself and, as it was one of my ambitions to see one of these perambulating works of art and to photograph it I said, 'let him do so'. And I must say that he was perfectly extraordinary. He unclothed himself completely excepting a loin cloth and there was hardly an inch of his body that was not tattooed in a manner quite out of the common. Even my guide was astonished. The song he sang was weird and ugly. He wrote his name and address on a piece of paper and asked the *geishas* to remember him if an opportunity afforded for showing himself.

THURSDAY JANUARY 5TH Was up tolerably early, feeling considerably better but still with a very bad cough and cold. I did a large variety of things in the morning including a call on Mitsui who, I heard, has been very ill since he landed at Kobe.

I went over a summer houseboat; it was a model of neatness but the roof rather low. However, I think a very

pleasant and economical summer might be spent in one of these and in one of the Inland Sea boats, and you would see a great deal of Japan which no one else sees, even according to Sir Ernest Satow's opinion, which I consulted later in the day when I called to say goodbye to him. I think it is, in fact, an expedition which I must make some day. And when I do, I shall apply to M. Mitsui, Esq., Mitsui Bussan Kaisha, Sakomoto-cho, Tokyo.

I was taken down to a great festival at one of the Shinto Fox shrines but such was the crowd that it was quite impossible to get in and I stayed outside viewing the acres and acres of cheap toy stalls. I saw a man looking at an English sporting picture of fox-hunting and his face at the awfulness of it was a study. No wonder we are looked upon as 'Foreign Devils', thought I, and I wondered if the *Graphic* had any idea of the awful desecration it was guilty of, enough to cause the death of many a European in any fanatical or troublous time.

The smells of Tokyo are ninety per cent stronger than any I have ever smelt elsewhere, and if compared with, say, Naples you may imagine what they are. I smoke incessantly. I went round to Ueno Park to get out of them for a bit and had a cup of tea on Lotus Island. There were no lotus plants visible now, but the teahouse was pretty.

I saw the grey goose, common mallard and what I used to know, upon the St Lawrence (Canada), as 'Blue Bills'. It is really strange to see these birds swimming about in peace, right in the middle of an enormous metropolis.

The temples in Ueno Park are, I think, the most impressive I have seen. This impressiveness arises from the fineness of the trees and the stone incense burners under them which look like so many knights of old – all of stone, so cold that it gives one quite a chilly feeling.

At a store I bought for 1 cent a facsimile of Japanese cards, forty-eight in number. They represent the seasons of flowers and game – practically an almanac, and thoroughly emblematic of each season. Everything is emblematic in Japan, and everything so represented takes its origin either in flowers or some other of nature's creations.

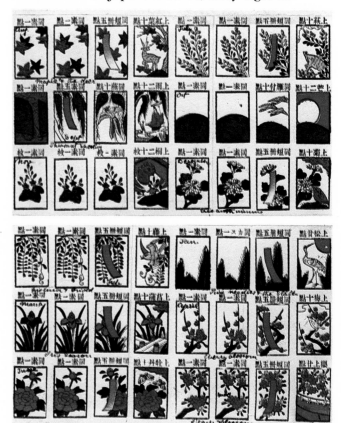

I wound up my day by driving to the Temple of Yanaka and then calling upon the Chilean Chargé d'Affaires, whose wife, fortunately, was better. They asked me to dine but I find my time sufficiently taken up in recording my impressions here, daily in the evenings, and therefore refused, for I hope my notes will some day be instructive to my children[5].

FRIDAY JANUARY 6TH After the most extortionate charge from the Imperial Hotel of 16 yen a day (4 of which were for my servant because life in his own country was not worth half as much) I left this city of Tokyo both with and without regret. Had it not been for the present climatic conditions it would have been simply and solely *with* regret.

SATURDAY JANUARY 7TH Not at all well this morning, renewal of ague and fever. K. Kaito, my new guide, is by far the best I have had – as a companion at all events. A keen fisherman and a great smoker he appreciates anything comical. In the morning I drove down to the Goto factory of cloissoné and bought many small things really cheap; also sent off and paid for three cabinets I had bought for my children.

In the afternoon I pottered about and met a charming Japanese girl called Yukari. I have pasted in this specimen of a pretty girl for she is so exactly like Yukari and dresses in the same style. In the evening I dined with the Russians who came up in the *Indus*. The husband is in the Russian Naval Guard. And a very nice fellow.

I walked several miles today hoping to get some information about the hire of a native boat of 30 or 40 tons for my future trip in Japan, but could get none.

SUNDAY JANUARY 8TH Drove down early to Kugenuma through several pretty fishing villages. The drive was really the prettiest I have had in Japan so far as scenery was concerned. At Kugenuma we had lunch in the usual fashion, regular Japanese. The cooked fish were good and so were some eggs cooked into a kind of hard omelette and eaten with dry seaweed-cakes; the seaweed is called *nori* and is largely consumed on the coast.

Great kite flying was going on amongst the boys, and I have found out today one reason for their excitement in this game: attached to the kite string are small knives (one or two) specially made and very sharp and cleverly set in wood. The object is to cut your adversary's kite string and thus become the winner of either his kite or something else. Intense excitement is worked up over this and I am no longer at a loss, therefore, to account for this absolute *rage* of kite flying.

I was presented with several branches of plum blossom, both pink and white, by various girls and saw many trees almost in full bloom. How these girls delight in them too, and in showing them to you out of sheer friendliness and the delight in studying you to see if you appreciate anything that they do. One feels deeply drawn towards all of them, both young and old, and I feel now that I shall be very very sorry when I see the last of Japan in spite of the rigours of its present climate. *Sayonara* (goodbye) will be quite hard to say to some, especially to Yukari, who does her best, daily, to instruct me in Japanese.

MONDAY JANUARY 9TH Busy all the morning, picking up the last of the photographs which I wanted – this necessitates hunting through many hundreds. I also had to go and order four Japanese oiled-paper lamps that I want for using in the Burmese jungle. They pack lightly, stand rain and the candles burn straight in them. They are white with my name painted on them in red Japanese letters and cost 30 cents each. I also went down to the ship *Rohilla* to make the necessary arrangements for embarking my luggage tomorrow.

In the afternoon I paid a few calls, and then went to tea with Yukari and furthermore stayed to dinner. The one drawback to these Japanese is they are apt to get sentimental which in other words means that they easily fall in love and get very sad, and so it was with this one who, before I left, gave me a long letter all in Japanese and which I was to open and read after I left Yokohama – rather embarrassing for me, generally. I was also given a piece of her *obi* which I had previously greatly admired, and several other small souvenirs which, she explained, she gave to one who had been so kind and good in trying to learn Japanese. She wished me to take them and 'please not forget her'.

40

This flirtation was really very wrong of me, but there it is. In Rome you do as the Romans do; in Japan, you do as the Japanese do and if you don't you are an ass and had far better stay away for you will be disappointed in yourself. *Sayonara* was sadly said and that was the last I saw of Yukari.

At 10 p.m. I went to a native theatre with my guide, Kaito, and there witnessed two pieces, the first one with rather a good moral called 'The Ferryboat that carried God's Spirit'. My guide explained it fairly well. The other piece was exceedingly vulgar, quite unfit for ladies to see (or even men for that matter) and was called 'Revenge of a Girl called Wabimi O-Ushi'. The acting in both was really not bad. The band consisted of a couple of *shaminsens* and the mode of shifting the scenery was rather clever, the whole of the visible stage revolving on a pivot. We had a little box about two yards square for which we paid 1 yen (4 s.); there were of course no chairs and we had to sit on the floor.

Two-thirds of the audience were as usual women and a large number of children. All evinced intense excitement and interest. On one occasion where a servant coming home at night finds his master murdered on the road, the servant bewails the fact. In the meantime the murderer is seen to be coming through some long grass with sword drawn to kill the servant also. At this moment a man in the pit shouted out at the top of his voice the Japanese equivalent of 'Look out man, the devil is going for you, turn quickly while you have the time and kill him, hey! hey! You will be too late. Oh, how I wish I could help you'. The poor fellow was completely carried away by the piece and no doubt it was a great compliment to the actor.

A good deal of interest was centred upon myself as being the only European present, but I am so thoroughly accustomed to this *everywhere* that I don't care an atom about it.

Cloth store

TUESDAY JANUARY 10TH   A lovely morning. Curiosity prompted me, early in the morning, to get my letter from Yukari translated. It was quite touching. She wrote how sorry she was at my departure and what a pity it was that it was not in her power to make me remain. She prayed to the Gods that I should travel safely. 'Two things I will ask you only, one not to forget me, a little girl in Japan; the other, to write whenever at leisure and return to Japan as soon as you can.'

At 10 a.m. I went to complete the embarkation arrangements, did a little more shopping for photos and saw the way boots or clogs were made. I also went to a silk shop where I might have spent hours but I bought nothing. Some of the silks and the patterns are truly marvellous. The production, the patterns, the embroideries, etc, are simply lovely, even to me.

After luncheon I went down to the ship and put Nicholais and my luggage on board and then returned to the town. I did not go to see Yukari thinking it much better to leave her to get over her little affair as soon as possible.

I dined alone at the hotel and went down to the ship later. Very few people were on board. The officers are an extremely nice lot and the ship, old as she is, a real treat in cleanliness after the *Indus*. Thank God, I always think, you are English.

Bootmaker

When a baby is born your best friend buys and offers one of the dogs to the temple so that the baby may grow strong and brave, like a dog

WEDNESDAY JANUARY 11TH Lovely morning but very cold as we steamed away from Yokohama. Passing out of Tokyo Bay into the open ocean, there were constant views across the range of Hakone mountains of Fujiyama. On our portside we passed Vries Island (Oshima, the largest of the Izu-shichito group), whose very high volcano, well outlined against the sky, sent forth a column of pure white vapour which added an air of mystery and majesty.

When we had passed the large peninsula of Izu we came to Suruga Bay and here we got the most wonderful view of Fuji that I have seen either in picture or reality. The base of the mountain ran right down into the sea and thus looked like some gigantic cone. Though no cloud was visible and the sky was blue, a curious bluish mist, the colour of both sea and sky, concealed the whole of the base of Fuji, while above, 12,550 feet aloft [actually 12,388], the top of this remarkable mountain is as clear as if the space between you and it had been polished and burnished crystal. It was enough to fill anybody with awe and to make one reflect that those born within sight of such a mountain must necessarily be born to art and its praises. No wonder, either, that these people venerate such a mountain, that many of their stories and much of their religion is centred upon it. As for myself it made me even more sorry to leave the country of which I have seen so little and liked so much in such a short time.

Today I had a long discussion on politics in the East with a Russian officer. Unfortunately it was suddenly stopped in the middle by a school of whales spouting around us. He told me much of interest, however, and the way in which Vladivostok is kept clear during the winter months with ice crushers of 6,000 tons.

A lady, a Miss Thompson of Kobe, who is on board did the coolest thing I think I have ever seen even a woman do. My deckchair has my name painted on it, also three yellow and blue stripes a foot wide all around it, two labels with my name and a strap around the whole. When I went on deck I found she had unpacked the chair, settled herself with her own cushions in it and never said a word in excuse or anything else!! D—— such women, say I; what a lesson the Japanese can give them in manners.

In a rhyme competition today, I made up the following which I thought rather good as it was impromptu:

> 'As we sailed away from Yokohama,
> And passed the Mount called Fujiyama,
> I thought of Yukari, my charmer,
> And prayed to the Lord that nought would harm her.'

It fetched the prize which was a cocktail.

On his way home Gordon Smith hunts elephants in Burma and it is not until May that he disembarks at Gravesend. Within two days he is shooting at Hurlingham. Evidently family life has not improved: July, August and September see him in Spitzbergen and by November he is 'off to the East again'.

He breaks his journey at Ceylon, for fishing, shooting and golf. In Singapore he waits to hear if he will get permission to shoot tigers in Jahore or Burma and whiles away some of his time with Rajah Brooke in Sarawak. Unsuccessful, he moves on to Hong Kong and Canton, finally arriving in Yokohama at the end of February 1900.

BACK FROM A SHOOTING TRIP.

Mr. Gordon Smith, who it, will be remembered, did some shooting here last year, arrived from Burma by the B. I. steamer "Fultala" yesterday morning, after a similar excursion of about two months, and is staying at the Galle Face Hotel. He is disappointed at the result of his trip, as he had been promised some tigers, but failed to secure any. He, however, managed to "pot" six elephants amongst other game. He is at the present time uncertain of his future movements and has not yet determined whether he will undertake another expedition here.

CHAPTER 3

The Call of the East

1900

*Second trip to Japan – comforts of Yokohama – enquiries for a yacht
– illness – the Japanese character – Tokyo and the Legation – artificial
pearls – an excursion to Miyanoshita and an encounter with Dragon
Cats – a theatre piece – cherry blossom and children – renting a house
at Kobe and hiring servants – Kuniko-san explains women's costume
– early callers*

SUNDAY MARCH 4TH Very cold in Yokohama and an earthquake at 10 a.m.
which was very distinctly felt. I went and inspected a native *fune* [boat] to see if
she could be fitted up as a cruiser-yacht but found her far too dirty and smelly.

In the afternoon Lockyer [captain of the *Rohilla*] and myself went for a walk
and then went up to the Hundred Steps Teahouse. The situation of this
teahouse on the bluff is perfect. It overlooks the town and bay and every ship
can be seen at anchor. It is the teahouse where the song 'O-Yuki-san' was
written and Yuki-san herself served us with tea and cakes, and though getting
an old woman now she still shows signs of good looks. The other little *musumes*
then led us at a trot into a charming little room, made us sit as close as we could

get to the *hibachi* [charcoal
brazier] and warmed our
fingers over it by throwing an
eiderdown quilt over all
our hands (Lockyer's and
mine, and the two *musumes*
rubbing them and squeezing
them as if their, or our,
very lives depended on it.
When this operation was
successfully completed,
O-Yuki-san brought in tea
and cakes and the *musumes*
showed us books with the
signatures of many hundreds
of people who had honoured
their teahouse, amongst them
Prince Henry of Prussia's.

Yokohama

WHITE PLUM

MONDAY MARCH 5TH Today it is almost warm again and the beach is full of shell and weed gatherers. A walk in the morning to the pier and lunched with the Walters where I met the Whiteheads[1]. The lunch was excellent and the best cooking I have had outside Europe. The table and drawing room were decorated with nothing but the yellow willow blossom and pink and white cherry; there were masses of them and very pretty they looked. Later Lockyer and I called on the Ushis and spent quite a merry afternoon.

TUESDAY MARCH 6TH I lunched with Lockyer on the *Rohilla* and then went to an insect and butterfly shop, where the only thing of any note was an immense sea spider whose legs alone were 2 feet 10 inches in length.
    Embarked on the *Rohilla* late for Kobe.

An ornamental stone lantern for holding a nightlight

WEDNESDAY MARCH 7TH Sailed at 4 a.m. Gale from the south, and unpleasant day generally, with no very fine view of Fuji.

THURSDAY MARCH 8TH Snowed this morning at Kobe, by way of change. It is a wonderful country for variety. Landed at 11 a.m. Went to see Mr Drewell, the agent for the *Snowflake* (auxiliary screw, yawl-rigged, 45-ton yacht). Found her too small. I also went to see some native craft but I was asked ridiculous prices, and they were quite uninhabitable as they were. Tea was given us at the Japanese junk broker's.

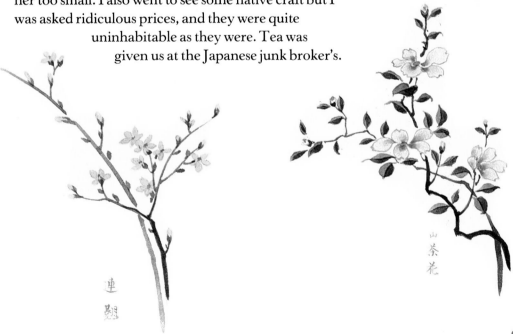

47

FRIDAY MARCH 9TH   Today a tattooer, Nakajima, came down from Kyoto with his son and my day was spent in tattooing[2]. He had placed dragons on the arms

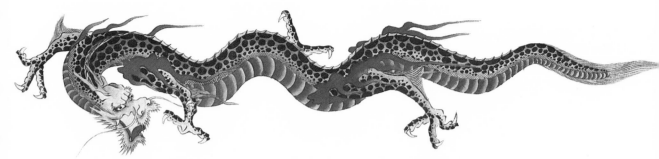

of Prince Henry, the Czar, and no end of others and had, besides, the names of many American and English ladies on whom he had tattooed storks, swallows and cherry and plum blossoms.

SATURDAY MARCH 10TH   Called on Sim[3], Drewell, and Dresser, all people of note in Kobe. The first is a sportsman and the owner of *Snowflake*, and the man who has travelled the Inland Sea more than any other man living. The second is an agent who will enter into negotiations for you, and the third is an agent for houses. Embarked on P.&O. *Rosetta* at 2 p.m. [for Yokohama].

SUNDAY MARCH 11TH   A full gale of wind blowing, high seas, and scud flying in a way I have not often seen before. Fuji was glimpsed at times but not to the best advantage. The sea was abominably rough the whole day and we reached Yokohama at 6.30 p.m. after a decidedly cold and miserable journey.

TUESDAY MARCH 13TH   Very seedy this morning and saw a doctor (the first I have really consulted since leaving England). Poisoned with something – either tattooing or prawns or both.

   I went up later to the Hundred Steps Teahouse with Pye, and O-Ushi-san's daughter was more full of fun and chaff than ever.

WEDNESDAY MARCH 14TH   Wrote letters in the morning. Took my diaries up to the Ushis in the afternoon which interested then immensely and especially Mataketchi, the little son. I am now teaching them English and they are teaching me Japanese with the result that we are all learning something and when O-Hama-san comes in with her full knowledge of both we progress still more.

THURSDAY MARCH 15TH   Still feel ill: gout, cold, fever and blood poisoning. Went to Tamamura (photographer) this morning for my coloured photos of Burma. They were badly done. The moment a Japanese leaves his own country he can neither paint nor think. He is a person, really, of extremely narrow mind, a marvellous ability to copy and to ape others, and also the brain capacity for remembering what he has learned; but of his own accord he can think out very little and invent practically nothing. The art in Japan is today all copied from the old things. No one devises even a new cabinet – everything is very beautiful but nearly all copied.

Isume, my rickshaw coolie's wife, died today. I sent 1½ yen for joss-sticks, which were so well received by the foreman of the hotel rickshaws and the men themselves that they sent their thanks as a body. This is a pleasing side of the Japanese character and, as is often the case, the lower you go in life the better the people.

SUNDAY MARCH 18TH Arrived at Tokyo 10.30 a.m.; very cold and snowing. Lunched with Sir Ernest Satow and found Churchill, the Military Attaché, still there and not yet tired of the country. Sir Ernest was as interesting as ever and, if possible, still more full of flowers and the spoiling of his dog. After lunch called on the First Secretary to the Legation and from there went on to call upon Mr Kentaro Kaneko[4], formerly Minister of Agriculture and, I hope, future Ambassador in London. He was most kind and gave me letters to Kobe, etc. His house was charming, half European and half Japanese – so that, though you took your boots off still you sat on a chair and had your tea put on a table. Some of the works of art in the house were very beautiful.

Street scene

I next went to see Mikimoto[5] of No. 1, Owari-cho 1-chome, Kyobashi-ku. Mikimoto is the first man who has successfully produced pearls or, as they might better be called, half pearls. They are of perfect colour and are solid pearl right through. Naturally, the process is a secret, and the pearls take from four to five years to mature. The shells are more full of lustre than any I have seen elsewhere hence the brilliant 'orient' of the pearls. A pearl as large as a marrowfat pea can be sold for about £2 10s. and would, if set, be sold for £30 in Bond Street.

TUESDAY MARCH 20TH Fine day, left Tokyo [for Yokohama] at 11 a.m. I know no people who stare at one like the Japanese do. I am pretty well accustomed to it from visiting strange and out-of-the-way places, but how a man coming from England via America must feel is a puzzle to me. Groups form round one at the station and stare open mouthed. They appear fairly astonished, there is no intention to be rude, they just look as much to say 'well I'll be . . .!! You are a rum 'un. How I wish my relations were here to see you'. Here again, the Japanese show their love of contrast, no one rivals them in politeness and none in rudeness of this kind which is, I believe, absolutely unintentional.

Oji, the first station outside Tokyo, is at present resplendent with white and pink cherry blossoms, and is well worth looking at. A pretty, smart English girl

Musumes amongst the cherry blossom

was in the train and when she got out here with many charming little Japanese *musumes* I thought she looked very much out of place, reminding me of a bouquet of snowdrops with a scarlet hibiscus in its middle.

WEDNESDAY MARCH 21ST Wet day. A letter arrived from Sir Ernest Satow this morning enclosing one for me in Japanese from Mr Sone[6], the Minister of Agriculture, to all the Governors of the Prefectures in Japan which ought to be extremely useful.

THURSDAY MARCH 29TH Went to meet P.&O.'s *Rohilla* and to my astonishment found my old friend W. H. Grove and his faithful servant Fowler – they were on their way round the world again. Strange to meet one of my old Spitzbergen companions here. There were also two Miss Huttons on board who said they knew me, but I failed to remember them.

I took Doctor Sheppard [ship's doctor on the *Rohilla*] off to the station at once and we started for Miyanoshita[7] by the midday train, reaching Kozu a couple of hours later. Here we got a new electric tram which was excellently arranged, and ran through the villages at a pace which was dangerous in such crowded streets. Crossing the Sakawa River I noticed several men catching fish which evidently ran up from the sea and which, I think, must have been a kind of sea trout.

We made our first stop of consequence (twenty minutes) at Odawara, a long straggling village, where I noticed some very fine Japanese magnolias in full bloom; the trees were covered with large white flowers but not a single leaf showed. The tram stopped close to a large school-feast in a kind of garden. I went to see it – much to the delight of the children, who crowded round and laughed right out at me: my waxed moustaches strike them as most comical. They were all enjoying themselves, eating sweet rice and bean cakes, buying toys that cost half a cent and were worth less, and playing games much after the fashions of our own. Nearly all the boys under ten had running noses which was the only upsetting thing to me, and it nearly made me sick.

Getting back into the tram we started inland through much prettier country and twice crossed a little river which came bubbling down over rocks and boulders and looked so like a trout stream that I got quite a fishing fever. We reached Yumoto (end of tram line) at about 5 p.m. and were here regaled with tea and sweet cakes. Yumoto is a pretty little place with several Japanese hotels and many teahouses. It reminds one of some little place in the Pyrénées, and is frequented in the summer by a Japanese family who, my guide tells me, do nothing but read and eat. It is a curious thing that the Japanese gentleman has so few outdoor pursuits. The middle classes and some of the nobility are very keen about shooting, but fishing and riding seem to be too much for them. From Yumoto one has either to walk or take rickshaws. I walked the whole way (six miles).

At the Fujiya Hotel I found Pye. The hotel is good but the weather intensely cold with a hard frost. The waitresses in the hotel are Japanese, two of whom I think are the prettiest girls I have yet seen. Daintily dressed with huge *obis*, they slide about chattering and laughing to each other; but what a contrast to the sour-visaged European females that were at the hotel. There were three of these latter at one table – veritable ogresses, bespectacled, loose-bloused, curled, broad-waisted women of the type whose sole mission, it seems to me, is to vulgarise the world at large (and do, wherever they go).

The baths at the Fujiya Hotel are delightful. Huge smooth wooden things let into the ground, polished wooden walls, and the hot water comes pouring in direct from the springs. One must add cold water because the spring water is too hot naturally, and thus the real effect of the strong sulphur is weakened.

FRIDAY MARCH 30TH   Up early and pretty cold it was, a hard frost being on the ground with ice whenever there was any damp to freeze. After breakfast I made inquiries about fishing. An old fisherman said the fish hereabouts were nearly all netted and you must go on a two-hour journey up the river for any trout, and even there they are small and difficult to catch. Judging by the flies they use I should say that nearly every fish was a 'pricked' one. The flies reminded me very much of the uncouth, rough ones used by the Basque peasants in the Pyrénées.

I borrowed a rod and fished most carefully with a worm for a couple of hours but never even saw a fish. The stream was one of those which almost made you think you could smell trout.

SATURDAY MARCH 31ST   I was up early but the 'Dragon Cats' left before I did saying, I was told, that 'they were unaccustomed to places where gentlemen talked to the servants'. What a victory for me!! I can assure you I felt more like Jack the Giant Killer than I ever did before and only distressed in mind that I had left these roaming females of repulsive appearance unburied and still at liberty to act as an emetic to anyone as susceptible to contrast as myself.

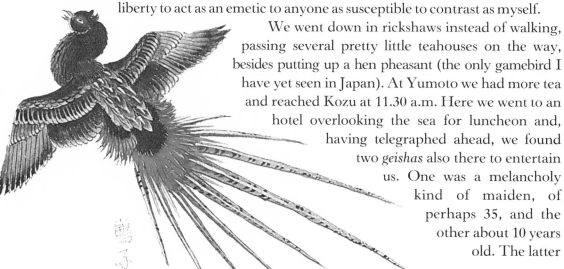

We went down in rickshaws instead of walking, passing several pretty little teahouses on the way, besides putting up a hen pheasant (the only gamebird I have yet seen in Japan). At Yumoto we had more tea and reached Kozu at 11.30 a.m. Here we went to an hotel overlooking the sea for luncheon and, having telegraphed ahead, we found two *geishas* also there to entertain us. One was a melancholy kind of maiden, of perhaps 35, and the other about 10 years old. The latter danced rather well but it was an exceedingly dull entertainment; the elder lady played the sweet *shamisen* with a force which nearly made you jump. The singing was equally harsh, and though I asked her to write her name in my pocket diary as a compliment it is as well, after what I have said, to leave it out of this one.

The bill for the whole entertainment was cheap and as our names were not known it was, as is often usual in Japan, made out to 'Mr Up', which means a gentleman from the upper-level classes – rather curious.

We reached Yokohama at about 6.30 p.m., pleased with our trip, but I, at all events, cannot help thinking that the only thing worth journeying to Miyanoshita for is the pleasure of being waited upon by such charming creatures as the two before mentioned.

SUNDAY APRIL 1ST   A lovely day which was wasted by me in changing hotel rooms. At low tide this morning the beach was a perfect sight: simply thousands of girls and women came to pick up the shellfish and by the time the tide was low there was scarcely a spare yard of beach visible. No gold or diamond rush ever equalled the density with which the people were here packed – grubbing away in the dirty black sand with a kind of small hoe made purposely. They were searching for small oysters and several kinds of clams, and those that found neither, contented themselves by laughing and picking *nori* [seaweed] which floated in moderate abundance. It was quite a pleasure to look at the lively scene, everybody absolutely free from jealousy and bent upon enjoying themselves.

Gathering shellfish

MONDAY APRIL 2ND   In the evening I went to the theatre with Pye and an Australian. The piece itself was uninteresting but I was intrigued by the various curtains drawn across the stage between the acts. They carried the gifts of subscribers who admired the actors and the names of the donors. The contributors are lady admirers of the actors and it might be supposed they would rather their names did not appear, but the Japanese lady in love with an actor sticks at nothing to gain his favour. I saw one such lady occupying a box this evening who had sat through the whole day from 10.30 a.m., when the theatre opens, until 10 p.m. I also saw her smoke eight pipes and pay her bill for food and fire – a *hibachi* is always put in your box. Her day's consumption cost 3 yen 4 sen. We made our exit before the piece was over and left her still there, sitting like a statue waiting for her actor to appear.

THURSDAY APRIL 5TH Spent all morning looking at the cherry blossoms. In the afternoon the Ushis came down to be photographed with me at Suzuki's. Kuniko wore a most enormous *obi* of steel grey with copper- and gold-coloured maple leaves.

In the evening Grove and myself took a walk round the Yoshiwara[8].

Yoshiwara at Yokohama

FRIDAY APRIL 6TH Went to the public park to see the cherries again, and watched the delight of the people looking at them – which is really the most pleasing part of the whole thing. Went up to the Ushis; took my camera as promised to photograph Kuniko. As an illustration of the extraordinary tender-heartedness of the female half of these people, when I cut my thumb, Kuniko-san promptly bellowed.

SATURDAY APRIL 7TH An idea of the ignorance of Japanese tradesmen when dealing with European goods can be obtained from the following amusing incident today. I went into a shop to buy some Bovril; while there I noticed a dozen bottles of brandy on a shelf with new labels dated 1845. I asked how much a bottle cost and was told 3 yen. 'It would be worth about £3 in England,' I told the man, 'if it were really 1845.' 'Ah, but this is the best,' he said, and fishing out another bottle, 'this is 22 yen.' I looked at the bottle and found the date to be 1891. The man was very much upset at the ridiculousness of his own prices, and said that he had never thought about the dates at all!

SUNDAY APRIL 8TH Up early and off to Tokyo by train with Pye. In Ueno Park *musumes* and children were out by the thousand, all in new clothes. The colouring in the dresses of the children was most gorgeous, the smaller the child the more colours and the more dazzling the patterns. Some of the pictures on the silks, like those on old willow-pattern plates were very pretty and entirely baffle description.

Under the trees were hundreds of picnic parties mostly composed of girls, for I noticed that the men leave the latter very much to themselves, and one saw circles of beautifully dressed girls all kneeling inwards with their nice little boxes of food, thoroughly and innocently enjoying themselves; their minds not bent on men or anything else but the pure and simple enjoyment of each other's company, of the cherries, and of the contents of their various boxes.

Here and there circles were formed and games played much in the fashion of some of our own English games, 'kiss in the ring', of course, being absent. Skipping games with boys seemed to afford much amusement. Fencers, boxers, jugglers, all were there just as at home – the fencers dressed in old Japanese warriors' armour, the wrestlers fat and practically naked. All girls from 8 to 14 or thereabouts had paper eye masks which they seemed pleased to walk about in and, curious to say, it did not disfigure their faces in the least. Their little mouths looked sweeter than ever.

> 'Oh for a kiss from the thousand lips
> Which I could have picked today
> But the laws of the country forbade
>   such tricks
> Though you be whosoever you may.'

Gordon Smith and Pye returned to Yokohama later that day and the cold weather prevented further excursions.

WEDNESDAY APRIL 11TH Laid up with cold and rheumatism and sent for a shampooer; the latter in Japan are blind[9] and their shampooing (50 sen an hour) is not vigorous enough to please me. Wrote all day.

THURSDAY APRIL 12TH Weather worse than ever and I feel really seedy again, in addition to which my room is wretchedly cold and I have to use an *hibachi* which nearly suffocates me.

FRIDAY APRIL 13TH Grove left on the C.P.R. [Canadian Pacific Railway] ship and I was too seedy to go and see him off in such weather.

When I went into luncheon I found a man occupying my table who was dining last night with a party of vulgarians, the like of whom I have never seen before, even on a bank holiday at home – drunk, bumptious and noisy. An expostulation with the manager: the latter refused to give me a table to myself. There were no alternatives but to lunch with him or remove myself from the hotel. I did the latter, and on his saying, in his usual familiar manner, 'My dear sir, you can't expect me to give you a table to yourself,' I told him to be good enough to keep his American familiarity to himself and to understand that I considered he had given me cause to be sufficiently annoyed to decry his hotel on every possible opportunity. I removed myself to the Oriental (a quiet place, an *hotel* however, and not an American 'saloon bar'). I deeply regret that I had not gone there from the start for I found the manager civil, the food good and a very superior tone pervaded the whole place.

SATURDAY APRIL 14TH A fine day, thank goodness. Bought a very old cloisonné photograph frame by Motomoto for 15 yen. Lunched at Hudson's bungalow, at the boat club later and Ushis in the evening. Rather interested in

Nobodji [he probably meant *nobinobi*], Kuniko's 14-year-old sister. On asking her, before her mother and family, what her name meant she said 'late, retarded, put off' and that she had been carried before birth for thirteen months. The word *nobodji* she hunted up in a dictionary and that is what it meant. It filled me with pity both for herself and her mother and thus left me no alternative but to give them a place in my diary, more especially because the elder sister, who is the more talkative one (and hence named by me 'O-Chatterbox-san'), confirmed the story.

O-Ushi-san

SUNDAY APRIL 15TH Opened with a violent earthquake, the like of which I never felt before in my life. I was awakened completely from my sleep, both by the rumbling noise and also by the violent, jerky, and peculiar swaying of everything. It lasted about thirty minutes and I was told afterwards it only lacked the final jerk which would have sent everything flying as it did in the big earthquake ten years ago.

Nobodji-san

O-Chatterbox-san

MONDAY APRIL 16TH A busy day packing for a move to Kobe on the *Rosetta*.

TUESDAY APRIL 17TH Dined at the Ushis. Embarked on the *Rosetta* afterwards and sailed at night.

WEDNESDAY APRIL 18TH A lovely morning but deadly passengers. There was a very ignorant German traveller on board who had a poor idea of taste. We were talking about military attachés to foreign countries, when a young American or Canadian asked, 'What are the duties of military attachés?' – quite a natural question. The German jeered and said, 'Ask your military attaché at Pretoria [an allusion to the Boer War] what his duties are.' I enlightened him by telling him that whatever Germany did, England never sent military attachés to unrecognised or dependent states. An argument followed which I am happy to say I got the best of, though some rather strong language had to be used.

THURSDAY APRIL 19TH Arrived at Kobe in drenching rain and was met by Kaito, who had come on by train. Evidently he had found bad friends for his

Kobe settlement

face was bloated and red and I noticed for the first time strong signs of *sake* drinking. He was if possible more stupid than ever.

I went to inspect my house, an exquisite Japanese one belonging to a Mr Yamamoto on whom I called to settle the details of rent, etc. All this conversation was listened to, much to my annoyance, by all the clerks in his office as well as by my rickshaw coolies – an indignity which I resented and showed by saying that I was unaware that Japanese gentlemen confided their

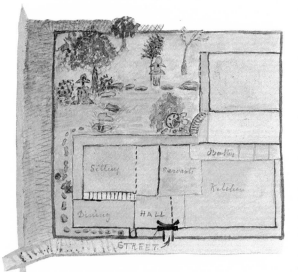

entire business to people in stations of lower rank than themselves and that we did not do so in England because we thought it rather undignified, but that I was delighted at learning the customs of Japan. I was thereupon shown into a private room amidst much blushing and confusion. I concluded one 'treaty' about the house provided that the laws of my own country were followed with regard to duplicating leases, etc. This led to nearly another hour's discussion but I got it and was promised that the lease should be signed in the presence of H.B.M.'s Vice-Consul at 10.45 a.m. the next day.

On getting back to the hotel two remarkable surprises awaited me; one was an utterly unasked-for love letter from O-Sai-san. She had to send me some of my plates and photographs from Yokohama and took it upon herself to write a most romantic letter the like of which I have never read before. It was written in good English and referred to the number of times I had passed her shop (rather, the shop where she was engaged as head person) and complained that

I never noticed her, that she strove all she could when I did go in not to show her attachment for me, and that now I had gone away she felt obliged to write and to send her photo, hoping I should sometimes think of her. It was really most embarassing. I left the letter unanswered, thinking that she must have written many other such letters. However, be that as it may, I never in my life said a single flirtatious word to that girl other than one day, while buying a photo of a Japanese *geisha* to send to England as a copy for a fancy dress and after having been shown four or five very ugly girls in good clothes I said, 'Oh, get a better looking girl than that – one more like yourself for instance.' Nothing more than that was said but the *imnbumi* (love letter) [he may mean *koibumi*] would have been ample to have satisfied the most romantic Lothario in Spain.

O-Sai-san

The second surprise was my meeting Surg. Col. H. R. Smith[10] and his wife from Southsea[11] – two of my oldest and dearest friends. The former I took to a Japanese theatre but we saw nothing of interest. Also, I picked up my old rickshaw coolie No. 25, of last year, or rather he picked me up, which meant much bowing and rejoicing on his part.

FRIDAY APRIL 20TH I signed the agreement for my house in great state at the consulate today, and subsequently called upon the Chief of Police to notify him that I had taken upon myself the responsibility of settling temporarily in native quarters (a previously unheard-of proceeding). The interpreter at the station, Mr K. Horiye, was most useful. Cigars and tea were brought in, as well as many other officials, and I went minutely into everything, occupying five men quite an hour and apropos of absolutely nothing. So much for red tape and officialdom in this country which sooner or later must lead it to ruin. Rules, laws, etc., are all good but the Japanese are decidedly unpractical in putting them into force.

My 42nd birthday today. Dined alone and as usual drank my own health. The only good thing of the day was a Mr Feareon, whom I met in the club. He was stuffed full of interesting information. He told me about the Naruta Passage in the Inland Sea where the Japanese dive for pink coral – also of where women, instead of men, dive for pearl oysters. He told me, too, how the Japanese put a seed pearl of perfect roundness into a sore eye and take it out twenty-four hours later three times the size, having collected bad matter from the eye (this is true).

He also told me of a way whales are killed when found asleep. A man with a long knife and a hook leaves a boat and swims in the direction of the whale's throat, where he fixes himself on with the hook and then he tries to cut the whale's throat. When the whale dives the man hangs on by the hook and travels with it – cases are on record of a man being under water thus for five minutes.

I visited a place where enormous quantities of large Venus's ear-shells from the Luchu [Ryukyu] Islands are on sale for making buttons.

FRIDAY APRIL 21ST Interminable bother about my house. Police regulations vexatious. My cook Gehei an ass. The rain shutters were all out of order owing to an earthquake shock, the curiously constructed Japanese bath (which has a fire under it and in which you feel as if you are being boiled like an egg) leaked; and a good many of the paper slides were burst while bringing in such large things as my leather portmanteaux. Kaito my only interpreting beast was drunk and altogether I had an unpleasant day, relieved, however, by the arrival of the rest of my household by dark: O-Suda-san and Kuniko-san[12]. With these and one more servant I shall be able to keep a Japanese house.

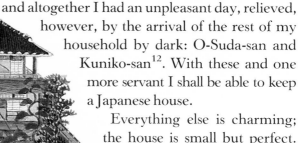

My house in Kobe

Everything else is charming; the house is small but perfect. Upstairs there are two rooms, which I call one, and a servants' room; downstairs there is a dining room, which divides into two, a sitting room (you sit on the floor everywhere), a kitchen with a well in it and a long bamboo pipe that takes the water direct from it to the bath, a larder, another servants' room, and the entrance where you take off your boots. (I have provided grass slippers for my European friends at 2 d. a pair.)

The whole place, were it not for the trouble, is most cosy and comfortable. On two sides there is a ditch 30 or 40 feet deep with unscalable walls. The garden is a gem with its huge stepping stones, stone lanterns, fish ponds, rockeries, an old stunted fir tree, a scarlet maple, and 101 odds and ends going to make a Japanese landscape garden – the perfection of an art. Not a stone could be placed or a tree planted by a European to such an advantage as these people do. My garden, which is 30 by 40 feet, is a park. Your eye can wander over rocks and miniature mountains, places to picnic, and water scenery. Going round the side of my house on a 5-foot-wide path over rocks you come to a goldfish pond, a diminutive temple and a dozen other odds and ends making the whole perfect. The house, excepting its disorder of rain shutters, is the same; the simpleness of the whole is astonishing: a bit of bamboo here and there, a wainscoting, a polished cherry- or maple-wood pillar with the bark on, and all the boards picked out, in the most beautiful grey wavy wood, unpolished and unvarnished. The eye wanders from point to point and rests at each in admiration – there is no *tout ensemble* about anything. The sort of thing you never tire of, and yet it is little else than the inside of an unpapered bandbox.

SATURDAY APRIL 22ND Busy with Japanese carpenters who, though perhaps the best in the world, are the slowest. Gave Kaito a good lecture on drunkenness and its results, and also notice to leave.

For breakfast my cook gave me about thirty octopuses, about an inch long and stuffed with rice; they were rather nice but very indigestible and the sauce spoiled them. I also had some scraped dry fish soaked in the sauce which was pretty to look at but as tough as cotton wool would be to swallow. I had an English luncheon of beef, potatoes, and jam, to make up for it, and dined off a *tai*, stewed rice, a couple of curious mushrooms and several vegetables – bamboo, raw turnip and a green thing like cold cabbage. My cook is an ass.

SUNDAY APRIL 23RD Got rid of Kaito for good and am now minus an interpreter which makes housekeeping somewhat difficult.

Kuniko very busy feeding goldfish in the garden and she also told me about the various garments worn by Japanese women.

First, *assima koto* – that is their overcoat [*koto* is coat but the meaning of *assima* is unclear]. Second, *haori*, a sort of outside *kimono* kept together by a silk tassel called *haori-no-himo*, and then the real *kimono* over which the *obi* is worn. Fourth comes the *juban*, also made like the *kimono* but of gorgeous colours, it takes the place of our petticoat; under the *juban* comes the equivalent of a chemise called *shita juban*. The white stockings [with the big toe in a separate section] are called *tabi* and the wooden shoes, *geta*. And that, with a parasol, completes the Japanese costume. No, I have forgotten the collar, *eri,* worn under the *kimono* and sewn on to the *juban*. Now you have the fully dressed Japanese lady, and I trust the above details may be of use for someone who wishes to dress herself correctly as a Japanese, for I have never yet seen a European able to look anything like a Japanese at any fancy-dress ball I have been to.

WEDNESDAY APRIL 25TH In the morning I went to call upon the Chief of Police, as usual; it is always advisable in Japan to ask their advice. You make friends with them, in as much as that they get to know you. You will have an ample fund of amusement in drawing them out, both for your information and your amusement. They carry out a sort of detailed examination of you which they consider very clever, and you may rely upon it that the more in-apropos questions you answer politely, the more will you be able to get from them. I wanted to know one or two things this morning regarding police laws and taking houses, especially as I was doing so in a Japanese quarter of Kobe known as Gochome, Shimoyamatedori. On arriving at the principal station I met several uniformed policemen and an office boy.

Of course, the Chief of Police was most civil. I was shown at once into his private sitting room, the interpreter, Mr Horiye, was sent for, as well as a messenger to telephone to my district and a police corporal to report upon all the houses surrounding mine. I was offered day and night protection (which I refused) and I was given three cups of tea, cigars and cigarettes. In spite of other pressing police business, I remained for an hour and a half with the Chief and the interpreter and we got on capitally. He told me all the ins and outs of police arrangements in Japan, asked me to apply to him for anything I wanted done or to know.

On arriving home I found a fat-faced girl called Ume (plum blossom), who had come to present herself as a scullery maid or its equivalent called here *gejo* [kitchen maid] or as the Europeans call it an *ama coolie*; she spoke about twenty words of English so I engaged her at 8 yen a month.

In the afternoon Bevington [a P.& O. agent] took me to call on one of the directors of Kobe pier who was very kind in organising a deer drive for me, and, as he was an ardent Japanese sportsman, I expected to see some fun.

THURSDAY APRIL 26TH Went to call this morning on His Excellency the Governor of Kobe and Hyogo, Mr Omori; luckily he spoke French. He gave me a 1 yen licence to shoot deer on the 29th, the last day but one [of the season].

I spent the afternoon at the Club reading old papers and looking at the wisteria both purple and white, the latter new to me and both perfectly lovely. No resemblance can be found in England of the plants here – they are all flower

with very little green until the flower is gone, and the masses are so thick as to render them impossible to see through.

FRIDAY APRIL 27TH I was disturbed this morning by two early callers, 9.30 a.m. is rather an alarming hour for formal calls, but the correct time here is from 9.30–10.30 a.m., the equivalent of the European 3.00 p.m. I had two callers, a Mr Kotsue and Mr Shikata, the latter bringing a beautiful basket of flowers from Mr Kanimatsu, who was too ill to call in person. They were handed to me amidst the peculiar hissings produced by a Japanese when addressing one for the first time and which reminds me of the sound produced by a turtle when he is out of water and annoyed. The flowers were most tastefully arranged in a finely made basket which completely covered a bamboo vase which contained the flowers. They were irises, which were now beginning to come out, and a large red peony.

Kuniko and O-Sama-san brought in a *kakemono* [a scroll painting] today for 2 yen that may be worth 20 or 30. They got it in a pawn shop. It is signed by the artist. It represents the sun and waves and is supposed to be one of a good taste and lucky. The sun means grandeur – there is nothing superior to it and the sight of it is a good omen. Sea waves mean longevity, unchangeableness, everlasting, freshness, and power and strength. The *kakemono* has also an ivory bar and the two golden cords which show it to be a superior work of art.

CHAPTER 4

Setting Sights – Setting Sail

1900

A Japanese deer hunt – the Emperor inspects the fleet – hiring a yacht and preparing for a cruise – sightseeing – old friends from Cheltenham College – first cruise in the Inland Sea: oysters and troublesome natives; fish and fishermen; the rudeness of the Japanese; restricted diet; collecting netsukes; visit to a shrine on Shikoku; Japanese fishing techniques – back to Kobe and a daytrip to Suma

SATURDAY APRIL 28TH   Up early. We met (Bevington, Kojiro and myself) at Hyogo[1] station and started for Himeji, a two-and-a-half hours' railway journey partly along the sea and partly away from it, but never free from things that please the eye. Suma is a charming place on the sea with fine palm trees, and hills running right down to the water, which is as blue and calm as the Mediterranean, and bordered by the most beautiful sand beach. Akashi is a larger place and frequented by many Japanese for sea bathing, but the place I liked the look of was Maika which resembled Suma but had fine pine trees, old and distorted enough to please the eye of the most fastidious of Japanese.

We duly reached Himeji where we found rickshaws waiting for us and also a friend of Mr Kojiro's who was going to shoot with us. After the brief stop at a teahouse we started for the village of East Sakamoto at the foot of the hill called Sashi.

Off Suma Beach

On the way we passed through a wonderfully well-farmed district, the rice and barley looking simply as if they had been grown in an orchid house. This farmland was of a deep emerald green, and here and there a perfectly pink field of a kind of clover gave it an almost 'impossible-to-imagine' kind of beauty.

We got to an inn in time for dinner. The place was very clean and neat, and the people most civil. A charming little garden and a fine old altar to

Drying rice with husk on

Buddha in the kitchen, and here, at last, I have ascertained that the straw rope seen on every *torii*[2] arch or temple is an emblem of cleanliness and purity for it supports rice and barley and prevents the grain from falling into the dirt.

Several local sportsmen of the farmer class came to see us after tiffin [a term, mostly used in India, for a light midday meal]. There was a great talk about the morrow. Guns were looked at and shown. They were principally flint locks of extraordinary construction and great length, some were fired with caps and some were richly inlaid with silver and brass. Great interest was exhibited in my Paradox[3] but more in the bullets.

We were to start at 3 a.m. so as to be at the top of the mountains by 4.30 a.m. 'All right', said I, 'I shall be ready'. As it was then 12.30 a.m. I went to bed, or rather lay on the floor. The men talked and smoked for another hour, and I thought as I lay unable to sleep: I shall be even with you at the getting up time, for how your heads will suffer.

SUNDAY APRIL 29TH As I made up my mind to, I awoke at 2.15 a.m. and rattled up all my friends of last night. There are no swear words in Japanese but the sounds which were made under the *futons* (cotton quilts) meant quite clearly: Oh d—n that fellow; however, I simply stood and shouted 'Out you get, out you get', and the noise obliged them to do so. It was beastly cold, much too early to eat; nevertheless, the Japanese sat down and stuffed themselves with rice; one just smoked – his head preventing him from thinking of anything in the food line. We got off at 3.10 a.m., not bad as these things go. People are not very regular as to time in these things, anywhere.

Our way led straight to Sashiyama and a pretty steep climb it was. The views of the sun rising were simply gorgeous – a crimson ball amidst such scenery, with a cloudless sky and a thin but transparent mist – and well rewarded the climb. We were hurried along and placed in our posts for the first drive.

I was there for an hour before I heard the beaters, and then they began to tumble in from all quarters. No attempts at a line and no more idea of driving deer than they had of ballooning. The less I say about it the better – no attention was paid to wind, noise enough was made to frighten even earthworms to the surface of the ground but the deer, alas, were far too clever. Two shots were fired at does, there was furious excitement but nothing was hit. The second beat was worse and the third, fourth and fifth worse still. I once caught sight of a fawn being pursued by a cur of a dog, and had much more of a mind to shoot the dog than the poor little fawn; but I shot at neither.

I had long since given up all idea of sport and merely considered myself an onlooker at a new kind of performance, otherwise I should have got very angry. Several more does were seen as well as two fine cock pheasants with tails about twice as long as those of ours at home – but they were out of season[4] and had to be allowed to pass.

We lunched at the fine old temple at Shakamirai where I was really interested in the pilgrims coming up the hill to pray: there were young girls with their mothers or elder sisters, and couples of the Darby and Joan description. The latter are most touching to see. Carrying their luggage they go on a four- or five-day pilgrimage travelling from shrine to shrine, sleeping where they may, and looking at all the special features of the shrines at which they pray. At this shrine for instance there is a holy tortoise pond with hundreds of tortoises, many of which can be seen piled up on the islands warming themselves in the sun. Also several heads can be seen sticking out of the water.

There is a lotus pond and perhaps a dozen other things of significance in the Shinto religion that require praying to, or looking at after praying. A big gong is struck and a bell is shaken while you pray. This went on at full swing with never more than ten minutes respite. All this was most interesting, even the veneration with which the pilgrims looked at the tortoise pond. There is a little fountain where the pilgrims wash. Our three mongrel dogs got in bodily.

We went back to the inn, paid our bill, and arrived at Himeji just in time to catch the 7.30 p.m. train back. It was crowded with country people going up to see the Emperor review the fleet; men and women of all sorts and classes – anything but comfortable to travel with, but instructive. An old swell in a *kimono* occupied the room of three; squatting on one seat he had three Japanese refreshment boxes opposite him containing fish, rice, octopus and fungus, and the bottles of his *European* dressing bag were filled with other delicacies. He was really very funny. There was the lover and his *geisha*, youths of all kinds, women with funny little babies, and healthy red-faced *yamas* (nurses) [perhaps he meant *anma* (masseuse) or *ama* (nun)]. One of the latter sat on my tiffin basket, much to the amusement of the rest. Smoke filled the carriage to such an extent that I heard a Japanese baby cry for the first time, and by gad it did cry, poor little thing. The atmosphere was simply foul. The trip ended satisfactorily if unsuccessfully.

MONDAY APRIL 30TH Awoke amidst a salute of guns for the Emperor as he arrived to inspect the fleet. There were about forty ships. Foreign countries were only represented by France and Russia – no encouragement was offered to foreigners to see anything and it was considered doubtful taste of the two powers mentioned to come at all. The illuminations of the fleet at night were good and reminded one of Spithead[5]. The show was a very fine one, the ships smart and trim, and the men on shore of good physique, sober and orderly.

A vile dinner of scraped salt fish, black beans and a mutton chop.

Snowflake

TUESDAY MAY 1ST Nothing of interest. It was a fine day. The fleet broke up and left. I went over *Snowflake*, my future home from May 15th, with her owner, Sim. She would be extremely comfortable if only I could talk to the crew of five men (captain, engineer, two hands, and steward).

Developed photographs with Tamamura[6]; the ass let in too much light and spoiled most of them. I would have given a good deal for the privilege of knocking him down, but here in Japan this means from between three and six months' imprisonment, without the option of a fine.

WEDNESDAY MAY 2ND I engaged a new interpreter today: Egawa, about 4 foot 6 inches high but talks English well and does not appear to be over balanced with conceit.

Egawa

67

FRIDAY MAY 4TH Called on His Excellency Governor Omori but he was too busy to see me so I left a message about the letter I wanted for the Inland Sea cruise. The letter arrived in the evening and now I can do pretty well as I like, I think, and get any assistance I may require from the police.[7] It says 'Mr G.S. is about to leave on a cruise on the Inland Sea in a hired yacht for pleasure. All police officers are instructed to give him any possible help he may require, to afford him every convenience and not to interfere with him in any way whatsoever. By order of the Governor'.

In the afternoon I walked up to my favourite shrine at Myokensama, the shrine of Inari or Fox shrine.[8] It is also a favourite of the pretty *musumes*; it is near for them, the views are lovely. There are teahouses dotted about all over

The kind of girl one meets at the Fox Shrine

the place where you can sit and drink tea and eat sugar-coated beans.

As I continually refer to Shintos and Buddhists I have stuck in two photos – one of each of the priests. There are women priests in both religions and there are girls who dance in the temples and I presume are, in a way, attached to them in much the way that our choir boys are at home.

Shinto priest   *Buddhist priest*

SATURDAY MAY 5TH Very fine morning. I paid an early call on Kanimatsu and was, as usual, regaled with biscuits and tea.

On the way back I went to the Somiyama sulphur baths and on looking into one of the baths, which I thought was the men's, I somewhat disconcerted two ladies who were bathing. Both of them had remarkably good figures.

In the afternoon I went with Egawa to the Nanko shrine to try and pick up some *netsukes*[9] from one of the cheap stalls there.

Heard a touching story at the Club[10] of getting an officer's Japanese sweetheart to India.

TUESDAY MAY 8TH   Sultry and earthquakey today but the latter, I am told, are never very bad here.

Men came to clear the water drains with long bamboos fixed, one socket in the other, until they are about 35 feet long. Egawa went to see a Japanese doctor who gave him, at most, six weeks to live with the result that I shall again have to look for an interpreter.

I engaged an old hag called Ogi-no-Shima in place of Plum Blossom but in the evening she bolted saying later that her husband was ill.

WEDNESDAY MAY 9TH   Sent Egawa to see Miller, the English doctor, who is to give an opinion three days hence.

I called on the Superintendent of Police at Kobe about putting a policeman in the house while I am away. I found him, as is usual with the Japanese police, most courteous and I pleased him by inquiring into his two medals, which are both decorations.

Engaged another servant, in place of the old hag, called Suige San who had a gold tooth right in the front of her upper teeth which gave her an air of importance.

THURSDAY MAY 10TH   In the morning I went to the big Buddha or Daibutsu at Hyogo. It is a disappointing affair, way down in the slums. It is made of bronze, of course, and I was offered the privilege of going inside it but said that I preferred to stay outside where the smells were already known to me – which remark was considered rather irreverent, I fear, in addition to the fact that there was no fee to be got out of me. I saw a model of Fujiyama.

In the afternoon I went over the *Snowflake* with Sim, and from there to the Club, where I met Prendergast[11], an old Cheltenham[12] pal, and also David Pakenham[13] who once practically saved my life in the swimming bath there. I was being half drowned at the bottom, sat upon by a big boy who would not let me up until P– gave him or threatened him with H– if he did not. After nearly thirty years it was a curious meeting. Saw a promising interpreter called Kamoda.

The Daibutsu in Hyogo

FRIDAY MAY 11TH First thing this morning had a letter of refusal from the promising interpreter. Luckily Sim found me another, and Dr Miller pronounces Egawa to be not so bad as the Japanese doctor told him. So I may take both. Two others came: one, an old man whose only recommendation was that he collected shells; the other who said he 'did not mind going'. I also had a visit from the interpreter of the Kobe police on behalf of Superintendent Misaki, who very civilly offered to put a policeman in my house night and day during my absence provided I would feed them. No tips allowed, which, of course, means that presents are.

MONDAY MAY 14TH Busy in the morning provisioning *Snowflake*. In the afternoon took her down as far as Akashi in lovely weather, seeing Suma, the spot I passed when going to Himeji. Steamed the whole way (7 knots) and came back under both steam and sail.

THURSDAY MAY 17TH Up early. A superb day to start anywhere but a still finer one to start a yachting cruise in the Inland Sea.[14] We sailed at 10 a.m. passing, as we left the harbour, H.M.S. *Endimion*, U.S. *Oregon* and French, Italian, and German men-of-war. The owner of *Snowflake* came with me as far as Iwaya, a fishing village on the island of Awaji where we anchored at 1.30 p.m. There is nothing particular about the place except some exceedingly picturesque rocks. There are, of course, no Europeans. I went ashore for a walk and found the people less trouble than usual though boys were a bother – they look upon you as sent entirely for their edification and amusement and are, in themselves, disgusting sights owing to the running of their noses and often their eyes as well.

In the evening an immense junk came down and anchored close to me which, because it came on to blow, filled me with alarm that she would drag her anchors and be down on us.

70

FRIDAY MAY 18TH Up at daybreak; the storm prognosticated last night did not come – it was dead calm when we awoke. No delay was lost in starting for we had kept steam up all night in case of accidents. The coast along Awaji was very pretty and the hundreds of boats with their peculiar sails were quite picturesque in the oily calm.

The entrance and little harbour of Eishima reminds me of a small Nagasaki, only very much prettier. The scenery in this group of islands is beautiful. Having safely anchored, I landed and went to call on the Mayor, Mr Mika, and the police to avoid any trouble and to ask them about any curious fish they knew of. The village numbers only about a thousand – that is, in fact,

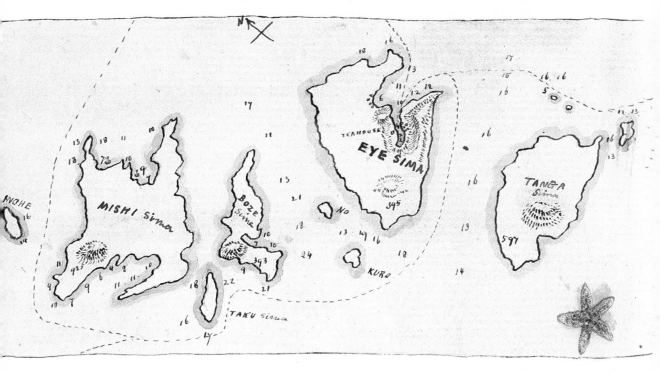

the population of the entire island. The people, who are, of course, quite unaccustomed to seeing European clothes, are a little troublesome but not so bad as many. On the opposite side of the bay is a little teahouse which is within a stone's throw of *Snowflake*, and it has a pond full of sea fish where you may try your luck for a few cents. I found I could buy only one live chicken in the whole place. People won't part with them because they produce their eggs. The women with children in arms walk about with their breasts bare and are not pretty sights.

SATURDAY MAY 19TH Perfect peace and quiet last night in this harbour. Up at daybreak, and went off with Inshie [interpreter] and the skipper. We got many blow out [puffer[15]] fish of two varieties, but it was impossible to photograph them in their blown condition.

When caught, the fish here are left alive in sunken boats and only taken to market as opportunity rises. They are bought from the fishermen by merchants who keep them thus, and all the fishing boats have a compartment through which there is a constant flow of sea water.

Weather looks set for rain. We are at anchor close to the village and about 300 people turned out this morning to see me in my bath and I could hear murmurs of approval that I was tattooed. It is mostly the women who cause this inconvenience, and the only thing to do, I find, after my Burmese experience last year, is to take absolutely no notice of anything. Behave exactly as if you were perfectly alone.

SUNDAY MAY 20TH Gale from the east with heavy squalls and rain. The little harbour had filled in the night with over forty boats and junks, making it unpleasant and, with the swinging on anchors, dangerous. I ordered the top-

mast down, as well as awnings, steam to be got up at once and to get over to Naba. We cleared the crowded harbour in fine style, touching nothing, and as we rounded the point of the island we had a lug sail and jib. It was rough enough to make me sick but did not. The crossing was worse and I was really pleased to get into smooth water.

Naba is a wild place with five old huts and a well, but it is worth landing, for opposite the huts are very small but delicious oysters. Naba Bay is over three miles long.

While getting away from anchorage the dinghy's rope caught around the screw and was broken. I was below at the time and for some time after and, wondering why the screw had stopped. I went up to see. My language became pretty strong when I understood the situation. The screw being temporarily jammed, it never entered the heads of anyone to put down the anchor, in spite of the fact that we were being rapidly blown on to a reef of visible rocks a mere 100 yards away. There you have Japanese yachtsman! The screw was jammed only temporarily, and the anchors had only just been hauled up, so why put them down again?!! That is very much their form of argument in everything. I had one anchor down at once, for had it not been down we would have drifted on to the rocks in ten minutes.

MONDAY MAY 21ST Fearful night with both wind and rain; the only problem, however, is one of my interpreters, Inishie, who is a conceited little ass. He asked me last night if he could go on shore to sleep – because of the weather! It is the first time that I have been able to get at him, but I did, though I fear he did not take it kindly.

TUESDAY MAY 22ND A beautiful day. Sailed at 7 a.m., stopping at a little village of seven cottages, most beautifully situated on the hillside and surrounded by nothing but rocks and bushes with two gigantic fir trees dominating the whole. Very few of the inhabitants had ever seen a European before, and in spite of this they were most respectful. Quite different from those in Naba, who had. They came out to be photographed and were generally polite. From here we steamed across to Mishishima, passing between that

The harbour on Eishima; May 20th 1900

The school and teahouse on Eishima; Snowflake in the background

and Inokeshima. These islands are all particularly barren, rocky and wild, and almost uninhabited. South of Mishishima were many rocks and small islands. There was a fisherman's cottage on one, and four on another.

We steamed into Eishima at sundown in a perfect calm having had what I consider a delightful day, glorious weather and delightful scenery.

WEDNESDAY MAY 23RD Left Eishima at about 8 a.m., took the eastern course between Ei and Tangashima and turned all the way down to Kazura

Karashima (one of a group of four small islands). Got the usual collection but with nothing new except a few bivalve shells. Landed on Kazura Karashima which is a rocky, cavey kind of a place inhabited by no one but it is visited by stone breakers and fishermen. Later we landed on the western side of Mishi in a big bay which, because of its barren wilderness, reminded me much of parts of Spitzbergen. During the day I nearly blew my forefinger off with my Mauser pistol by holding it wrongly.

THURSDAY MAY 24TH
Left Eishima
at 8.30
a.m.

Naba Bay, from Kimishima; Snowflake at anchor

Nishishima – my uninhabited island

for
Sakoshi,
the most pretty
place I have ever
been to in Japan, with a
small island opposite which is
a mass of timber undergrowth and
big trees – the government allows none
to be touched.

Anchored at Naba at 7 p.m. Very hot, fireflies to the fore. Later in the evening I went to the fish sale held in a curious open building right on the water, where fishermen bring their boats right alongside with their live fish – as the turn of each arrives he flings his live and wriggling fish, between rows of excited men, along the stone floor up to the foot of the auctioneer, where a large pine-log fire is lit. There, the fish stop with magical abruptness so dexterously are they handled. In two seconds, before you have time to think, they are sold and in less than another second the purchaser has poleaxed them with a kind of hooked hatchet which he uses as a lifting instrument. You can hook on to anything with this Japanese tomahawk – and I intend to get one.

FRIDAY MAY 25TH Fish selling went on all night for I was up twice and saw the lights and heard the noise. Got the Kobe paper and heard of the Relief of Mafeking[16]. Busy taking in water and collecting bait and got away at 10 a.m. I went straight for Amani Karami Island (a small island off Morotsu Bay) and owing to the inattention of the helmsman very nearly slammed into a sunken reef clearly shown on the chart and of which he was perfectly well aware. I was writing at the time and just happened to look up in time to go full-speed astern. I only mention this to show how utterly unreliable these people are if you take your eyes off them for a moment.

Went back to Naba Bay at sundown and anchored at a little place near the entrance called Tsubone.

SATURDAY MAY 26TH Up early after a miserable night of heat and mosquitos. I landed, took a photo and renewed my acquaintance of the few people. They asked many strange questions but generally pleasant. A few bits of chocolate went a long way with the children and, if you take an interest in them, the people generally like you. We sailed for Shozushima (Cape Kanega) at 10 a.m. and came up to it at about 1 p.m.

The entrance of Shozushima is truly magnificent and might comfortably anchor thirty men-of-war. All round the edges are delightful bays with rocky islands here, and caves there. The coastal strip is fairly well populated and highly cultivated with wheat and beans and rice. In the rear of these magnificent crops the fine hills of wild-looking rocks and forest rise abruptly from the sea. We anchored at the extreme southern end at 6.30 p.m. and made ready for the coming storm. Two of the men went ashore to order their sauce which is made in a celebrated factory here. They brought me back two quarts for 11½ cents.

SUNDAY MAY 27TH Was up twice during the night fearing anchors would drag; it blew and rained as it had never done before but our anchors, buried in mud, never stirred. In the early morning all the crew excepting one went ashore leaving me practically alone. I was very angry and sent two of them off for a two-hour row (as they were so fond of the small boat). They were to take a letter to the mayor of Kasakabemura asking him to send me two boats and nets by

2.30p.m. – the weather permitted of nothing else. It was rather a dictatorial way of doing things, I thought, but I often found it best as it prevents refusal and puzzles the person to whom you give the order. They don't have time to think and it never occurs to them that you would have the cheek to order these things without some extraordinary power. At 2.30 p.m. ten men and two boats were with me, my own two men having had all the rowing they required for some time – in spite of the fascination of the soya sauce factory and its attractions which had been the cause of the trouble.

The most curious fish caught was the *tanago*, a fish of about three to the pound, a light-green cross between freshwater bream and sea perch. It was very fat and at first I thought they were full of sperm. Imagine my surprise when, on handling the fish, I found young ones to the number of fifty-two crawl out as lively as crickets. They came in twos and threes as you pressed the mother and invariably came tail first. In addition I took forty-eight from another. I put the young fish in water where they lived for about half an hour. Had they been put in the sea I believe they would have lived. They were thin, delicate, and beautiful to look at but did not really resemble their mother. They were transparent pink with their veins and bones showing. When brought to light they wriggled and jumped about in the most lively way. I took a photograph of a parent with its young which I doubt will be successful. The

The tanago and her young

fishermen told me that there are two or three other fish which also bear young in the same way. I have never before heard of this, and had I been told, I should have entirely disbelieved it as, no doubt, others will.[17]

TUESDAY MAY 29TH   I got up in a bad humour ordering five boatloads of fishermen, who surrounded the yacht, to clear off at once; I had a quick shot at one boatload who did not, and had them told that I did so because they were the ugliest men I had ever seen (and so they were). Their idiotic and insolent staring is at times most insulting. They think nothing of laughing at you yet they, themselves, have positively diabolically ugly heads and are more vulgarly clad than the naked savages of the tropics. A blue shirt comes only to their hips leaving bare all that is supposed to be covered; it is almost impossible to imagine what low looking beasts they appear.

WEDNESDAY MAY 30TH   The gales in the night necessitated our taking down the topmast and doing the various other unpleasant things a gale necessitates at 1 a.m. in one's nightclothes. It was finer in the morning and I took a long walk, calling on the mayor, who was collecting taxes on boats amongst other things. The villages are clean and the crops simply splendid. The people are civil. At the inn I bought some fine mackerel, six enormous shellfish for the crew and two venerable chicken for myself.

Over the whorehouse was hung a Venus's earshell with its mother-of-pearl side facing inwards. On inquiring about its purpose I was told that it was to keep away rats, etc. On turning the shell I found *tora* (tiger) written in Japanese. It is said that the curiosity of rats is great and that when they turn the shell and see *tora* inside they immediately run.

THURSDAY MAY 31ST   Lovely morning but cold. Left Shozushima at 6 a.m. and steamed at seven knots all day passing hundreds of islands, each better than the last. Before we cleared Shozu we passed H.M.S. Peacock which returned our salute, and I could see an officer, telescope in hand, wondering no doubt who we were. I should very much have liked to have stopped them and borrowed some bread for I am beginning to miss this commodity very considerably. Seaweed soup, fish and an occasional crustacean may be all very well for the slow-combustioned Japanese interior, but I feel mine getting very tired of such diet and there is a sort of craving for meat and bread that I have not felt for a very long time.

A bento, or packed luncheon box

We passed Cone Island at about 9 a.m. It is an island of curious construction – a perfect green cone arising abruptly out of the sea to the height of, I should say, 800 feet and a perfect land- or seamark for ships in these intricate passages. From here to Takamishima and then on down to Tadotsu which is on the island of Shikoku.

Tadotsu is a village well worth visiting: from its temples on the hill the most lovely views can be had and the village itself is unlike any others I have seen. The streets are narrow and quaint with awnings of straw and matting hung across them in order to keep the goods in the shops from being damaged by the sun. The girls struck me as being particularly good-looking and, though poor, well dressed. I fancy there is a large congregation of fifth-rate *geishas* who now, as I write, are giving one of their infernal concerts on a large junk close to where I am anchored. If it lasts much longer it will drive all the fascinations of Japan from me, for a more diabolical and infernal row I have rarely heard. Tom-toms and *sake* and the noise of drunken men are incessant.

With the assistance of the mayor we picked up some cheap *netsukes*, old sword mountings at dirt-cheap prices and four very curious old pieces of stamped leather covered with hieroglyphics and coloured beasts. I had letters from home and a few newspapers which were a godsend.

FRIDAY JUNE 1ST Up early, having had four hours of excellent sleep for, in spite of the noise and the *geishas*, the Japanese have one very good law – there is to be no music or noise after midnight. So well is this law enforced that Europeans in Kobe and Yokohama have to ask permission before they can give a ball lasting beyond that hour.

Konpira, looking towards the first gateway

I took an early train and went to Konpira (eight miles away), passing through country with the finest crops of wheat and barley I ever saw, much resembling an over-prosperous country scene in England. At one of the temples there I was interested in three horses belonging to the priests. Three holy horses, in fact. They were in their own temple with heads facing outwards – like the elephants in the zoological gardens at home. Opposite each is a table with small dishes of cooked beans. As I approached, the three horses went through some extraordinary antics with their heads which I did not, at first, understand. They were taught to bow in a succession of rapid nods of the head much after the fashion of the people themselves. If you are generous you give them each a very small dish of beans – perhaps eight beans in each plate for which I paid two cents. The money, I suppose, buys the beans, and the horses thus get kept for nothing. There are also some gigantic holy fowls which pick up the crumbs and made me feel quite hungry.

Another side temple also interested me; it contained a wooden stallion, a pony with his mouth open, and a bull.

The wooden pony at Konpira

78

I could not get at the full meaning of this, but you are supposed to throw rice into the pony's open mouth. The hotels are splendid and the Toraya, to which I went, can put up 700 people (Japanese, of course). There is a Japanese garden which is out-and-out the most artistically arranged one I have ever seen. I had a pint of sake which astonished the girls for I drink it cold and in a tumbler. The shops and booths contain just what Murray says: prayers, miniature temples and praying beads; there are pawnshops, curiosity shops, booze shops and a hundred and one other things.

I came back to Tadotsu in a carriage containing four charming *geishas* who were most friendly and smoked nearly all my cigarettes.

Found the *Snowflake* ready to leave, and in an hour we were steaming away for Tomo in the Province of Bingo. We passed about thirty islands, large and small, the last a particularly pretty one where the men were nearly black, and not over polite, almost insolent, in fact, when I tried to buy some fish from them. In their boats they appear the wildest looking savages imaginable, stark naked, without straw round their middles. As they haul in their *tai* nets they intone a low monotonous chant which is rather musical for Japan but utterly barbaric. We anchored at Tomo at 8 p.m. and crowds of boats came out to see us. Two contained boys beating large drums – it being the last day of the boys' fête.[18]

Pines on the shore of the Inland Sea

SATURDAY JUNE 2ND Lovely morning; a quiet night but the people of Tomo came off in boatloads at 7 a.m. making a horrible noise around the yacht. On my men telling them to be quiet and clear away, they were hooted and laughed at, so I was told, but I was below shaving at the time. I steamed away at 10 a.m. making first for the large steamer passage south, taking the Bingo Sea and skirting every island on my port side. Later we got amongst crowds of fishing boats, some of them containing twenty men, all naked and of a deep chestnut colour, resembling Red Indians more than anything else. Six or eight boats are required to haul the immense nets: two with twenty men gradually hauling at the ends, the other boats are used to bring round the ends gradually, to form an immense circle about a quarter-of-a-mile in diameter. The nets are the largest by far

I have ever seen, the previous largest being on the Irrawadi River in Burma, but these treble them in size and wide areas of sea are enclosed making one wonder how there are any fish left at all.

Koyoshima harbour

SUNDAY JUNE 3RD As usual up early. Glorious calm morning. Started from Koyoshima at 7.30 a.m. and made straight for Cone Island and, passing south of this, anchored on a fishing bank in eight fathoms, but had no luck. I bought my bait (prawns) from an old woman, naked to her middle, in a boat with her five children. She was a widow and lived in this way with merely an awning or straw over her – a hardy, rough red-skinned old hag whose hide would have made a good saddle. We reached Naba harbour at 7.15 p.m. and anchored for the night at my favourite little place, Tsubone.

TUESDAY JUNE 5TH Cloudy day. Left Nabamura early. Landed on Okino Karamishima for the first time and secured a couple of dozen splendid oysters, and about six quarts of periwinkles. From there we trawled north of Eishima. Anchored for the night at Naba.

WEDNESDAY JUNE 6TH Up at daybreak but it blew half a gale from the east so I made up my mind there was nothing to do in the fishing line and headed for Kobe (fifty-one miles). We had, in fact, a weak wind the whole way and though we started at 7.30 a.m. we only got to Kobe at 6.30 p.m. having had the most uneventful day.

Tsubone, in Naba Bay

SATURDAY JUNE 9TH Blew a gale so I spent the whole day writing letters on the *Snowflake* (Ethel, Mabsens, children, mother, *The Field*, H. Cox and others[19]). After this I called on the old Indus and her officers, and from thence to the Club.

MONDAY JUNE 11TH   Started at 11 a.m. with *Snowflake's* owner. We stopped and landed at Suma and went up to the fashionable Kasuga Hotel (Japanese) and were entertained by the hostess, whom Sim had known since he was 16-years old, now some twenty years ago. She was very hospitable and showed me over the hotel which, in some ways, reminded me very much of an old well-kept English country inn, both owing to its cleanliness and the general pleasure it gave her and the staff to receive you. Even the pretty little servants, of whom there were about two dozen, were all beautifully dressed and their hair absolutely irreproachable. I took three of them out to the fine pine trees to make a [photogenic] foreground and very pretty they looked, sitting on the old tree roots. As usual they made me promise to bring them their photos, and, as usual my moustache caused them much amusement.

On the way back Sim told me there were many deer on Shozushima, also boar and pheasants, and that he had seen them dead there, and that the people lied to me when they said there were none. He told me much about the shooting around Kobe. With a good yacht, Kobe is not at all a bad place to live in, and sport can be had in plenty.

Satisfied with the potential of Kobe as a future home, Gordon Smith makes preparations to return to England via New Guinea and Fiji. On 31 July 1900 he sets sail on board the S.S. Eastern. The summer heat is now over-powering and throughout the next few days the temperatures remain firmly in the 90s. By the time he arrives in Hong Kong he has been without sleep for several nights and is laid low with fever.

Realizing that a cruise through equatorial waters in his condition would be 'madness', Gordon Smith abandons his proposed trip and, through the good offices of the captain of the Eastern, he secures a refund on his ticket. He books a passage back to Japan but must wait several days in Hong Kong for the C.P.R. ship, the Empress of China. While there he develops some particularly virulent and painful boils and during the return journey his health deteriorates badly. When the Empress docks in Kobe, Gordon Smith is fever ridden and can barely walk.

CHAPTER 5

A Home for the Hunter

1900/1901

Sickness and ill-health – a nurse arrives – shooting must go on – the insect seller displays his wares – sport in Osaka – Kuniko-san returns – inspection of a crematory – the old man at the waterfall – choosing a plot – Kuniko-san asks to stay – the Japanese perception of nature – a new signature – death of A.C. Sim – keeping warm with kairos *– New Year and sayonaras – April in England – a new endeavour*

WEDNESDAY AUGUST 15TH   I arrived at Kobe at 8 a.m. and was met on landing by Egawa. On getting through the customs, who were most polite, only charging me 75 cents on twelve pints of champagne, I went straight to bed and sent for Dr Miller who said I was pretty bad and did more lancing.

The hotel unbearably hot, and I can get no attendance. The thermometer reads 90°F. I sent Egawa to see if I could get my old house and succeeded.

THURSDAY AUGUST 16TH   At 2.40 a.m. there was a very serious earthquake which left all the pictures in my room at different angles. I really thought the house was coming down and don't think I should have said d——n if it had; at all events, such was my pain with twenty-seven boils, the excessive heat, and no sleep I never dreamed of getting out of bed.

By midday the thermometer stood at 107°F, but the heat was not nearly so oppressive as at Hong Kong where it had been 93°F. I was in bed all day, the doctor came and cut three new holes in my head, four on my right leg, two on each arm and two on my ribs. Tropical boils are horrible things, and grow deep into the nerves. The cores remind me of cricket bat pegs.

FRIDAY AUGUST 17TH   Still worse, three new boils. I was practically carried into my house from the hotel. No nurse to be got. O-Suige-san, however, did all she could by way of propping me up with pillows, etc., but she is very stupid at thinking of what to do, utterly unreliable at cutting up lint and binding and bandages never can be explained to her. Besides, I have such a loathing for pimples and boils that I should never let anyone but a nurse attend to them. Consequently, I attend upon myself. I talk to myself, too, but it must be remembered that I am absolutely alone, with a Japanese household and I can only lay and think and curse my luck.

SATURDAY AUGUST 18TH A long dull day. I lay in bed watching the butterflies in the garden all day, feeling very sad and miserable.

SUNDAY AUGUST 19TH More monsoon. No one called today. I lay and watched the butterflies again. I had nothing to read. Thermometer 94°F.

MONDAY AUGUST 20TH I felt so much better this morning that I got up, to the astonishment of the doctor who found me with my boots on ready to walk up to the waterfall. He said various things: 'marvellous healing powers; must usually be in remarkable health', etc. He cut open three more 'affairs' on my arm and told me to keep quiet. However, I was not to be done out of the Waterfall Teahouse, and I crawled up there and spent quite a happy hour, talking to O-Tsune-san, the proprietor's daughter, and one of the prettiest girls I have ever seen in Japan.

The Waterfall Teahouse at Kobe

TUESDAY AUGUST 21ST I had many little servants sent to me this morning but they all seemed very nervous and frightened of the foreigner and could not speak a word of English so I sent them away. Several were quite pretty. Their wages ranged from 3 to 10 yen.

WEDNESDAY AUGUST 22ND Down at the club in the afternoon reading the papers. Egawa's wife brought a young lady called Tsuru (stork)-san. She spoke English and professed to be able to nurse, do up bandages and so on. I engaged her at once and she proved herself not only good at this but amusing as well, and quite clever. She took the greatest interest in singing insects, could imitate

O-Tsuru-san, my nurse

most of them and delighted in butterflies. She sewed buttons on my clothes and made herself generally most pleasant. She came of a good old *samurai*[1] family called Takikaoncho [Takenouchi?] of which she was very proud. One of her brothers was at the Relief of Peking[2], another a priest, and the other a good-for-nothing who made her mother's life a misery. I sat and talked to her the whole afternoon, and though not a beauty, she could call the insects and was really entertaining. The temperature was 91°F.

THURSDAY AUGUST 23RD At home all day. O-Tsuru-san was most attentive at bandaging me. I have dispensed with the doctor at 10 yen a day for the 'Stork' at 5 yen a week.

Sheppard arrived, and we had a regular Japanese dinner, some of the things being quite excellent, the rice and eels in soy sauce particularly so. At 85°F it was decidedly cooler though it rained all day.

FRIDAY AUGUST 24TH I taught Tsuru halma[3] today and after three games she could play as well as I could. It may seem that teaching your servant to play halma was an extraordinary thing to do but if you live as an ordinary Japanese there is nothing extraordinary about it. You are as polite to your servants as you are to the upper classes. I walked up to the waterfall in the afternoon to sit in the pool.

SATURDAY AUGUST 25TH Seven new boils today but much smaller. I had to engage a new servant for extra help – the bath and the well necessitating much labour. The new arrival's name was Fuji-san, a good looking little grass widow, her husband having gone to Peking.

O-Tsuru-san with the halma board

85

The new shooting club

SUNDAY AUGUST 26TH Crawled up to the new shooting club to have a try at the gold medal, which I eventually won. There were eighteen shooters, about nine Japanese and nine Europeans. My score was 21 out of a possible 25. The next best score was 17. I was told that in the future I must give three dead birds [as a handicap] to everyone. What extraordinary ideas the Japanese have of shooting. If there is any doubt why a sparrow fell, it is retrieved and carefully examined. If the wound is not in a vital place it is scored against you. It will not be long before they require a board of surgeons to give its opinion. I noted this as a new rule for Hurlingham!!

The European people receive an invitation to the Osaka Gun Club and I also got one to Tokyo.

MONDAY AUGUST 27TH Very hot again but not so damp. In the afternoon I called on Mr Horiye, and in the evening I went to the temple bazaar where the promenading crowd of Japanese always interest me. Not a single European was there, of course – they don't like such shows, beneath their dignity! To me, however, these crowded night bazaars always afford interest. The ordinary people of the town go there. On a fine night they consider it a sort of religious duty to turn out with their lanterns, and to look at the hundreds of stalls of cheap things. The stalls are set up by folks too poor to have a shop but who can afford to pay 10 or 15 cents a night for the few yards of space which the display of their goods necessitates.

On this particular evening what interested me most was a *suzu mushi* (singing insect) stall in full swing. The *kutsuwa mushi* was making enough noise to drown the voices of all the rest and those of the people surrounding the stall. I promptly made arrangements with the owner of the stall to bring the whole thing up to my house on the following day.

O-Fuji-san asking Nakashima how much his insects cost

TUESDAY AUGUST 28TH K. Nakashima, the insect man, came to the house at 10 a.m. and, as he brought his entire stall, afforded me much interest. At the bottom is a cupboard where the insects themselves are kept in jars out of sight, only a cage of noisy *kutsuwas* are visible on top of the whole show. Over the cupboard there is a place to keep spare cages, repairing tools, etc., and above this cages of varying prices, sizes and shapes, and above this again a white-painted panel on which the hieroglyphics represent five of the favourite insects. Behind this is a lamp, and the roof is of black-and-white paper squares.

The prices of the common cages vary considerably: if they are wanted for really small insects such as *kusa hibari* they are more expensive because they require very fine workmanship – 11½ yen, say, for the small square kind, which is the most common. The same cage for a *suzu mushi*, which is larger, would only cost 70 cents.

I myself bought *matsu mushi, kutsuma mushi, kusa hibari, enma korogi, kin habari, kirigirisu*, and a sword-tailed green grasshopper called *monin*. He sang, I found later, between 9 and 10 p.m. a rather quiet, mournful little song, about life or love. I found no traces of this insect in any book I had. In fact, I know of no English books on the subject, only a chapter or two in Lafcadio Hearn's book[4], which is well worth reading.

A singing toad I refused to buy at 4 yen. I thought he might not sing. He did not look like it.

FRIDAY SEPTEMBER 7TH A lovely day so I took a long walk up to the waterfall, where I sat and talked to Tsune-san for some time, and then went on to the lake above. The views were lovely, as were the wild flowers of which, it appears to me, there are more kinds than in any non-tropical country I have ever seen. Butterflies appear to be finishing up their season.

I felt better today, and believe this is due to the many lily roots I have been eating lately. The temperature was 84°F both day and night. Kuniko arrived at last [presumably from Yokohama].

87

SUNDAY SEPTEMBER 9TH Up all night with diarrhoea but I went to the Osaka Gun Club. A vile brass band played all the time. On arrival you pay 2½ yen which includes three tickets: one for entrance to the teahouse, one for a cake, and the other one for a bath.

Some of the costumes and attitudes of the shooters were remarkable. One man shot in white tights with elastic-sided boots, a frock coat of antique pattern, a broad-brimmed straw hat, and thick brown woollen gloves.

Osaka, through which we passed in a rickshaw, is an immense place – the Manchester of Japan – cut up by canals everywhere. They are well arranged and at right angles to each other with the result that things can be taken to or from the merchants' and manufacturers' doors with great facility. I passed through one street which was apparently employed exclusively in the edible seaweed trade. The smell was quite a delicious contrast to the surroundings. I noticed innumerable good-looking girls, some beauties.

WEDNESDAY SEPTEMBER 12TH Typhoon announced. I feel worse. The doctor orders me to bed for a week, or else I am to have dysentry – well, if I must have it, so be it.

One of my insects (the female) ate her husband this morning. This is the second she has eaten. I let her out in consequence as it offended me looking at the beast that reminded me so much of married life in England.

THURSDAY SEPTEMBER 13TH At home all day; 85°F again. I gave lessons in English and took Japanese ones from K[uniko].

FRIDAY SEPTEMBER 14TH Still ill. I could not operate on my leg so I sent for the doctor who said I am not far from blood poisoning. Altogether I am in a damnable state, the whole of it coming on from the minute I boarded the S.S. *Eastern* and went to Hong Kong.

Home all day. Kuniko a blessing – she plays draughts, halma, and double dummy and never tires of doing what I like. It seems that her greatest pleasure is to please.

SATURDAY SEPTEMBER 15TH Still the same, in bed all day, too weak to move, leg very painful.

SUNDAY SEPTEMBER 16TH I had a ring with some writing on it as a present today from K. A Japanese ring of 24-carat gold, a very soft and simple piece of gold just turned over and not joined. I shot at Tenno [the Imperial Shooting Club] and came second.

MONDAY SEPTEMBER 17TH Did nothing but walk to waterfall.

TUESDAY SEPTEMBER 18TH In bed again today; I really see no end to my troubles this time.

FRIDAY SEPTEMBER 21ST 'When in doubt play trumps.' I feel so doubtful about myself that I went up the hills to the crematory to see how it worked, and looked for a personal spot. The morning was spent with the solitary man who does the burning. He and his wife are a half-clad, yellow-bodied, ghoulish-looking pair. The whole thing is primitively done: a few pine logs in an open oven to make the bodies burn. They are forced into a small cask by the usual method of breaking the knees, and so my friend burned from eight to sixteen a night. Ashes are not often taken away, but if a tooth or a bit of bone remains it is buried in about a square foot of ground, and some three weeks later the little grave is decorated.

MONDAY SEPTEMBER 24TH In bed all day with gastritis. Kuniko was rather pleased as she says she can now nurse me.

The human ash pit is under the shed that looks like a cucumber frame

Father, mother and son with human toasting forks

Some desultory outings are made during the next few days while Gordon Smith's illness continues.

THURSDAY OCTOBER 4TH In bed all day and was well nursed by Kuniko. I lost a good deal of blood.

MONDAY OCTOBER 8TH I was ill again, and went up to the cemetery and took a photo of the father, mother and son who spend their nights doing this gruesome business. I saw many queer graves, one with a pair of crutches on it – the man buried there had been lame. Over many were *sake* cups and bottles, denoting their love of this wine. It is a pretty and interesting cemetery, and I chose a place for myself, should I die here, which does not seem at all improbable.

SATURDAY OCTOBER 13TH   I had a long interview with Horiye and Kuniko-san, who wished never to return to Yokohama. Mrs Tamamura [the photographer's wife] came to tea in the afternoon.

SUNDAY OCTOBER 14TH   In the morning I went up to the waterfall. On the way there I could not help admiring the ideas of some Japanese boys in front of me. They were hunting for autumn leaves, not to pick, but merely to look at. They stopped long to admire a tree turning pink, and evidently discussed its beauties amongst themselves. A view down the gorge next impressed them, and one boy was particularly interested in the outlines of the rough bark of the large pine trees, outlines which appeared to him either artistic or fantastic in shape. Here, in Japan, it is the *fantastic* which is artistic. Dull as their power of vision is, they see what, to us, is almost impossible.

A stone of which you take no notice will catch the Japanese eye at once; it will be taken home and, with a little sand on a dish, it will be transformed into a rocky sea beach and, what is more, you will see it then yourself. But, hunt as you may along riverbeds for such a stone, *you* will never pick one up.

MONDAY OCTOBER 15TH   Off to Osaka early to pay official calls on the Governor, the Chief of Police and others at the Kencho [prefecture office) of that district, the object being to obtain permission to shoot in a forbidden place near there. All were most polite, and I was eventually sent off to the head of the Dock and Canal Company where, after half an hour's diligent telephoning, the Governor's permission was granted. It is the first time such permission has ever been given, the British Vice-consul having been refused.

As I have for some time found *kimonos* infinitely more comfortable and less expensive to wear while in a Japanese house, I have pasted in a photo of one of my most gorgeous costumes. It cost 7s. 6d. and, with blue crows on white cotton, it is enough to startle anyone.

TUESDAY OCTOBER 16TH   The Japanese Crown Prince went through Kobe this morning. All the people were asked, as usual, not to look at his train from above the level of the railway line. For modernised Japan this appears to be rather absurd, for anyone might do so quite unintentionally and, not knowing how offensive an act he was committing, be set upon by the mob and done to death.

WEDNESDAY OCTOBER 24TH I set off for Osaka early. There were very few snipe about and all I could get were fifteen, plus one duck, one teal, one rail. A poacher fishing was fool enough to bring two dogs which ran over the whole ground. I was so angry I nearly shot them both, but one has to be careful what one does in this country.

FRIDAY OCTOBER 26TH I still have lumbago. The Fiji mail arrived in full but it was very disappointing. I had a letter from Ernest Lawrence[5], dated Bulawayo May 7th. Letters from England had dates up to June 11th so many may be lost.

SATURDAY OCTOBER 27TH Took Tomiya into the mountains to try to feed the copper pheasants. I carried 15 lb of raisins, he carried 25 lb. I see no reason why they should not be drawn to baited spots – the cover is simply too thick to get through more than a few hundred yards; besides which there are precipitous sides to the mountains, earthquake cracks and holes, everywhere covered with a dense mass of grass and stuff 3 feet high, and over all there is scrub, creepers and thorns (simply damnable).

WEDNESDAY OCTOBER 31ST I went up to my pheasant baits but nothing was touched. It was very hot in the mountains.

THURSDAY NOVEMBER 1ST I had a walk with Egawa in Hyogo and bought some curious Japanese pictures of the war or rebellion in China.[6] Japan is in each shown as the leader – England and America coming next. The other countries *nowhere* – not even represented in the pictures.

SATURDAY NOVEMBER 3RD Tenshi's birthday.[7]
Kobe was all flags, and even I have borrowed
two Japanese flags to hang out and please the natives.
There was no noise or drink, the only
drunken man I saw was a European.
The streets were crowded and those
who could had a new *obi* or dress.
My servants' attire quite startled me:
Kuniko had a remarkably pretty
dress of a coarse grey silk and a black
obi with a bow more like a dragonfly's
wing than anything else and a collar
with autumn leaves on it.

The beaters

TUESDAY NOVEMBER 13TH I took the
9.30 train to Nishinomiya, where I
hoped to get some woodcock but
found none. The beaters were no use
so I had a real row with them and made them go full lick to Itami, across
country. They did this well and in splendid time, taking only thirty-five
minutes for nearly four miles. We lunched in a very pretty place, alongside a
deep, clear pool which was as blue as turquoise. The blue sky and light-green
bamboos on each side of the pool made quite a contrast and there were a
few trees, now red with autumn leaves, hanging over the water.

WEDNESDAY NOVEMBER 14TH I read the papers in the morning and played bowls
in the afternoon. I had some of a new kind of lily roots for dinner; they were
very excellent. It is a plant which the Japanese have nearly as much respect for
as they have for the bamboo.

    My stamp, or Japanese signature, arrived today and here it is. The small one

is of my initials and the large one is my
name. Both the Chinese and Japanese
use these seals, stamps or signatures –
even in their banking affairs. Forgery
is said to be nearly impossible unless
you lose your stamp. They are officially
registered by the government and any forgery or use of another person's mark
is heavily punished, the minimum, I believe, being two years.

THURSDAY NOVEMBER 15TH Off again to Itami by the early train. The train at
Kanzaki Junction was full of people, all bent on picnics and orange gathering. I
saw no less than five picnics even on my own shooting grounds, and one party
of men joined me at my lunch to see, I believe, how I eat with a knife and fork.
They were intensely interested in that as well as in my patent frying pan, which
was full of bacon, rice, and lily bulbs.

Egawa cooking lunch

FRIDAY NOVEMBER 16TH I went to the club to read the papers. A notice had been issued saying that a typhoon is approaching – probably the same one as at Hong Kong.

SATURDAY NOVEMBER 17TH At 2 p.m. the typhoon arrived. It blew down about 150 houses, all the telegraph poles, and ships were swept ashore. My own experiences were at home, where I remained all day, expecting everything to collapse but beyond losing about twenty roof tiles and having a number of leaks, we survived. We shut all the shutters and lit the lamps to turn night into day. Do I like typhoons? No, I don't, though I like excitement.

The next few days are spent on uneventful shooting expeditions.

THURSDAY NOVEMBER 22ND I bought some furniture to send home. The truly Japanese furniture is very simple and beautiful; I also bought a lacquered food box. In the afternoon I played bowls with Dimock and during the game a woodcock flew right over my head – bang in the middle of the town!

WEDNESDAY NOVEMBER 28TH A great gloom was cast over Kobe this morning when it became known that Alexander Cameron Sim was dead. The loss of such a man was felt equally by both Europeans and Japanese. Typhoid fever and eating oysters ten days ago at Osaka was the cause. Seeing his crew on the *Snowflake* and the old boat herself made me feel quite sad.

SELTZER WATER
MINERAL WATER
MANUFACTORY
No. 18.

MEDICAL HALL KOBE, JAPAN.

A.C.SIM

FRIDAY NOVEMBER 30TH   The funeral of poor old Sim was quite an impressive affair. An Austrian warship lent her band and all the Japanese authorities, from His Excellency the Governor down, attended the ceremony. Pigeons were released from a cage at the graveside and many other Japanese customs carried out. Sim was cremated and I heard that most of his ashes have been sent to Scotland, only a small amount being buried here.

The weather becomes brighter and Gordon Smith fills most of his days with shooting around Akasaki and Itami, often with his friend Kronenberg.

WEDNESDAY DECEMBER 12TH   I went shopping in the morning and tried everywhere to buy a few plain pots for stones and rocks. No demand for them from Europeans, I was told, unless they were decorated with patterns. (Beastly looking things they were, too.) Ten years more of European requirements will kill all the Japanese ideas of simplicity, and ruin them as an artistic people. I had to send to the slums of Hyogo to find the things I wanted.

I bought some of the small finger warmers, *kairo* as they call them. They are little copper cases, the size and shape of a cigarette case, in which you put a lighted charcoal cigar that burns for two hours. They are really most ingenious and useful little things which I should never have known of had it not been that on one of the cold day's shooting I ordered Egawa to get into shelter. 'Never mind, sir,' he said, 'I got two fire in back', and sure enough he had and felt as warm and as comfortable, no doubt, as he might have done in a house.

THURSDAY DECEMBER 13TH   Today I went to Itami with permission from the Chief of Police that I might sleep, if I chose, at my favourite teahouse, in spite of its having no licence [for overnight guests]. I thought this was extremely civil. Moreover, he telephoned the Itami police and asked them to help me in anything I might need. The shooting was about the same as usual but I lost four snipe, which I could not find. The island, 'Egawa's Island' I call it, produced two woodcock and four quail. It is a wonderful little spot and is always sure to produce something. The peasants about Itami are I find, the most polite I meet, and altogether it is quite my favourite place to visit.

When we got back to the teahouse we found a hot bath, towels, and dinner all waiting for us. I made Egawa dine with me, of course. In fact, what I should do without him I don't know. He is as well and strong now as he was weak and delicate when he came to me. He attributes his recovery entirely to the life he leads with me, and is as keen about the shooting as I am; also he gets quite as excited as I do when the beating is badly done. He swears, for a Japanese, splendidly, and there is no doubt that it does the men good to be sworn at. *Baka* (fool), I understood was the worst thing you could call a man. I know this to be untrue for Egawa gets fifty points worse than that when I tell him to. It is just like setting a terrier at a cat when I put him on beaters who are beating a good place badly. Egawa I look upon as both my cook and companion, whether yachting or shooting. I shall be very sorry to return to Japan and find him dead.

SHINTO FUNERAL.

BUDDHIST FUNERAL.

During the intervening days the shooting season continues to dominate Gordon Smith's life, but he does find time for some photography.

TUESDAY DECEMBER 25TH I went to market with Egawa and bought some fish. Later I played battledore and shuttlecock with K. for about an hour and lunched with the Pakenhams. I dined at home. How I hate this season.

TUESDAY JANUARY 1ST, 1901 Don't forget to say *Omedetashi* [A Happy New Year] to everyone you see. It was said to me, almost before I awoke, by two servants who came into my room with a cup of *fukucha* which I had to drink at once. It is a sort of weak soup with radish stems tied into the same bow that, in Japan, is almost the emblem of a gift. There were also strips of seaweed tied in the same way and three preserved plum blossoms. The contents of the cup were certainly prettier to look at than they were nourishing or agreeable to the palate.

Before my customary egg-and-fish breakfast, I was given a cup of *toso* [a spiced *sake* drunk to celebrate the New Year] and then a lacquered case containing quite five-and-twenty different kinds of delicacies, none of which I liked at all.

After breakfast a couple of men came and played an old-fashioned string instrument and a small drum, and wished me *banzai* [good luck, and a life of 10,000 years], for which I had to pay 50 cents. Shortly after this my rickshawmen called. Then the young friends of the servants and the neighbours called. It was these visits that really interested me. There were thirteen children callers, all dressed in new clothes, gorgeous in colour, and each group bowing themselves insane, saying *Omedetashi* as if they had been old ladies accustomed to court manners all their lives. Egawa's

O-Sei-san and O-Suzu-san in calling costume

96

children came with the rest, but the best-dressed two were my neighbour's children, O-Sei-san and O-Suzu-san – two dear little sisters, each carrying a little bag in case they were to be given a present. Five or ten cents is quite enough to give, but I had entirely different tactics and gave them chocolate creams wrapped in silver paper.

After the visits are over, all the men go to the temples. The women do this on January 2nd, after the men have been. After praying you may continue to drink sake, and by the evening fifty per cent or more of the men are drunk. This virtually finishes the New Year's celebrations.

MONDAY JANUARY 7TH Arranging many things about leaving [for England].

TUESDAY JANUARY 8TH I took some men and beat the mountains in the rear of the waterfall up to Futatabisan. Beating on the hills was nearly impossible, especially with town men.

WEDNESDAY JANUARY 9TH Packing.

FRIDAY JANUARY 11TH The break-up of my household, amidst general regrets on all sides. I, myself, candidly confess that I have never been more contented than I have here. One can slide through one's life here, without trouble, I feel sure. The *sayonaras*

My two smallest servants, Egawa and O-Miyo-san

to the servants were quite sad, and the contrast and vulgarity of the Oriental Hotel got on my nerves before I had finished my first dinner there.

I wrote farewell letters to Governor and Chief of Police and made out my game list:

289 snipe, 63 woodcock, 48 quail, 5 pheasants, 4 pigeons, 2 hares, 6 rails, 12 plovers, 6 ducks, 2 teal, 10 bitterns, 5 hawks and owls, 7 various. In addition I lost, for want of a dog: 129 snipe, 5 woodcock, 7 quail.

Gordon Smith leaves Japan in January 1901. As his ship clears the harbour at Hong Kong he hears the guns signalling the death of Queen Victoria. He stops off in Burma for what proves to be his most exciting and dangerous elephant hunt and, though he gets his 'tusker', he incurs injuries which will trouble him for the rest of his life.
Reaching England in April, he finds the contrast with the East thoroughly distasteful: the people, the climate and culture have all become unpalatable.

On April 25th of the present year [1901] I landed in Southampton and found our customs officers at that port still upholding their reputation for incivility. Our dock-landing arrangements are as bad as ever, and I thoroughly thanked God when I and all my luggage were safely on a train bound for Portsmouth. Returning to one's own country as often as I do, it is curious to find much to compare unfavourably. Apart from family ties and things of that sort, there are so many *absurdities, snobberies and official laws* here that it positively renders one's country ridiculous in one's own eyes. Apart from seeing my family and some other people, all I look forward to in England are railway comforts, the commonsense shown among railway servants, finnan haddies for breakfast, and the pleasing appearance in the youth of the land. Apart from these things and sport, or so-called sport, there is very little pleasure to be derived from arriving home.

Having returned from the Far East after nearly two years absence, I was nearly overcome by the utter ignorance of my countrymen of the whole Far Eastern situation – political or otherwise. They had almost ceased to look upon the Boer War as worth talking about;

Photo sent to me by my friend Arnold White

the still larger, almost daily deathrolls remained unperused; they were sick of it. Some two or three days after my return, I wrote to my friend Arnold White[8], more or less expressing these sentiments. His answer was so characteristic and so true that I now write an epitome of his letter.

2 Windmill Hill, Hampstead.
April 30th.

My Dear GS. We shall be delighted to lunch with you. Don't say the British nation is ignorant on the Eastern question, say rather, they are totally and absolutely ignorant of every single topic except racing and football!!!'

That is how I find them – devoid of life's interests in any way. And that is the one thing that has decided me to leave the country again, as soon as possible, for scenes where, at all events, the mind is fed. To this end I busied myself with the British Museum[9] authorities, whom I knew wanted fish from inland Korea. They were kind enough to make me one of their collectors, and gave me a letter to this effect. They also supplied all the necessary material for collecting, and sent it to Japan. Their letter ran as follows:

'This is to certify that Mr R. Gordon Smith of 84 Jermyn Street [a private hotel], Piccadilly, London, has undertaken, at the request of the officers of the British Museum of Natural History, to collect natural history specimens for the British National Collections, in connection with a scientific expedition which he is making in Japan, Korea, and Russian Siberia. He is desirous of thoroughly exploring the Inland Sea of Japan in order to collect specimens of the fishes or other fauna of the sea, for which purpose he wishes to dredge. Amongst other animals, it is hoped he will secure a specimen of the long-haired tiger, a skull of which would be a valuable acquisition for the British Museum Collection.

'The spirit which has been supplied to Mr R. Gordon Smith by the British Museum is wanted for the preservation of the specimens which he is sending to London. Any facilities which may be afforded to Mr Gordon Smith in the prosecution of his researches, and in furtherance of his desire to benefit the British Museum would be gratefully appreciated by the authorities of the institution.

C. Ray Lankester, Director, British Museum, 19 July 1901.'

Always a sportsman and a countryman, Gordon Smith's everyday interests are leading him into the pursuit of a new role: that of the naturalist. The following winter he spends several cold and dreary weeks amongst Korean villagers in a vain attempt to find a long-haired tiger. Despite the native testamonies, he finds no sign of one and he must be satisfied with catching little more than bronchitis.

The spring of 1902 sees him hiring the yacht Tommy Atkins *and trawling extensively in the Inland Sea. He collects many specimens of fish and small mammals and consigns them to the containers provided by the British Museum. Amongst his haul is a small stripey dab which proves to be new to science and is named after him:* Synaptura smithii. *He finds this a tremendous encouragement for his work.*

Autumn 1902 is taken up with shooting and in the spring of 1903 he returns to England by way of Penang and Colombo. Back in Japan in the autumn of that year, the noises of war are beginning to be heard. Russia and Japan have long held conflicting interests in Korea. After the Boxer Rebellion, the Russians took the opportunity to extend their influence in Manchuria. Meanwhile, the 1902 Japanese Alliance with Britain is threatened by Britain's entente with France who, in her turn, is allied with Russia. If war comes, will Britain honour her commitment to Japan? As an Englishman living in Japan, this thought is uppermost in RGS's mind as he goes about his activities in Kobe.

CHAPTER 6

The Edge of War

1903/1904

Rumours of war – lunching on dojos – head-dresses of the Japanese girls – to Tokyo for permits to dredge in the Inland Sea: an audience with the Minister of Finance – Professor Ijima at the Imperial University – a carriage accident – two new kakemonos – an incident in Theatre Street – gardening in Kobe – a temple in Kyoto – idle gossip – a fine teahouse – Japanese military preparations – painting fish – the first naval action and a declaration of war

SATURDAY OCTOBER 10TH There are thousands of war rumours and the most creditable way of dealing with them is, like the Japanese people, to pay no attention. The long and short of the whole thing is that the situation is most precarious. The Japanese recognise fully the danger, and are calm and confident in the wisdom of their Government. Even the Jingoists, who want immediate war, behave quietly presenting petitions to the Government, instead of howling and creating the scenes which we do. There are no 'pro-Boers' [enemy sympathisers] in Japan.

SUNDAY OCTOBER 11TH A fine day. Lunched off *dojos*, done in several ways, at an eating house especially set aside for that purpose, which is not in the least like anything else. My lunch was partaken of in a beautiful clean Japanese teahouse, with stone and moss rockeries, stone lanterns, bronze lanterns, and stunted pine trees, not in the least, however, like the romantically situated *dojo* house with which my painter's mind was evidently associated when he painted his idea of what a *dojo* eating house ought to be. The four *dojos* are, however, true enough to life, especially the two which have come up to take air (a peculiar trick which these mud loach have). There are poems, and songs to the *dojo*, I am told, much as there are to *suzu mushis* but so far no one has been able to tell me one. Amongst the various ways of cooking them, *dojo nabe* is the best. The fish is boned and then thrown into a pan full of beaten egg and onion, fried for a minute until the egg is set and then eaten with soy sauce.

The top ridge of the thatched roof on the house is planted with lilies. These often portend fortune or otherwise, depending on their annual flowering.

MONDAY OCTOBER 12TH   The mail and news arrives but there is little of interest except that about the children. Knowledge of the situation in the Far East, our interests and duties to Japan as allies seems to be almost unrecognised by all our papers except the *Globe*[1] for which I have always had admiration.

WEDNESDAY OCTOBER 14TH   Took dogs to mountains for exercise, but sent Carlo to a doctor who recommends tonic and quiet. He sulked in consequence and would not look at me all day. In the afternoon I was much amused in the town by the procession of a quack dentist who marched solemnly through the streets preceded by a drum and brass band, and two flag bearers – the latter speaking of the wonderful rapidity with which the dentist could pull teeth. I followed until he was called into the house of a vegetable seller, whose tooth he pulled out in a couple of minutes surrounded by a gaping but sympathetic crowd. The band played as the tooth came out. The dentist bowed as he picked up his ten cent fee, and stalked after his band with an air of gravity which can only be assumed by a Japanese who is impressed with his own importance and wishes to impress others.

THURSDAY OCTOBER 15TH   The news today looks better owing to Baron Hayashi (Minister in London) having said that he knew of no danger which might precipitate his country into war with Russia. Poor Baron Hayashi, he has my deep sympathies ever since I met him at the Navy League dinner. He is persecuted with dinners, speeches referring to the strength of our alliance, of English admiration and sympathy for Japan and by newspaper representatives. What is he to say? What is he to think of this almost Judas betrayal of his country, since our cowardly and suddenly grovelling friendship for France? The more one thinks, the worse our appearance in the present political situation.

FRIDAY OCTOBER 16TH   Laid low today by a sudden attack of fever and ague which came on suddenly and with more violence than I ever had it before. No control over teeth or limbs which shook and chattered like those of a frightened ape. Temperature 103°F. Dry skin burning like fire and my head quite incapable of thinking straight. My men catch a badger in the graveyard and bring him to me. Got out of bed to make a cage for him out of a wine case and put him away in a shed.

SATURDAY OCTOBER 17TH   Badger escaped in night having eaten a hole through the wine case. Fever still on but not so bad (temperature 101°F). In bed all day.

SUNDAY OCTOBER 18TH   Very weak but better. I spent the day in the garden.

SUNDAY OCTOBER 25TH On going down to Motomachi (the main street) it occurred to me that I have never said in all my writing a word about the small cheap shops where things are made for girls' hair: flowers, toothpicks, coloured paper for tying their hair – an endless profusion of coloured things which dazzle the eye and make one extremely curious to know what they are all for. As Pierre Loti says 'a Japanese will almost carve a flower or pattern on the inside of a keyhole on the chance that somebody may look through it' or words to that effect. It is true: a Japanese will take trouble to decorate that which requires no decoration, and often leave that which does, undecorated. This collection cost a little less than a penny: two whalebone hair decorations, five toothpicks, the papers used by children for tying in their hair. Notice the care with which the toothpicks are bound with silk. *Why*? With me, it is always *why* with these people. The unnecessary care they take in the minute things of absolutely no value, and practically of no use, must be a loss to a nation – so much energy ill expended.

MONDAY OCTOBER 26TH War news decidedly bad today. Telegraphs from the speculative and lying Europe declare that Lloyds [insurance brokers] have doubled their premiums on Japanese ships coming out. I decided to go to Tokyo by the *Empress of China* on 28th [to obtain permission for a cruise in the Inland Sea].

TUESDAY OCTOBER 27TH A new servant arrived who had never before been employed by a European and knew nothing of our ways of eating. On my telling her in bad Japanese to fetch a bit of ice for my whisky and soda, instead of putting it in my glass, put it on my plate, just as I had succeeded in making a beautiful arrangement of woodcock's trail and liver on toast.

WEDNESDAY OCTOBER 28TH I embarked on the *Empress* at noon and sailed at 2 p.m. The same officers were on the ship who were aboard two years ago and the captain was kind enough to put me next to himself.

THURSDAY OCTOBER 29TH I arrived in Yokohama at 2 a.m., where it was cold and wet. I was met on the steamer by Yamaguchi, my guide, whom I immediately despatched to Baron Sone at Tokyo with a letter from me, and my letter of introduction from Sir Ernest Satow, asking for an interview but affording him an opportunity of refusing should his business as Minister of Finance be too great to allow time. Yamaguchi returned to Yokohama at 10.30 p.m. having seen the minister who was quite pleased to hear from me and made an appointment for 9 a.m. on 31st. In the Club I saw many old friends. The new Palace Oriental Hotel is a great improvement on the old one which was burned down, and I was glad to see the French manager back again. It is the only hotel east of Ceylon fit to live in.

FRIDAY OCTOBER 30TH Wet miserable weather. I spent the morning hunting for Ethel's [his wife] tea service and at last bargained one down from £55 to £40 for cash. It was by far the best I saw but, I feared, difficult to keep clean.

SATURDAY OCTOBER 31ST Up early, and donned frock coat, tall hat, etc. I had quite a long interview with Baron Sone who was most kind, even taking an interest in what I was doing and in one of my diaries which I was taking to show Dr Isao Ijima. Baron Sone said it would take some days to get all the documents necessary and that there would be some difficulty about Yura [on Awajishima] and obtaining permission to anchor there. I asked His Excellency to say [to those concerned] that if there was any difficulty about this I should prefer not to ask for it at such a time and wait until things had assumed more peaceful aspect. We spoke French as Baron Sone couldn't speak much English.

After this interview I drove to the Imperial University and was fortunate enough just to catch Professor Isao Ijima, whom it is always a pleasure for me to meet as we have so many ideas and interests in common. As usual, I went through the University Museum with him. There was little that was new but I was much interested in some deep sea fish which came from the area between Japan and the Bonin Islands. One was a most extraordinary beast – white as ivory, long and narrow with projecting eyes – and which Doctor Ijima promised me should be copied for my book by his best man. He gave me a stuffed rat as an example for a Japanese artist to copy for my collections, and was generally most kind.

The deep-sea fish painted by Prof. Ijima's artist

After leaving the university we had a serious carriage accident. While going downhill through narrow streets at full tilt, the horses bolted. The old closed landau lurched about in such a way that it was a marvel it hung together for a dozen seconds. Luckily, because of heavy rain, the street was empty of children otherwise we should have killed a dozen. There was nothing for it but to sit tight and hang on. Yamaguchi and I did so, for all we were worth. After some 600 yards had been covered in this mad flight the driver shouted to us, 'Look out!' and in a second drove the whole left side of the outfit into a deep ditch, which had a strong stone wall beyond it. The wall was on my side so I

got the worst of the broken glass, and the whole landau was smashed to pieces. One horse lay in the ditch injured, the coachman was chucked out against the wall, while his assistant received a bad kick from the other horse. Yamaguchi scrambled out without a scratch despite the fact that part of the wall had come through the window and dented my tall hat. A sympathetic crowd assembled (but no police) while I was made comfortable in a vegetable shop – I in a tall hat and frock coat, a landau and pair of horses were strange objects to the onlookers, but I was still more a subject of interest when I asked that my stuffed rat should be repacked.

At last rickshaws were found and I proceeded – slow and stately – to Baron Kaneko's house, and was sufficiently lucky to find him at home. We had a long and interesting talk. I gathered he had not such an opinion of British politicians that he used to have. What wonder!! I learned that my letter of two years ago had been instrumental in getting *dogs taxed* and, instead of causing offence as I feared, it had been handed to the minister whose business it is to deal with such things.

After luncheon at the Imperial [Hotel] and changing into ordinary clothes I called on Sir Claude Macdonald[2], but he was out, and then the First Secretary to the Legation, Barclay[3], whom I saw. He gave me the Admiralty warrant to fly the Blue Ensign, which I had asked for and which had been sent to the Legation.

I next went to the annual exhibition of *kakemonos* and paintings in Ueno Park. I bought seven very cheap and really pretty *kakemonos* which appealed to me. There was one in particular, a carp painted by an 'RA', as it were, and another of maple leaves and distant mountains in a grey tone giving a misty effect, an indescribable softness to the whole which pleases the eye, and yet resembles neither nature nor anything else.

SUNDAY NOVEMBER 1ST Up at Legation early. There were invitations to a ball given by the Foreign Minister on behalf of the Government and much squabbling and fighting to go, but I would not have gone myself for £20.

It was much too cold for me to stay a day longer than necessary in Tokyo so I decided to go to Yokohama in the afternoon and leave the following day for Kobe by train.

Next I went to Theatre Street where a girl, looking at a show, accidently shoved her bamboo umbrella spoke up my nose which caused much bleeding and amused the people in a kind of hysterical way. However, they were kind, and when they saw that it was unpleasant I was asked into a theatre free of payment but I went instead to a fishpond where my nose could bleed, and fed the fish.

Left in the evening in time to get my dinner at Yokohama.

MONDAY NOVEMBER 2ND I got up early and decided to start for Kobe. It was, as usual, cold and wet in Yokohama and too European for me. There was nothing to be seen or learned.

TUESDAY NOVEMBER 3RD Reach Samomiya at 9.20 a.m., dusty and tired not having slept owing to a company of Americans in the next compartment who drank and played a flute up to 3 a.m.

Theatre Street, Tokyo; from left: the fishpond, a rifle-shooting stall, and the entrance to a show

Today was the Emperor's birthday (*Tenno Heika-no-Tanjobi*) and there were flags everywhere, more this year than usual due to the many thousands of troops all converging on Himeji for the manoeuvres. The billeting system in Japan appears simple. So patriotic is the nation, and so well behaved the troops, that people almost consider it an honour to have the privilege of putting them up! Not a case of *drunkenness* or *assault* or *disorder* occurred to my knowledge by one of the many soldiers who were billeted or passed through Hyogo or Kobe. So impressed was I after a few days of these passing troops that I thought I should in no way be inconvenienced had ten or twenty been billeted with me. Of course, foreigners do not get asked to billet soldiers. If I am here another year I should feel inclined to take in ten or twenty soldiers, *free*, just to see if my ideas are correct, I should do so without the slightest fear and a firm conviction that the soldiers would go to bed and keep quiet just at the time I suggested.

WEDNESDAY NOVEMBER 4TH The Governor sent for me this morning to present the first of the letters which he had received from Tokyo. One was important and an immense concession – a permission, in fact, to anchor at Yura while fishing the outer waters between Tokoshima and Awajishima. I called on Mrs Pakenham and then went to the Club.

THURSDAY NOVEMBER 5TH   A quiet day spent in the garden with my gardener. I find great difficulties in getting manure. It cannot be bought, and there is only one road in the mountains where it can be picked up. Consequently, we deputed a collector for 25 cents to bring back two loads; eventually this arrived and we laid the train for fruitful productions in the spring. My gardener is a dear old man who not only takes an interest in my learning about Japanese gardening but also is determined to teach me. He refuses to waste a foot of ground in which anything can be grown.

SUNDAY NOVEMBER 8TH   I watched soldiers being billeted and noted the excellent arrangements, such as signs in large letters at street corners indicating where the different houses are.

MONDAY NOVEMBER 9TH   A lovely day with one of those magnifying atmospheres I have attempted to describe before, and which often turn into rain squalls from over the hills. Today's scene my painting friend has attempted to describe according to my directions. The effect of the rainbow and black cloud coming over the hills was more beautiful than usual. Today I shot a fair bag: 8 woodcocks, 2 pheasants and 1 bittern.

The rainbow at Itami

TUESDAY NOVEMBER 10TH   I am making some progress in the moss and stone kind of gardening which appeals to my senses more than any other. Moss and stones please my eye and remind me of a thousand things – trout streams, climbs after various animals. Moreover there is always an element of wildness about this kind of gardening which fascinates those who have a true love of nature. The Japanese, as we all know, are past masters at this kind of thing and the effect which can be produced from small and insignificant things to the Englishman's eye are truly wonderful and afford me much interest not only in trying to reproduce them but also in discussing them with my old gardener.

SATURDAY NOVEMBER 14TH   Lovely day again but cold. My rock garden is now assuming the shape of an island in the Inland Sea.

My 'island' rock garden

FRIDAY NOVEMBER 20TH Yamasaki today by the early train. The day's shooting was not bad: twenty-one head. That is very good for Japan. I left my men and dogs at Yamasaki and went to the Miyako Hotel at Kyoto. It is an uncomfortable barrack of a place, cold and cheerless, with formal European meals though the people, as usual, were very civil.

SATURDAY NOVEMBER 21ST First thing I called on my old friend Mr Omori, now Governor of Kyoto Fu. He was very kind, and gave me a letter to all the police in his *ken* (Prefecture) to help me in everything I wanted, and a letter of introduction to the Governor of Otsu on Lake Biwa.

I then went to the Kiyomizu Temple – the name means the Temple of Clean Water. We climbed the steps of the temple with weariness, knowing it as well as I did, but on gaining the upper terraces and looking down, an entirely new scene met my eyes. The small rockery roads, leading here and there through miniature gardens, were crowded with people in holiday costume. This was pretty enough in itself but added to this was the spectacle of the maples, perhaps 40 feet high. Seventy per cent of them were blood red and light scarlet, while the remainder were lemon yellow to orange. Above, and all around the area the dark gloomy green of the pine trees formed an extraordinary contrast which baffled my limited powers of description. One felt well when looking at it.

More than ever I was impressed with my idea that nearly everything in Japan requires looking at in the four seasons of the year – principally spring and autumn. But the half seasons also have their fashions.

MONDAY NOVEMBER 23RD [Back in Kobe] The *Kobe Chronicle* quotes a piece from an Osaka newspaper in which I am referred to as 'the Director of the British Museum' and, as such, having been provided with letters from the Ministers of Agriculture and Finance to the various Governors, etc., all over Japan. I note this in my diary for the reason that it shows leakage somewhere amongst the clerks or secretaries of government offices who should be above that kind of thing. It is a known fact, I believe, that clerks and secretaries supply news to papers for cash in Japan.

Though the *Chronicle* referred to it only this morning, Newnham told me in the Club that Barclay[4] had mentioned it to him four days before, thereby showing the extraordinary amount of interest the latter takes in me. 'He got no change out of me, G.S., I can assure you', said Newnham, by which I gathered he showed considerable spite. Why, I am unable to guess for I bother myself little enough about him.

The following month Gordon Smith shoots in the districts around Kobe and waits for further reports on the deteriorating relations between Japan and Russia.

SATURDAY DECEMBER 19TH I went to an exhibition of water colours, where I came across my old friend Yamamoto whom I long since thought dead. I took him off to my house at once. Gave him an order to paint me several water colours of scenes that I wanted, and a specimen of his art in my book [diary]. Yamamoto, after a small whisky and soda, wished me to allow him to draw 'something besides' as he called it. 'What was it?' I asked. 'Give me a looking glass. I am going to paint myself to show you I am not dead yet.' And so he did with a very excellent though not flattering likeness. Yamamoto's history I was unable to get out of him. His pictures, all original ideas except where painting landscapes, are quite unique.

Fudo has copied him unsuccessfully. Watanabe has had sense enough to stick to his own line but I never saw a picture of his that pleased me in the way that Yamamoto's do. Five years ago I got as many of his pictures as I could. He painted them for Kuhn and Kumor [curio dealers]. Suddenly he left them and disappeared and, though I made several enquiries, I was unable to find him.

Yamamoto – 'not dead yet'

At the small exhibition at Kobe I was talking to the manager about Yamamoto's pictures, and what a pity it was that he was dead when the manager told me 'Why, he is here, he paints for me.' In came Yamamoto and explained. The fact of the matter is that whenever he had painted a dozen pictures he used to go off on a *geisha* spree and not recover for months. Seeing such talent being lost, he was taken in hand by his manager and is only allowed so much [money] now and then, the rest being put away for him in his old age. The picture here does not do him credit – how should it considering he borrowed a child's paints and brushes?

110

FRIDAY DECEMBER 25TH   I spent Xmas day alone, writing in my paper house. I had a cheap American tinned plum pudding but it was a filthy mixture – the only beastly item on my menu. On non-shooting days I always dine at 1.30 p.m. and have eggs in the evening. Today my menu was twenty oysters, seaweed soup with oysters in it, my own private sole *Synaptura smithii*, a woodcock, lily roots and rice and the plum pudding (an evil-smelling mass of Chicago refuse in a tin).

I sent away my old servant, Yoshi-san, as she has become more and more idiotic as New Year approaches and today she forgot to cook any breakfast.

Barclay returned, I hear, yesterday, with two [Korean] tigers. Lucky man, I envy him, but he deserves his tigers as he has been most persistent about them.

SATURDAY DECEMBER 26TH   War rumours even worse.

SUNDAY DECEMBER 27TH   I took the 9.17 a.m. train to Yamasaki where, as usual, I was met by the innkeeper and his wife. First they hoped I was well and then informed me, with real Japanese politeness and smiles, that a man had just been run over and cut in half by the train. Most people would have thought from their smiles that they were delighted but as a matter of fact it was the reverse, for the coolie was one they knew well and liked. A Japanese smile is a truly desirable thing to possess – never to look *harassed*, or be bothered by anything. I must say that I do like smiling faces, myself, even though there is a bit of humbug about it. 'Would you like to see the man?' I was asked, with renewed smiles as if it were quite a pleasant thing to see. 'No thank you, I think I will hurry off and kill something for myself', I answered.

A good day's bag at Yamasaki – thirty-four head

I had an excellent day's shooting, and killed all I saw with the exception of three quail. The woodcocks I shot in an entirely new place across the river, as well as most of the quail – my old grounds were pretty well shot out.

The train was over an hour late coming from Nagoya. Consequently, we had a long wait at the teahouse where I discussed the future chances of finding some deer in the mountains west of Yamazaki, and inquired into the various interesting details of an old

The old inn (teahouse) at Yamasaki

inn. The picture gives a fair idea of the place. The biggest man is myself; also in the picture are my three dogs and my interpreter. We are ready to start just as soon as our coolies have arranged their straw footwear.

MONDAY DECEMBER 28TH A gloomy day. There is very bad news or, rather, warlike news. Transports are all ready and waiting for the troops. Of course, the Japanese *must* be ready, but much is made out of all these small things, such as 200,000 fur caps ordered. The same with boots, beef from America, as well as 200,000 barrels of flour. The Japanese authorities are not like ours and will be found *ready*. Moreover, they do not shirk their business as ours do and are patriotically energetic. Their early preparations no doubt astonish England and the newspapers, which fly into a kind of hysteria, and consider war inevitable. If any one country's policy was likely to bring about a war between two other countries I think England has proved herself entitled to that unenviable reputation.

The street scenes now are very bright in the evening, and the picture gives a fair idea of Motomachi at about 8 p.m. People are rushing here and there buying all manner of things, paying their debts [compulsory at New Year], making arrangements for the decoration of their houses, and the filling of their stomachs.

TUESDAY DECEMBER 29TH This morning I received the first newspaper for three days and the news looks better. I am sure the suppression of newspapers, or rather of what they are

Motomachi at night, before the New Year

allowed to print, would reduce the number of wars, and consequently increase the world's prosperity. Why do governments put up with newspapers?

THURSDAY DECEMBER 31ST   I visited the club both morning and afternoon. The news looks about the same. English telegraphs to the *Kobe Chronicle* show that a considerable proportion of the English at last recognise our duty towards Japan. There are reports that they are going to mobilise our Naval Reserve. I shall believe in nothing sensible, however, from our present Government.

Looking for the New Year, 1904

I took a photo of Egawa's sister by day and made it into a night picture called 'Looking for the New Year', and for my first attempt at a night scene it is, I think, not bad and apropos before I commence a new volume of my diary.

The extended Japanese New Year celebrations always disturb the pattern of Gordon Smith's domestic life and the bitter January weather affects his constitution.

WEDNESDAY JANUARY 13TH, 1904   I am still seedy with asthma and bronchitis and all my old pains are back. I can't sleep in spite of Dr Francis's seven operations last summer in London – I wrote to him accordingly today. I don't think doctors should be allowed to charge for these kind of operations which, after all, are purely experiments for their own benefit. Unless, of course, they effect a cure. The same rule might apply to lawyers with their attendant bloodsuckers, greatly to the good of the country at large.

First rain today for three weeks.

THURSDAY JANUARY 14TH   More rain. My right lung is bad. A large mail for me, including a nice letter from Baron von Pawel-Ramnengen[5] with a photograph of H.R.H. Princess Frederica of Hanover and himself, signed by both and both, I was pleased to see, looking in robust health. Arnold White sent a photo of last summer's Naval League dinner, and I had quite a number of Xmas cards.

EXTRA

TO THE

"Kobe Chronicle."

TUESDAY, JANUARY 5TH, 1904.

JAPAN AND RUSSIA.

IMPORTANT NOTIFICATION.

As indicating the critical nature of the situation, we are officially informed that the War Department has to-day issued instructions to all newspapers prohibiting them until further notice from making any statements regarding movements of troops or strategical operations of the Army or Navy likely to disclose military plans.

FRIDAY JANUARY 15TH   Asthma and coughing kept me awake all night, so I got up early and caught the train to Yamasaki [northeast of Osaka]. On reaching there I was dismayed to find the little place all upside down. Special trains from Osaka and Kyoto, arriving every half hour, were disgorging crowds of people. There were also crowds of pedestrians. Huge barges were bringing down hundreds from Kyoto – in fact, there were said to be some 8,000 people in this place already.

It was the first of the four great days of the shrine of Hachiman at Otokoyama. This old shrine, situated on the mountains across the river, is dedicated to the Shinto god of war, Yawata, who is said to be the son of Empress Jingo who carried him in her womb for three years while making war on Korea.

My shooting was not much of a success. In fact, I devoted much of my time to watching the people crossing the ferries. Here, indeed, some fault might be found for the large flat boats were well overcrowded, and it is quite marvellous to me that not a single accident happened. At a teahouse I was presented with a red paper fish on a bamboo, brought it home and sent it to my friend Arnold White whom, I am sure, will use it under his mattress when suffering some of his worst pangs of gout.

SATURDAY JANUARY 16TH   I was worse today, of course, having started a new cold yesterday. The war news seems better and I still hope for peace.

SUNDAY JANUARY 17TH   Not well enough to start with Dr Sano for a three day trip down the Inland Sea for deer. It is very cold and my paper house is practically unwarmable. I sat by the small stove most of the day trying to write. But it was almost impossible even to keep one's hands warm enough to do this.

SUNDAY JANUARY 24TH   Very cold again. *Fukojuso* [*Adonis amurensis*] bloomed today. This is a particularly weird yellow flower which is planted in every *shochikubai* [a planted container] kept in all households around the New Year, comprising always an old pine tree, small bamboo, a plum tree and a plant with red leaves called *naten* [the sacred bamboo, *Nandina domestica*]. Each of these plants are emblematic of what may be called the very first signs of nature coming to life again.

TUESDAY JANUARY 26TH   Half an inch of snow on the ground this morning and it remained

all day. The first time I have seen it in Kobe. I went to Yamazaki and had what may be called a lucky day getting a woodcock twenty minutes after leaving the teahouse, a pheasant in the next five minutes besides two quail and a snipe.

THURSDAY JANUARY 28TH Packing fish for the British Museum, while Baiho comes to paint more for me.

SUNDAY JANUARY 31ST Quite warm today. I went to have a lesson in gardening and in plum-tree tying. I doubt whether peace will be kept much longer now.

WEDNESDAY FEBRUARY 3RD I had a letter from Heneage[6], now a major in 5th D.Gs. [Dragoon Guards] and a D.S.O. Who would ever have thought it in our old days at school, college, and army crammers? Always one of my favourites, I never expected him to shine, but he has. Instead of 'Old Chang', as we called him, he has grown full blown. I wonder if I, the indolent but truthful 'ass' I was credited with being, would have bloomed had I had the chance. I wish I had had the chance and had been watered instead of being left to work or not, as I chose.

Today is the day on which devils ought to be turned out of one's home, but it is too cold to open all the *shojis* [paper screens].

I contented myself with allowing my servants to throw around a few peas and beans, which were subsequently collected to be eaten on the first thunderstorm's appearance in the summer. These peas and beans are supposed to be *strong medicine*, as it were, having been used to throw at and cast out devils, and well may they be able to cast out the headache devil which proceeds from early thunderstorms. I suffer from them myself and I shall swallow a pea at the right time. I have left a space for Baiho to paint his idea [of this episode] which is partly copied from a wood carving of mine.

FRIDAY FEBRUARY 5TH The Japanese Government have today recalled their minister from St Petersburg. They are right – for there can be no two ideas as to Russia's intentions. Great excitement – a newspaper reports that 6,000 Russians on the way to Chemulpo [Inch'on, the port for Seoul]. Heneage and Pakenham came to dine and we talked about our days at Cheltenham.

SUNDAY FEBRUARY 7TH I am glad to hear this morning that the rumour of 6,000 Russian troops having been sent to Chemulpo was all nonsense.

Shooting in copper-pheasant country

TUESDAY FEBRUARY 9TH I went to Itami where I found my men ready, and one extra who said he was coming to beat for nothing as there was so little game. And they were genuinely afraid I should get nothing.

Kosa overslept in the train on the way back and went on to Hyogo. The news on my return was that the Japanese have sunk two Russian cruisers at Chemulpo – one, the *Varyag*, being a good ship of 6,500 tons and twenty knots; two ship-loads of troops were also captured.

WEDNESDAY FEBRUARY 10TH Capture of Russian ships confirmed. Later in the day there was a rumour of a naval engagement at Port Arthur[7] in which the Russians lost the *Retvizan*, 12,700 tons, the *Tsarevich*, 13,100 tons, and one cruiser, besides seven other ships badly damaged[8]. Japanese damage slight. Everyone was delighted, so much so that a drunken coolie thought he would like my cigar and went for it. That is the only thing I hate about this country: no matter how you are insulted you may not strike. If you did, you would have everyone on top of you at once, and get imprisonment without the option of a fine. I telegraphed my congratulations to Baron Sone and Baron Kaneko, stood Egawa a pint of champagne, and my coolies a blowout of *sake*.

THURSDAY FEBRUARY 11TH A great day today. Rumours that altogether twenty-three Russian ships have been destroyed or sunk and that 60,000 troops have taken Port Arthur. I fear that this is almost too good to be true. The people are quiet. In the evening there was a great torchlight procession to the Nanko shrine – the crowds were immense, and the cheering the loudest I ever heard anywhere. It rose and swelled and could be heard five miles away, the cry of *banzai, banzai, banzai* echoing and re-echoing up the mountains from the throats of at least 60,000 men and boys. Old Harishine made more noise than

Baiho's interpretation of the naval engagement at Port Arthur

any, I am told by someone who saw him in Motomachi.

FRIDAY FEBRUARY 12TH   Off to Yamasaki. I took a bottle of whiskey so that the men could drink to their army's and navy's success. The figures in the official report, given in the papers, are considerably less than yesterday's wild rumours made them out to be. Nevertheless, there are altogether nine Russian ships damaged and one sunk. And that is a very good commencement. The casualties were slight, considering – Japanese: 4 killed, 54 wounded; Russians: 19 killed, 64 wounded. The Russians have done a decidedly outrageous thing off Hokkaido – they fired on and sank a small Japanese passenger steamer without asking it to give in first.

Today I never found a woodcock but I saw a pheasant, did fairly well with quail, and missed two duck.

I shot Kosa while he was in the bamboos, much to my regret. I put five No. 8 shot in his face. It was not my fault – he was invisible in the low bamboos. He never said a word and behaved with the same fortitude that he did last year when a bamboo spiked his foot; he really is the most extraordinary man I have ever met for bearing pain.

War was declared formally, I believe, yesterday. I got back late but found no fresh news. All the trains are now to be altered. There are to be no sleeping or dining cars anywhere, and trains are to be reduced to less than half the usual number and I fear it will be difficult to get my quiet little shooting days with the ease that I did.

117

CHAPTER 7

National Service

1904

The British Museum cuts back – troop trains on their way to Hiroshima – historic flags – Shojos – action at Pingyang – the intricacies of flower arranging – nets delayed – tittle-tattle at the Kobe Club – Sir Ian Hamilton – peculiar characters of Japanese myth – master netsuke carvers – Harishin's country house – the death of Admiral Markaroff – the nets arrive – battle at Yalu

SUNDAY FEBRUARY 21ST Letters from the British Museum announcing that the nets etc. cannot be sent off so as to reach me until at least end of March, also that they were unable to send me an otter trawl as well as a beam trawl[1] because the Museum's vote of money was not sufficient. How truly British and mean. Here am I risking some £400, if not more, in this undertaking while the

Museum's spent about £60 – and this only to provide me with apparatus to catch the fish which eventually benefit the nation.

Kobe streets are rather interesting now: all along the railway tens of thousands of Japanese flags and lanterns are hung across the road; the scene at night is charming, illuminated as it is with thousands of red lanterns. All this is for the fourteen train loads of troops who pass between 12 in the morning and 10 at night. They are cheered by the whole population from the entrance of Kobe to the end of Hyogo.

Talking of flags: how different must the gorgeous old flags of the past have looked if hung out in the profusion that the 'poached egg' – the round scarlet ball on white – is today. I have had some of them painted in my book – copied without leave from *Transactions of the Asiatic Society of Japan*, Vol XXII. These flags are truly interesting, particularly Nos. 6 and 7 – the flags of the *Sun and Sun Crow* and of the *Moon and Hare*. It is a curious fact that there should be

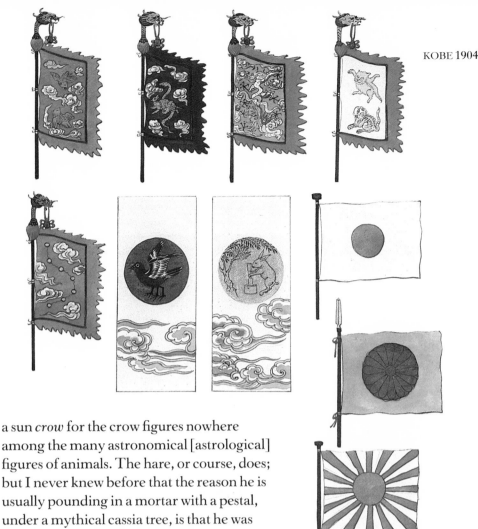

a sun *crow* for the crow figures nowhere
among the many astronomical [astrological]
figures of animals. The hare, or course, does;
but I never knew before that the reason he is
usually pounding in a mortar with a pestal,
under a mythical cassia tree, is that he was
manufacturing drugs, viz. the Elixir of Life.
Flags, 1, 2, 3, 4 and 5 are undoubtedly copied from
Chinese flags but they have been used since about the year A.D. 700. At all
events the Sun Crow and the Moon and Hare flags were, according to Aston[2].

The five flags are: the Red Bird, which was carried in front of a host of men;
the Dark Warrior comes behind; the Azure Dragon on the left; that of the
White Tiger on the right; the Northern Bushel (Charles's Wain) should be
hoisted high in the centre to excite and direct the fury of the troops. There is a
note also in reference to these flags or banners by Doctor Legge[3].

'The Red Bird', he says, 'was the name of the seven constellations of the
southern quarter of the zodiac. The Dark Warrior embraced those of the
northern quarter, the Azure Dragon those of the eastern quarter – and the
Tiger those of the western quarter.' In 1859, when Japan became open to
foreign commerce, the need of a national flag as distinguished from an imperial
flag became felt and the Hi-no-Maru, a red ball on white ground, was taken,
representing, of course, the sun. The army and navy flag have the sixteen rays
of the sun (Figs. 8 and 10), the emperor's flag is the sixteen-petalled gold
chrysanthemum on purple. Some say that the chrysanthemum ought really to
be the sun and that it was meant to be the sun. I don't myself believe this for,
besides being on the flag, the chrysanthemum is the royal crest. Although why
it should have sixteen petals is not quite clear.

MONDAY FEBRUARY 22ND Down to Harishin in the morning to see if he could tell me anything more about Shojos [red-haired sea monsters] than I knew. The story goes that at one time, some 1,500 years ago and up to within about 100 years ago, there lived in the sea people whose bodies and hair were red. Red of the most perfect scarlet. They were so strongly given to *sake* drinking that the farmers and fishermen used to put a barrel of *sake* on the beach, another higher up and so on until they were sufficiently far inland so as to ensure capture of even the Shojo most impervious to the effects of drink.

Shojos drinking sake left for them by a farmer

I have also heard stories of Shojos who lived in the mountains and were considerably more trouble to capture than their sea relatives. There was nothing against these mythical people beyond the fact of their theft of farmers' *sake*. It was impossible to keep this wine while there were any Shojos in the district. Their capture was always considered valuable because their hair made the most beautiful of scarlet dyes, even the flesh, they say, was of value. The arrival of the Dutch [*c.* 1609] put up the price of the dye and consequently the Shojos were hunted more than ever.

My own ideas are that, as drunkenness makes the face red, the most drunken got redder and were termed Shojos; or perhaps the Dutch brought the red mias gorilla [orang-utan] from Borneo; or, again, a shipload of these were wrecked on the coast and hence the story arose, for all monkeys, like tortoises and badgers, like *sake* and hence this reputation of red-haired people coming out of the sea. There are so many things in Japanese stories that are in the sea or come out of it that [the myths are] difficult to follow. Sea spray is said to be the hands of the ghosts of shipwrecked people. The old-fashioned way of drawing breaking waves certainly forms the spray into hands. Lafcadio Hearn says, 'Some hold that the drowned men never journey to the Meido [Hades]. They quiver for ever in the current. They billow in the swaying of tides. They toil in the wake of junks, they shout in the plunging breakers, it is their white hands.'

SATURDAY FEBRUARY 27TH Fine day, quite springlike in fact. The morning papers brought unpleasant news, quoting the report of Admiral Alexieff [Russian Viceroy of the Far East] from Paris saying that on 23rd four Japanese battleships had been sunk. I never believed it – and later came the news that the battleships turned out to be only four old steamers[4] filled with stones, which the Japanese had very pluckily attempted to sink in order to block Port Arthur.

My special permisson to go to Yura has been cancelled but there is nothing wonderful in that – the place being considered as in a state of siege and, no doubt, mined.

SUNDAY FEBRUARY 28TH
Went up to the mountains to look at traps and got two more small mammals for the British Museum.

MONDAY FEBRUARY 29TH
News this morning of a skirmish between Japanese troops at Pingyang [P'yongyang, 150 miles north of Seoul] and some 200 Cossacks. The latter retreated. This is the first meeting. The Japanese opened fire, so the newspaper says, at 700 metres. Don't believe they can have been so foolish as to do this considering that they were behind walls and in strong force.

There is a subscription ball at the Club tonight. Considering that only about eight of the [European] merchants in Kobe who make their business and daily bread out of the Japanese have as yet subscribed to the fund for 'widows or orphans' or those in necessity owing to the war, I think the ball showed a want of taste to say the least of it.

WEDNESDAY MARCH 2ND Pouring wet day, so I have devoted myself to sit down and roughly explain the little I can about flower arranging according to Japanese ideas. I am taking some of my notes and most of the drawings from Conder's [Josiah Conder, F.R.I.B.A.] papers to the *Transactions Asiatic Society of Japan*, Vol VII. Conder goes into every detail, both scientific and otherwise. I wish merely to enter here enough for my children's guidance in art, and therefore to add to their pleasures in life – just enough to show how horribly wrong we are in our mode of arrangement, and how utterly vulgar and inartistic.

To learn flower arrangement fully, takes the average Japanese three years. There are volumes of writing about it and schools by the hundred for nothing else. It is part of the higher education of the Japanese to understand flower arrangement, not only the women but also the *men*. To an Englishman it may seem absurd for men to be interested in such. Indeed, the younger Japanese men under 20 do not often study flower arrangement but probably forty per cent of them do afterwards, no matter what their profession. And to older men, men in declining years, flower arranging is one of their gracious pleasures.

Certain Japanese writers attribute their art of flower arrangement to an Indian Buddhist priest who forbade the people to destroy flowers any more than they should life and, indeed, to preserve all the most delicate by arranging them in their houses or in the temples. If this be true, it is probable that flower arranging came to Japan with Buddhism.

Conder says that 'symmetry, which has come to be the byword of the ignorant in matters of art, is after all a highly unnatural and mechanical method of balancing forms in a composition. In nature, the great model of all art, symmetry nowhere exists. *Harmony* is the leading principal of Japanese design.'

Take Figs. 14–20 as lessons in curves: these are the ABC, as it were, to arrangements and should be fully studied. The bends are made in various ways – by wire, by warming over a charcoal fire and by rubbing gently with *sake* in

Ship homeward bound.   2. Stationary ship.   3.   Outward bound.

26.

27.

28.

29.

30.

31.

the direction you wish the plant to bend, never pressing so as to disturb the circulation. It is a long business and requires infinite patience and very careful and delicate manipulation with the hand. The next thing of importance is to study the vases of which I have given a fair number of samples. As will be seen by Figs. 26 and 28, it is essential that the stems of your flowers should appear to be growing out of the vase itself; that is, that the end of the stems must start straight upwards from the centre. In Japanese flower arrangements water is the mother earth as it were – thus in a shallow dish of 1½ inch in depth you may have a branch growing which looks like a tree (see, for instance, the bamboo in Fig. 27).

To bend stems, wrap in paper, soak and then burn with a flame when it will be found that the stems can be easily bent to the required shape. They are then tied with string and put in water for some time.

Of how to mix the various flowers and plants I have said nothing, for it would take at least fifty pages of my diary to do justice to that subject.

MONDAY MARCH 7TH   Fine and cold. Wrote to the Minister of Finance (Baron Sone) regarding [fishing in] the Bingo Channel. Kobe again a mass of coloured lanterns and flags. More fireworks and enthusiasm than ever.

WEDNESDAY MARCH 9TH   English mail came via Canada. The British Museum sends letters announcing that my nets are delayed and will leave on the *Sado Maru* on February 12th (that is four days after war had started); the spirits were shipped a week earlier, also on a Japanese boat. All these things which are necessary for my fishing must now arrive a full month later, while I have to pay £3 a day for the museum's stupidity – for certainly there is nothing to excuse them given their knowledge that I had bound myself to pay for the *Snowflake* from April 15th. If anyone in England on January 30th, the date of the Museum's letter, imagined that it was safe or wise to ship things on a Japanese vessel, things which were known to be *urgent*, then all I can say is that it reflects very poorly on their intelligence.

FRIDAY MARCH 11TH   Poor Carlo ill again. Shall hang on to him all the same in spite of his disreputable appearance.

SATURDAY MARCH 12TH   Inter-port football match today, resulting in a draw. I watched it from the window of the Kobe Club with a few of the older members of that institution, and a more spiteful, evil-tongued lot of gossipers I have never heard.

'Mrs so-and-so has got a new dress – who paid for it I wonder?' said one.

'Do you see that young fellow walking with her – is he going to marry her?' asked another.

'I don't know,' said another old beauty, 'perhaps it won't be necessary'.

'He was divorced in Australia three months ago', said number one.

'Oh, you don't say so' replied number two.

'Yes I do, I have kept cuttings from the Sydney papers just to show people – here they are – you read 'em', said number one.

'Lor, the young blackguard' said a chorus of Kobeites.

'Wish I had black-balled him for the Club', said number one again and continued, 'but, my goodness, look at Mrs Blank – did you hear what she did after the ball the other night? I can't tell you now because there are strangers here, but come and have a drink and I will'.

I was the stranger. Number one was an old man who ran away from his first wife, who subsequently died; he then ran away with someone else's wife, left her and took a Japanese wife, and since then has had two more.

SUNDAY MARCH 13TH Wrote letters. Baiho came to paint me a curious fish known here as *anko* (frogfish), I think a new specimen. The development of the arms [fins] are remarkable, and there are two curious holes under the fore fins the use of which I fail to understand.

I went to see the manager of the Nippon Yusen Kaisha [Japanese Mail Steamship Company] who tells me the *Sado Maru*, whereon are said to be my nets, dredges, etc., is perhaps going around the Cape [of Good Hope]. In any case she is only to come as far as Nagasaki. He fears greatly that the nets cannot reach Kobe until a month late. Surely it cannot be expected that I should add to my expenses by being obliged to pay for the *Snowflake* which on April 15th will have become a useless appendage without the nets etc. To make matters worse, my wife sent by last mail this picture which is enough to bring forth the following wail of rebuke:

Oh Lankester, Oh Lankester
You have filled me with dismay,
By sending off my fishing nets
Most truly, the wrong way.

For science deep, all know full well
Great talent you display
But when it comes to simple things
You flounder like a Ray.

MONDAY MARCH 14TH   Went down to the Club, where the Consul introduced me to General Sir Ian Hamilton[5] who had arrived on the French mail *en route* to Yokohama. Marquis Ito[6] also went off to Chemulpo [Inch'on] in the *Hong Kong Maru*, which is now painted grey and carries small guns – the first merchantman, in fact, I have ever seen fitted up for war.

TUESDAY MARCH 15TH   A splendid specimen of a parrot fish was brought to me from the Island of Akashi. It was about 7lb in weight – and the turquoise blue was perfect in colour.

hato (parrot fish)

maibaru

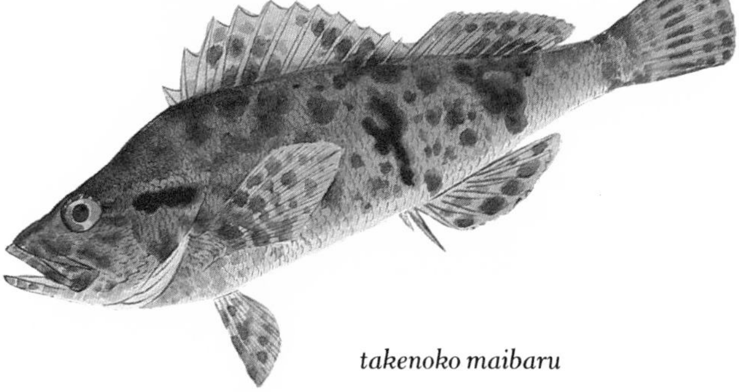

takenoko maibaru

I can only hope it is a new one. Too large, of course, for the British Museum tanks, so I went to the expense of tinning it. I also got another kind of *tai* with fifteen gold stripes along its side; also a remarkable *maibaru*. This kind is called the *takenoko maibaru*. It was brought to me at 9 a.m. but was probably caught the afternoon of the day before. During the whole time, up to 2 p.m., it remained damp, alive and was breathing regularly. At that time I put him into water with some salt, and in half an hour he was as lively as when he was caught. After this I consigned him to the 'morgue', Museum Tank No. 1.

SATURDAY MARCH 19TH   Pouring wet day. No news. A telegraph from Baron Sone saying he would do all he could to facilitate fishing now that war restricted matters.

When reading old books of research such as Colvin's catalogue[7] of Japanese paintings in the British Museum one comes across quantities of creatures

Long-nosed Tengu and Karasu Tengu

Kappa

which it is most difficult to learn about from the Japanese. There are enormous serpents 800 feet in length which eat elephants, the nine-tailed fox, which assumes the form of a Chinese concubine, and Ta Ki, the four-eared monkey that heralds a deluge; fish with ten bodies and one head, whose flesh is good for boils; the two-headed sow whose duplicate head takes the place of the tail; the dog-headed fish with a voice like a child's whose flesh cures madness.

The two Tengus were mythical persons of a very popular order, being the teachers of *jujitsu* (wrestling) – expert swordsmen are said to have learned all their fighting from them. The Long-nosed Tengu is the master Tengu, who lives high up in the mountains. Karasu (crow) Tengu is his servant. The latter flies down to the villages and carries off promising boys, who are taken up to the master Tengu who teaches them all the arts of becoming strong and fighting, and generally paves the way for their becoming heroes.

Another fabulous creation enveloped in mystery is called Kappa. Colvin says of him: 'The Kappa, Kawataro or Kawatochi Otoko is a creature of amphibious habits, infesting ponds, lakes, rivers in the various parts of Japan, but with a special preference for the island of Kyushu. It is usually figured with a tortoise body, having scaly or batrachian limbs, and a head of a somewhat apish character, whose crown is hollowed in the centre to form a cup-like receptacle for a fluid in which the power of the creature is supposed to reside. This not very impressive animal is of a malignant and quarrelsome disposition but polite withall, and is wont to challenge to single combat any wayfarer who may approach his haunt or retreat.

'The man who is unfortunate enough to receive such an invitation, which leaves him no option of refusal, is counselled to preface the conflict with low obeisance. The well-bred Kappa feels bound to acknowledge the salute, and the inclination of his head causes the strength-bearing fluid in the cranial cup to spill over, leaving the monster as feeble as Antaeus when raised from his mother, Earth. The Kappa is believed to adopt a peculiar mode of attacking unwary bathers and the method of catching the creature with human bait has been founded upon this tendency. Drawings of the Kappa *guaranteed* from nature are occasionally met with in the natural history manuscripts, and even in a sober guide book is inserted a story of a certain individual of the species which inhabited the Tone River and has given its portrait. A scientific roll in the British Museum collection discusses the matter with due gravity, and presents us with a circumstantial account of a Kappa, 4 feet 9 inches in height, that was caught in the year 1830 by drawing a pond in the grounds of the *daimyo* [lord] Matsudaira in Yedo. This specimen had the reputation of a propensity for killing and eating human beings.

For my own part I have seen many a labouring coolie in the summer come out of a paddy field with a huge straw hat strung on his back completely devoid of clothing, looking exactly like the Kappa which Baiho has drawn for me, and which resembles all the other drawings of Kappas which I have seen.

TUESDAY MARCH 22ND News of capture of Port Arthur this morning, though later it turned out, unfortunately, to be untrue. Snow and cold. Studied a bit of Japanese mythology again. O-Tafuku, the Goddess of Pleasure, who always interests me has a history of more antiquity than I thought. In the corner of the picture is the well-known mask of O-Tafuku. To all who know Japan it represents folly – according to Japanese ideas of such. Fat, small-eyed, and smiling. This important person has several names: Okame, Uzume-no-Mikoto (Mikoto is an honorary title given to gods and goddesses; 'no' means and) or Ame-no-Uzume-no-Mikoto. Here, in Kobe or central Japan, O-Tafuku is all that is necessary to say when speaking of the lady. She was one of the primitive Shinto divinities, and is regarded as the embodiment of the Spirit of Folly. It was O-Tafuku who danced and sang before the cave to aid her associates in enticing the Sun Goddess to emerge from her retirement and who sought to propitiate the long-nosed Sarutahiko-no-Mikoto by a lavish display of her physical attractions when he appeared likely to oppose the passage of a divine exploring party.

O-Tafuku, Okame, or Uzume-no-Mikoto

Amaterasu, the Sun Goddess, was born out of the left eye of Izanagi-no-Mikoto during his purification of the sea after his return from the infernal regions. Her sire, owing to her beauty, selected her as the ruler of the heavens, while her brothers Susano and Tsukiyomi, who were born from the nose and right eye of Isanagi, were placed in dominion of the moon and sea.

Susano was a *mauvais sujet* of a not very happy family and neglected his charge; he cried incessantly and clamoured to join his mother Izanami in the regions under the earth. At last, going to the place in which his sister was spinning, he cast a flayed horse at her, causing her to hurt herself with a shuttle. The indignant goddess, with a spirit more feminine than divine, immediately responded to the insult by shutting herself up in a cave, and so plunged the world into darkness. The devices of the gods to lure her from her retirement were many. Fires were lit on the beach, mirrors were held opposite the cavern, but it was O-Tafuku-no-Mikoto's dancing with a spear covered with bells, complimentary speech and final display of her charms who caused Amaterasu to leave the cave, and fill the world with warmth and comfort once more.

Decorations to cheer the passing troop trains

WEDNESDAY MARCH 23RD Lovely day. I go to see some troop trains pass through – mostly artillery. Great enthusiasm shown both by population and the troops who all seem in excellent *spirits* – indeed, it would be a disgrace to a Japanese soldier, if he were *not* in good spirits when such good fortune lay in his way as might lead to his death while fighting for his Emperor and his country.

SUNDAY MARCH 27TH   Tired out; stay at home writing, and gardening with Masaki the old gardener, doing a great deal of pruning, and clearing away pine needles. I had a letter from Baron Keigo Kiyoura[8], Minister for Agriculture and Commerce, and another from Baron Sone, Minister of Finance, both giving advice regarding the fishing and regretting their inability to give a scientific permit to kill animals out of season – therefore I am sorry but the South Kensington Museum will have to go without them.

MONDAY MARCH 28TH   Went down to see old Kobayashi who has at last succeeded in getting me a *netsuke* carved by the most celebrated of all *netsuke* carvers, Miva. Louis Gonse[9] says of one of Miva's, *c'est presque une jouissance du toucher, tout les accents en sont fondus et assouplis* [it is a joy to stroke, all its edges are as if one], and that there are only half a dozen of them in the Paris collections. According to Gonse, Miva came into prominence about the middle of the 18th century at Nara and, being his own master, started a style entirely of his own.

All other *netsukes* after this one seem, to me, to look dead – as a real artist no doubt Miva was the first. No. 3, the old man reading a book, also beautifully executed, is carved by a pupil of Miva's. The latter was no doubt responsible for the original, as it is in just his style. Nos. 1 and 4 are two ivory carvings (never so valuable as the wooden ones) by Hidemasa, who is also mentioned in Gonse's book as one of the great old carvers about Miva's time or slightly after.

At that time there seems to have been considerable rivalry among a remarkably clever lot of carvers, and each of the leading men stuck to his own style – for instance Miva carved almost entirely in wood and his subjects were fancies or persons. Hidemasa carved mostly in ivory though sometimes in wood; his subjects were historical and animals. Konaiguiokou carved only in ebony, coral, and amber; Sessai, Kisoui, Tôoun, Tomotada, Masa-tsamé, Masafoussa, Tomotshika, Jiouguiokou, Masakadzou, and Hidemasa stuck almost exclusively to ivory.

In *netsuke* hunting, nowadays, it is very difficult to pick up real old ones, carved by *masters*, for the Japanese collect them themselves. Sometimes, in fact, there are none to be found at all. Harishin tells me he has given up hopes of finding any – it is only at the sales of gentlemen who have lost their money that a few may be found.

The ideas used by these *netsuke* carvers in olden days often made their names as much as their carvings and, of course, every man of consequence had his own speciality. Isthimin, for instance, carved the larger animals; Tadatoshi, snails; Ikkonam, mice, and so on. If you required a *netsuke* made to order, say by such a man as Miva, he would charge you 400 or 500 yen and take a month or two over it, probably only looking at it for a minute or two each day and if he did not feel like carving he would leave it alone and wait until he did. Thus it is that there are, comparatively speaking, so few *netsukes* carved by the real swells of the business. At present thousands of modern copies can be bought but they are not purchased by the Japanese, who only value the *real, original, old ones.*

FRIDAY APRIL 1ST   Somewhat relieved today by a letter from Mr Fagan [of the British Museum] in which he says that the nets, instead of leaving on the Japanese *Sado Maru*, sailed in the *Ben Lawers* and should reach me in the middle of April. In any case there must be a fortnight's loss of rent [for *Snowflake*] to me before I can get the nets on board and in order – for which I think the Government ought to refund me.

SUNDAY APRIL 3RD   Jimmu Tenno's death[10] and a great Japanese holiday.

There was an exhibition (Japanese) of art paintings for which Baiho sent me tickets. Each Kyoto, Osaka, and Hyogo artist had contributed a painting on silk, a *kakemono* to be sold for the benefit of the war fund. I went rather late and bought two kakemonos – one of Kajiwara defending himself in Ikuta temple against overwhelming odds at some ancient battle and the other of Fudo [waterfall deity]. The former done by Bunko of Kobe and the other by Sawun of Kyoto. They were about the best pair there.

SATURDAY APRIL 9TH

Wet day. Went down
to Harishin's country house, where he entertained me for two hours or more,
showing curios of real genuineness and value. A real museum he has here, and
no less than five houses wherein his family dwell. The gardens are delightful
and much improved since I last was there with Sir George Warrender[11].

THURSDAY APRIL 14TH Exciting report came out in a special which says
Admiral Makaroff and all his staff blown up in an engagement at Port Arthur
yesterday. The wire is from Berlin and unreliable but there is no doubt that
something has come off.

FRIDAY APRIL 15TH Yesterday's news about sinking the *Petropavlovsk* is true
and judging from the morning's rumours it seems that the Russian Admiral
Makaroff ran into a Japanese mine and not one of their own, as was supposed.
News also of the burning of the palace at Seoul. Poor Emperor of Korea, what
will be left for him soon? Wet day. Went over *Snowflake*.

SATURDAY APRIL 16TH Yesterday's report of the new Russian disaster is quite
true. It appears that the Japanese laid a string of mines with 'destroyers', then
drew out the Russians to chase them out to sea where there was a fog and, upon
reaching this, to the Russian's horror they found themselves steaming straight
at the whole Japanese fleet. In making for the harbour, the flagship
Petropavlovsk struck a mine forward, blowing up the ammunition. She sank
with Admiral Makaroff, the whole of his staff and over six hundred men. The
Pobieda also struck a mine but got into harbour; there were several other losses.
The Japanese took this victory *very quietly* making absolutely no fuss over it.

MONDAY APRIL 18TH A holiday today [the Girls' Festival, Jomi-no-Sekku]. On this day women and children drink white *sake shiro* – a sticky sweet mixture made out of rice powder, sugar and just a touch of *sake*. Horrible stuff to my mind. All women and girls are allowed to do as they like, and go where they please; some go to the theatre, some to picnics, others to a favourite temple. All are dressed in their best clothes.

The *Snowflake* begins to look like a yacht, but the crew are a trouble, and rarely on board. Shall have to alter this.

TUESDAY APRIL 19TH The *Ben Lawers* arrived from England with my nets etc.

THURSDAY APRIL 21ST Lovely weather. I was much annoyed to have to spend it running about from one agency to another to get my nets. Late in the evening I was successful, but too late to examine them.

FRIDAY APRIL 22ND Find the winch and line together too large and heavy for comfort on the *Snowflake*. Finding Nickel and Co. an utterly hopeless firm to deal with, I went to Kawasaki Dockyard where I was met with civility, and prompt and effective help from Mr Yamagata and Mr Yotsumoto, the secretary. They really were very kind, practically volunteering to lend me the lead ballast which Nickel even refused to produce for hire. Kawasaki Dockyard requires no recommendation from me but, should it ever do so, it will certainly get it.

FRIDAY APRIL 29TH Wet day. *Snowflake* under trawl repairs.

MONDAY MAY 2ND Great battle announced this morning at the Yalu[12], the Japanese taking a place called Kuilien-cheng, or in Japanese Karenjo, and losing 700 men while the Russians lost over 800 and 28 guns, besides a number of prisoners. In wading the Ai Ho [a tributary of the Yalu] the Japanese showed great pluck, and altogether it was a most successful day.

Once the preparations on the Snowflake *are complete, Gordon Smith sets sail in earnest to collect new fish from the Inland Sea. He travels as far as Hiroshima Bay where he visits the celebrated Shinto shrines on Miyajima, but war regulations restrict his photography. He returns to Kobe to trawl in the Harima Nada.*

CHAPTER 8

The Enthusiast

1904

*Victory shoot planned – trawling in the Harima Nada – catching eels
at Typhoon Lake – sing-a-long sea shanty – the other Gordon Smith
– conservation policies – a few minutes in the Club – night vigil at
Shodoshima – trawling continues – ice shops appear – Russians sink
a British ship – death of Plehve – mountain pools – news runners –
Battle of the Yellow Sea – beriberi strikes – typhoon and dragon flies
– Liaoyang captured – suppon soup – Kiyomori's grave – dinner with
the Governor – the shoot*

SATURDAY JUNE 4TH   There is to be a large shoot in Osaka for gold medals, when
Port Arthur falls. Of course, I put my name down at once and paid 12 yen
entrance fee as they say it is to be limited to twenty people.

SUNDAY JUNE 5TH   Started rather late towards Akashi, passing the *Korea* still in
quarantine at Nada Point with plague. The passengers seemed lively enough,
however, playing games. Had two unsuccessful trawls but think I got a new
kochi [flathead fish].

No war news except that Kuropatkin[1] seems to have started the relief of Port
Arthur, a feat which he is not likely to accomplish, if the Japanese have
established themselves in the fort around Kuichan which they took from the
Russians. The papers say 80,000 troops are with Kuropatkin.

THURSDAY JUNE 9TH   Trawled and dredged in the neighbourhood of
Nishishima all day, getting a quantity of prawns and small fish of many kinds.
A good breeze blew back into Naba Bay so I went there for the night.

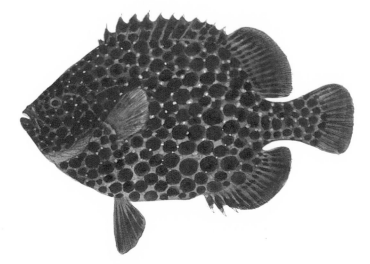

FRIDAY JUNE 10TH   All traps sprung by crabs except two, one of which contained a mountain rat with his tail bitten off by crabs, while another had one whose ears had been eaten (D— the crabs). Trawled about Soja and Nishi. At the south point of Takashima (a small island near Eishima) I pulled up two dredges full of magnificent shells of Hiroshima oysters – empty but larger than those from Hiroshima itself. There were also shells of the Akashi oyster.

Late in the afternoon, I went into the bay where the Typhoon Eel Lake is. The water was shallow, not more than five inches deep throughout the pond, and very clean. There were dozens of eels visible, all the same size, about 18 inches long, though there appeared to be no food for them. From what I could see, they were much the same as other eels though perhaps lighter in colour.

Set some traps at Typhoon Lake and also in Raspberry or Turtle Bay [RGS's names] where I anchored.

SATURDAY JUNE 11TH   Vile morning with pouring rain. Sent [Kojiro] off to inspect traps; crabs again had robbed and sprung them all. However, Kodjiro brought back an eel from the mysterious lake. We could see no differences between it and the other eels, as I thought, though its head may be longer and slightly larger.

Later anchored in my favourite bay, and fished from the rocks seen in the photo; got about fifty wrasse, some shells and barnacles. Ducks flew all around the *Snowflake* in the evening and weather cleared up wonderfully.

Oyster rocks in Raspberry Bay, Nishishima

SUNDAY JUNE 12TH   The first of my hauls was a failure owing to the men sulking but the threat of empty bellies if they failed in their next haul brought up enough, though nothing [of interest], except the biggest red mullet I have caught in Japan. It was with deep regret that I cast him into a British Museum tank, but very large prawns (about 9 inches) made up somewhat for the loss. Anchored at Eishima.

MONDAY JUNE 13TH   Started early in the direction of Matsushima taking a trawl each side. On the inside – that is the west – we brought up shells, various small fish, cuttlefish and octopuses. A high wind sprung up from the west which obliged me to heave my anchor and make for Eishima which I reached after dark in half a gale of wind and blinding rain.

TUESDAY JUNE 14TH I went and presented the priestess and her five acolytes at the Kami shrine with their photographs [taken on June 2nd]. The priestess was particularly delighted with hers. They were all pleased but more especially the man on the priestess's left, and the old man sitting on the lower step in the corner, he fairly gave 'tongue' with delight.

Remained at Tsubone and reset a few traps.

WEDNESDAY JUNE 15TH After getting up steam I went to the end of Naba inlet and trawled three miles out to its mouth, with the most disappointing results.

At Tangashima I tried my trawl again and got a 4lb flat fish, and a variety of small fish, and then returned to Tsubone in a strong wind which came up from the southeast, towing for a part of the way a *saba* (mackerel) fishing boat. I brought out the gramophone on the way, placing it so that the fishermen could not see it, and started 'Owakabushi' the great fishermen's song in Japanese. The effect in the fishing boat was truly funny. They jumped about to see who was singing so, as soon as I noticed this, I opened and shut my mouth as if I were, until the whole boat declared it to be most wonderful that the foreigner could sing their language so well. They asked for another song and I gave them the same one again, finally singing an English one, and then a band which puzzled them more than ever. Eventually, on leaving them, I showed them how it was worked but even then I think they thought the sound came from some part inside me. We parted the best of friends, I getting a huge 15lb *saba*, worth 250 yen, for 1 yen.

The most picturesque sailing boat I ever met

THURSDAY JUNE 16TH Left by train for Kobe on receipt of a most extraordinary letter from the manager of the Hong Kong and Shanghai Bank at Kobe. He said, 'We have received the following cable. "Please inform us what you wish done in the matter. A T.T. for £300 required immediately by Russell. Tell Gordon Smith.[2]" ' As I did not then know what a T.T. was and knew no Russell likely to call upon me for such a loan, I went to Kobe by train to tell the manager so. A T.T., I found, meant a Telegraphic Transfer, and the manager immediately wrote home to say that the message did not refer to me. This is another of the many cases where the Gordon Smiths who turn up all over the East are an infernal nuisance when they do not use initials.

FRIDAY JUNE 17TH Called on the Governor and had a long talk about the fisheries in the Inland Sea, strongly advising the suppression of prawn-exporting to China. Food for fish is getting exhausted in the Inland Sea and is quite one of the things which should be taken seriously in hand by the Government. Besides this, the prawn fisheries benefit only a few merchants, who pay the very poorest of wages to the people employed by them – they range from 13 to 17 cents a day to the divers and so much a basket to the fishermen.

Today has brought bad news in the attack (cowardly attack, one may fairly say) made by the Vladivostock squadron on the *Hitatchi Maru* and *Sado Maru*[3]. It is to be hoped that all Europe will cry out at Russia's barbarous conduct at giving so short a time to the men of the troop ships to escape.

MONDAY JUNE 20TH The *Sado Maru* had not gone to the bottom after all, but this is due more to Russian fear of being caught by the Japanese fleet than to intention. Kobe is full of khaki-clad soldiers, who look strong and fit to go anywhere. They practise a sort of 'sentry-go' in the streets and appear busy all the time; their orderliness is splendid.

WEDNESDAY JUNE 22ND Went to Club, but there was an extraordinary general meeting there – on such a ridiculous subject that I came away disgusted and went to the German Club [Club Concordia]. The meeting was called in order to oppose what appeared a very wise precaution on the part of the committee, viz. that gentlemen signing chits after 1 a.m. should do so on red forms and be charged a higher rate so as to pay more for the servants. For some extraordinary reason this suggestion produced a revolution. The committee were beaten. The president and committee resigned *en bloc*. The only thing that

surprised me was that members of the Club could recognise red chitts after 1 a.m. – perhaps the red, curved and twisted letters reminded them of 'snakes'.

THURSDAY JUNE 23RD Sent *Snowflake* to Naba, and went myself by train. At Himeji we drew up alongside a train full of wounded soldiers. They were dressed in white *kimonos* with a red cross on each. I never saw soldiers look so clean – one might almost say smart. I spoke to several through Egawa. They had been in the last fight of Tokuriji only six or seven days before. All looked well but were mostly wounded in arms or legs. There were no 'pale' men amongst them.

FRIDAY JUNE 24TH Left Naba early and trawled along the north-west side of Shodoshima about two miles from shore. Reached Hiki at 5 p.m. where my friend Umahara, the policeman, promptly came to pay official respect and to accompany me around the village, for he delights in the salutes he gets from the people who all turn out to have a look at me.

139

Umahara and his man

SATURDAY JUNE 25TH Umahara called at 6 a.m. and we started at 7 a.m. for Terashima, a small island to the north of Naoshima, towing his boat as we went.

We landed in a little bay to visit the curious rock which is said to be the shape of a cock's head, and crows at midnight on January 1st each year. Many fishermen come to hear it. No one lives on this small island, though an old fisherman comes and plants a small rice field there annually, which will be noticed in the picture with the policeman's boat, and *Snowflake* in the distance. After leaving Terashima we went to Kyonojuro Island, after which we took the policeman back to Hiki passing through a fleet of *hara* boats which always seem to be in these waters. After farewells and a present of loquat fruit, which the policeman produced from the interior of his boat, I left for Shodoshima, having three trawls by the way.

Anchored at Shodoshima at 7 p.m., but weather was too bad to go ashore with both rain and wind. By not going ashore, however, I was rewarded by one of the most interesting and beautiful sights I have yet seen in Japan. At about 9 p.m. I was sitting on deck, smoking my last cigar. It was still raining, but an easterly breeze was blowing the clouds away out into Harima Nada so as to cause the moon

Torchlight procession on Shodoshima

to show itself over the wild rocks which, from the summit of the pine-clad mountains, have always fascinated me in this place; strange and mysterious-looking rocks they are, almost inaccessible, and full of oblong upright caves, which in days gone by were the homes of thousands of large apes, and still are for a few. One very large ape, indeed, has been killed there this winter – so an influential soya-sauce maker told me next day.

While watching the moon coming out of the clouds, and listening to the boom of the temple bell away up on the mountainside, we suddenly saw the whole of the village of Nouma blazing out into the light of lanterns – paper lanterns carried on bamboos – each person having, as usual, his name painted on. At the same time dozens of trumpet-shell horns were blown. By degrees the lanterns formed a procession in single and double files, fully a mile long. This gigantic fire serpent wound itself around the mountain and by 10 p.m. it was, as it were, a complete serpent on a background of black with no light anywhere visible except its own and the moon just peeping over the rocks. The procession was an earnest and patriotic crowd of villagers, wending their way up to a mountain temple to pray that their soldiers, gone to Manchuria, should fight well. There was no prayer for a safe return, only that if they must loose their lives that they may kill more than their own value. There is no noise, no disorder, the only sound being, here and there, the sound of the trumpet shells being blown.

The Harima Nada from the deck of Snowflake

SUNDAY JUNE 26TH A terrible day of wind and rain. Trawled as far as the SE point of the island but there the heavy seas from Harima Nada met me and I was compelled to return to Shodoshima instead of getting to Naba as I had hoped.

MONDAY JUNE 27TH Left Shodoshima at 6 a.m. and at 6.20 a.m. we struck the submerged rock called, on chart, Hiranga Hikujiro but we slid over it undamaged. Before we got to Eishima we had a bad time again with heavy seas – as may be imagined by the fact that we took five and a half hours to do twenty-seven miles, in spite of having the current strongly in our favour. After getting my mail from Uranuma, I crossed over to Tsubone, where I anchored.

Sakoshi Bay from Tsubone

TUESDAY JUNE 28TH Up very early, having a busy day before me. First, I went up to the village and took my favourite view of Sakoshi Bay, as seen from Tsubone, showing Holy Island. I returned here to fulfil the promise of photographing the children, whom I have now taken photos of for the past three years, on my visits to this place. All put on their best clothes and I promised to make them look beauties in their pictures. The three photos show the result.

They are not a pretty lot at Tsubone, but are honest, kind, hard-working, poor, and always trying to find something that they think it will please me to eat. I would rather live amongst them than amongst many other communities that I know.

WEDNESDAY JUNE 29TH Started at 6 a.m. and had three trawls off Matsushima, the most southerly of my little group.

After finishing the trawls I went to Kashima, a small pair of islands, where I have not hitherto landed, and I was well repaid, for a more beautiful lot of holes and pools I have never seen, and they were simply crammed with fish,

Tsubone's best tree and some of the Kishimotos

principally of the wrasse kind, but there were also numbers of small perch and bream.

The seaweeds, when looking down into the deep clear water of this island, were beautifully coloured: blue, brown and green. There is enough water under the rock with the pine tree on it to tie up a yacht the size of *Snowflake* alongside.

The absolute belle of Tsubone

Kishimoto's brother's wife and baby, and cousins

The curious single pine tree on this rock is what first attracted me to the island, and I now bitterly regretted that I had not gone there before, for there must be good rod-fishing off those rocks. The arch at the end of the island is not at all a usual thing around the Japanese Inland Sea.

THURSDAY JUNE 30TH   I left for Naba to catch the 8.40 train to Kobe.

FRIDAY JULY 1ST

The heat was simply devilish.

Iced-drink shops or stalls are in full

swing – I counted fourteen in my own street

of about 500 yards. If nothing else, these stalls are always

cool to look at; there is ice somewhere but it is invisible. You can

have an iced lemonade, by paying 4 cents, instead of paying 3 cents for a bottle, which looks cooler from being placed in a tub of clean water – but that is left to boil in the sun. The Japanese are impressionable people, however, and would sooner pay 3 cents for a bottle which looks cooler than for a bottle that is cooler, but from its invisibility not appreciated. Flags bearing cooling titles – 'Ice', 'Iced water', 'Iced pudding', 'Ice cream' – flutter from all over the stall, but there is always one big flag with 'Ice' written in large letters in blue, and surrounded with red. The coming of the ice stalls always means 'now we are in for heat' and so we were. I don't think I have ever felt Kobe so hot and oppressive.

THURSDAY JULY 7TH P. & O. steam launch collided with *Snowflake* last night at 11.30 doing some damage above the water-line, but the agents still allowed me to sail. I took Jensen, a very nice, quiet German submanager of some firm here.

I found a small striped *tai* (black and white) which I had never seen before. He is copied exactly the size he was when found. Got the usual fish, and plenty of prawns.

SATURDAY JULY 16TH Started early again, taking Baiho to paint. As I had kept several of the fishes alive from

144

yesterday, he was able to commence operations at once. Off Wada Point the wind came a bit fresh and rather upset Baiho's interior, but half a dozen yawns and one attack of seasickness put him all right again.

At about 1 p.m. we came to a regular island of weed and wreckage. Some parts of the weed were so thick that it was as much as we could do to get through, and many times our screw got covered, necessitating our pulling out the boat to clean it. The island proved prolific in fish, but the smells were abominable, a drowned man contributing very considerably towards this. My skipper, as usual, steered appallingly, making it most difficult for us to manipulate the hand net successfully. He seemed to have an absolute fear of the dead man, so I determined to make him stay near it, while I had my luncheon and the men caught fish. Curiously enough, there was a remarkable collection of dead things grouped about: two cats, three dogs, a mole and a weasel, besides the man. Mostly attributable to the recent typhoon. The mole and weasel were no doubt out of some river. The dogs, cats and man I put down to shipwreck.

> Of fishing grounds and many
> I'd bet you my very last penny
> That never so smelly was any
> And gruesome and almost unkenny

SUNDAY JULY 17TH After reporting yesterday's drowned man to the police, I left early in search of 'Weed Island' and all its unpleasantness hoping to get one more haul of surface fishes, which I am sure will be of value to the Museum. It was, however, no use – we could only find small patches here and there with very few fish under them and nothing new. The Japanese call all these rough-skinned fish *kawahagi* [leather fish]. The Smithsonian papers make them out very rare in Japan, so I fully hope that my collection, which amounts to about 130 specimens, will be of value.

TUESDAY JULY 19TH Call on H.E. the Governor, hand over my cruising licence, subsequently pay off my crew. The captain and the bosun were the only two fined. Except for the former, the crew were the best I have had in Japan.

Sent off a collection of 102 war postcards at the request of Mr Fagan [of the British Museum] for our national collections. This is in addition to the following expenses:

	Yen	Cents
Charter of *Snowflake* for three months	2,700	—
Commission on charter to A.G. Drendl & Co	150	—
Coal	185	—
Presents to crew for extra work	225	30
Oil, ropes, lines, etc	50	—
Total	3,310	30

I wonder how much of this I shall be refunded!!!

WEDNESDAY JULY 20TH Take inventory and get rid of *Snowflake*. Very hot day. In the Club I was introduced to three or four correspondents for English and American newspapers. I am sorry, as I told them, that the Japanese authorities have allowed them to go [to the front]. They are *most dispensable* for Japanese successes especially now.

SUNDAY JULY 24TH No news; Vladivostock fleet still at Izu, between here and Yokohama.

Meanwhile some relics of the unfortunate *Knight Commander* have been found. Fishermen of Izu picked up at sea on the 25th instant and brought to Tago three boats marked *Knight Commander*. They contained about a hundred suits of clothing, some Mexican dollars, some gold and silver watches and a quantity of books. All these articles were handed over to the local authorities—another illustration of the remarkable honesty practised by the lower orders in Japan. It would seem that these are the boats in which the crew of the steamer made their way to the *Gromoboi*, or whichever of the corsairs picked them up, and that the Russian pirates did not even allow the men to take their belongings out of the boats but sent the latter adrift at once. We trust that Russia may pay dearly for this lawless conduct.

MONDAY JULY 25TH Vladivostock fleet have sunk the British steamship *Knight Commander*. As a true Englishman I am pleased, because the utterly unjustifiable way in which they did it may possibly twist the lion's tail until the joint cracks. I can see no way of England feeling the necessity of activity until nearly *every* joint in the lion's tail is disjointed. The Russians know it, so does France, Germany and Japan.

Busy with fish. I find I have 1,002 to send off to the British Museum.

THURSDAY JULY 28TH Great heat again. Rumours of battle at Newchwang [now Ying-k'ou] and Tashicaio [now Ying-k'ou-hsien], the Japanese losing heavily but winning.

FRIDAY JULY 29TH News that Admiral Kamimura[4] has met the Russians and has sunk two, and is chasing the other. Another report says that H.M.S. *Ocean* and four destroyers have left Hong Kong for Yokohama. The best news of the day seems to be the death of Plehve[5], the Russian Minister of the Interior, to whom the world owes the present war with four or five others, such as Alexieff and Bezobrazoff[6].

THURSDAY AUGUST 4TH Went off to Osaka on a regular *netsuke* hunt, picking up the seven best in the whole town, but they had to be paid for rather heavily at an average of 12 shillings a piece.

Osaka appeared to me to be much improved. Police boxes are neat and everywhere. Dust is kept down and some of the streets are comfortably shaded by awnings, especially in Shinsai-bashi Street, the appearance of which, for Japan, is quite gay and gorgeous. I returned by a train, half full of khaki-clad troops, going off to the front or to what I am beginning to consider the boundary of a new Japan.

SUNDAY AUGUST 7TH No sleep owing to heat. Thermometer 89°F but I nevertheless took dogs and the pup for a mountain walk, following the stream in the Valley of Lakes up to the top one. We spent about an hour at the pond for the benefit of Ruby and Nelly, who swam about the whole time. There were several bathing parties on the way up – children, whose village is at the foot of this valley. The flood having washed away all the banks, with the exception of the top one some 900 feet up, there remains only the stream, and the places where the lakes existed. Every available place that looks as if damming would make it a bath is taken by a party of children. Some of the baths were really quite pretty or so well chosen that, had it not been for two bashful young maidens, whom we surprised with very few garments on, I think I should have ventured in with the small children.

However, the confusion to which the two maidens were put by our presence was such that I hastened away, sooner than let it be said that the uncouth foreigner was bad in his manners or a nuisance to the natives.

MONDAY AUGUST 8TH Today is one of wild war rumours. General Stoessel[7] is said to have shot himself; Port Arthur is said to have been captured; the Russians have ceased fighting anywhere etc., etc. I wish it were all true, but fear the end will not come without the loss of much life. Thermometer in my room today registered 96°F and one feels rather like shooting oneself.

WEDNESDAY AUGUST 10TH
Vague rumours of the fall of Port
Arthur, but there are no Japanese
Government reports, which are the
only ones to be believed. There are
reports and 'specials' by the hundred,
the very life of the newspapers, but
no one believes naval news which does
not come from Admiral Togo, or
military news which is not *official* from
Tokyo. *Gogai* (special
news runners) are not
like those in England.
They howl out no exciting or
vulgar ear-catching sentences, but simply jog
along through the streets with a little bell tied
to their sides, dropping the little bits of
paper inside the doors of subscribers,
free of charge, and thus, quietly, is the
news of victory circulated.

FRIDAY AUGUST 12TH   One of the
teahouses sent this specimen
of a war fan [opposite] this morning, with
some quilled prawns in soy sauce, which
were as excellent as the fan is pretty. I think Japan is fully entitled to draw this
picture now.

SATURDAY AUGUST 13TH   Good news today. The Port Arthur fleet came out, we
are told, on the 10th and got what 'Paddy gave the drum' – Hell. One ship
appears to have run on a mine or been torpedoed at the start and returned to
Port Arthur – the *Potlava*, they say; later four or five others followed, much
knocked about. Two or three broke through and got away – the *Tsarevich*
[flagship of Rear-Admiral Vitgeft] to Kianchan with three torpedo boats, the
battleship a wreck. Others have got to Chefon and Nosung. This must be about
the last we shall see of the Russian fleet fighting, I should think, and the more
one thinks over it the more wonderful it seems[8].

SUNDAY AUGUST 14TH   Thermometer goes down 1° today to 92°F and the
Kamimura sinks the *Rurik* of the Vladivostock fleet[9]. A *banzai* day, in fact,
all round.

MONDAY AUGUST 15TH   Not feeling at all well, I sent for Doctor Sano who, after
an examination, said that I had a regular case of beriberi[10], but very slight and
that it would go with the cool weather. Doctor Kilpatrick confirmed the

opinion. Very little walking allowed, no standing in water; and altogether all pleasantnesses of life are to end. I have only got it in the calves, shins and stomach as yet, and they say it is really nothing. However, after reading the home newspapers and their accounts and discussions of South Africa, I do not look upon beriberi as nothing. The tests for beriberi are strange. If you press the flesh on the inside of the shinbone it leaves a hole. You are next told to sit on a table and you are struck below the knee. If the leg hangs dead, as it were, it is sure you have the disease.

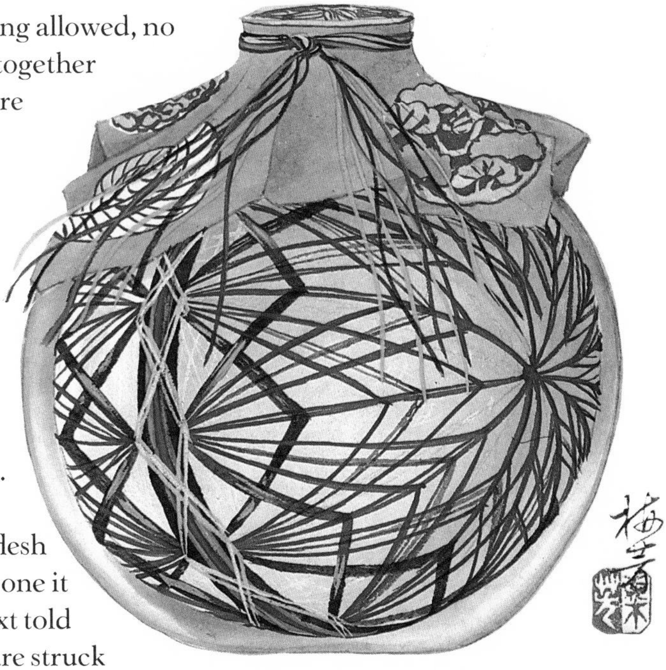

A glass vase with a ball of silken thread worked inside

Ten days later . . .

THURSDAY AUGUST 25TH Still lying down, legs a bit better, but the rest bad. Weakness is the worst part of it. Two destroyers sunk by the Russians at Port Arthur. A confounded bore, calling himself Professor Pfoundes[11], makes a call, but I do not see him, having heard enough.

FRIDAY AUGUST 26TH More trouble with Pfoundes who, the police say, is crazy. Why is it that, when one is abroad, and any *loafing ruffian, plausible humbug,* or *drunken blackguard* is found, he is invariably and without exception, in my experience, an Englishman!! It is a positive fact all the same.

WEDNESDAY AUGUST 31ST Thermometer down to 76°F today. Typhoon blew all day from northwest and towards evening hauled round to southwest, consequently Kobe got off cheaply. Liao-yang is beginning to be fought over. Japan had a victory. Announced today.

149

THURSDAY SEPTEMBER 1ST
All the small boys are out today playing a new game in catching *tombos* (dragonflies). After a typhoon, dragonflies come out in increased numbers – today there are simply thousands. The game consists of tying a female dragonfly to a thread, 4 feet long, which is attached to a bamboo about 10 feet long, sometimes with bird lime at its end; more often, however, and with the more sporting boys, the bamboo is not limed, but the female is moved about quietly over the water, while the boy sings a plaintive wail, 'ya-hor-ra, ya-hor-ra, ya-hor-ra', which means nothing in particular, but it has a wonderful effect on the *tombo*, who comes innocently to look at the captured female. On his approach, the artful youngster allows the female to rest on the ground. The male comes down and in the blitheness of his amours is promptly pounced on and transferred to a cage. When a male has to be used as a decoy, the song is, for some reason, different – it consists only of 'tombo, tombo, tombo', which seems to have the desired effect on the female.

Today, the whole air resounds with these cries. They are a beastly nuisance – fifteen or twenty boys are within fifty yards of my house and at it all day long from sunrise to sunset, so long as the flies are about.

SUNDAY SEPTEMBER 4TH   News this morning is that Liao-yang has been captured by the Japanese. There is great rejoicing in consequence. No sooner had the news come out than the population was busy decorating its houses with red lamps and flags. All the streets are hung with these lamps, and over the entrance of each house are two large white lamps, 3 feet long with the words 'victory' and 'rejoicing' written on them.

THURSDAY SEPTEMBER 8TH   Processions again last night; emphatically I think the money wasted on them is a mistake with so much suffering going on amongst the poor, especially amongst women and children of the bread or rather ricewinners, who are dead or wounded.

SUNDAY SEPTEMBER 11TH   Baiho came and painted a snapping turtle or, in Japanese, *suppon* (the Latin, I think, is *Dogania subplana*). I killed one this morning but, because of its ferocity, with difficulty. The turtle whose life I had resolved to sacrifice, allowed me in no way to seize him properly. His neck came out like lightning, and twisted equally rapidly round to any direction in which my fingers were over his back. It must be understood that if he can once lay hold of you, off comes that part of your finger; he will hold on even though you cut his head off. I drove the point of a large steel kitchen fork through his head as he ran, pulled his body back and Kosa chopped his head off in a second. There was not much blood. The mouth continued to open and shut, while the eyes turned to anything which you put near them. The headless body walked about five yards and stopped. The head was biting sticks hard and broke off pieces. It lived, so to speak, for twenty minutes. Ten minutes after the decapitation I turned the body on its back and so frantic were the efforts made by the legs to regain its position that it nearly succeeded in doing so. There is no doubt in my mind that had it a head to think with, or other thinking apparatus in its stomach, it would have got up and gone off – blindly, no doubt, but a long way.

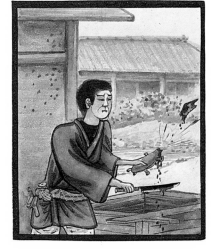

The strength of its legs appeared as great as when its head was on. It was an unpleasant sight, and it was only reading the experiences given in Wood's *Natural History*[12] that made me try it. I brought the head within two feet of the body, then poured scalding water over the latter so as to loosen the horny parts from the flesh. As soon as the scalding water was poured over the headless body the head became renewedly active and the mouth opened and shut more quickly than ever, though I heard no hissing sound. Finally, I gave Kosa the head to put on a plate and eat; he said 'it lived for twenty minutes, and was not a patch on viper to eat, no taste'.

Suppon is, in Japan, as in China, a great delicacy and very expensive. My cook prepared it in two ways. Soup is made from the fat, feet, liver, heart, and tripe, and to this was added pounded ginger, and a small amount of chopped leek with a little water pepper. The soup was peculiar in flavour but it grew to become pleasant. The second course was the remainder of the tortoise (for that is really a more correct name), blood, hindlegs, bits of meat and fat, cooked in soy sauce and served cold with no garnishings whatsoever. The tortoise cost about 3 yen. I ate him all and had not enough though the Japanese eat only fragments of him – as a dish, he would have fed twenty of them. *Suppon* is recommended to invalids as it is a most digestible food and, according to the stories, which I believe, there is, due to its ferocity and vitality, much medicine in the beast.

MONDAY SEPTEMBER 19TH   Once again Dr Sano came and absolutely forbad my walking. He stayed quite a long time and we had much talk on one subject and another apropos of religion and shooting.

WEDNESDAY SEPTEMBER 21ST   Another three weeks' mail arrived this morning, via Canada, and all in a lump. My mother wrote a lecture on the advantages of Roman Catholicism. Altogether a dull mail, the only redeeming feature being a letter from Arnold White in which he says that gradually I am 'drawing him out of the mud hole of Russianism into which he had fallen' by what he chooses to term my 'buffalo strength', by which he must mean my strong and forcible language.

THURSDAY SEPTEMBER 22ND   Still bad with beriberi but I went down to Hyogo to see Kiyomori's grave. Kiyomori may be said to be the founder of Hyogo, to which he came from Kyoto at the latter end of the 12th century. He removed himself to what was then known as the Fukuwara district, where there were but few houses and large marshes caused by the overflow of the River Minota. Kiyomori decided to reclaim the marshes and tried time after time, but without success, for the river always burst its bounds. At last an old plan was resorted

Kiyomori, struck by fever, fancies the mountains to be ghosts

to: the burial of living persons. He buried thirty-six fine strong men, not with pleasure but with remorse felt so severely that it brought about a fever. Kiyomori, in his delirium about to draw his sword, fancied the Hyogo mountains to be ghosts, as well as the pine and plum trees and the *toros* (stone lanterns) in his garden – all, in his mind, were the ghosts of those thirty-six men whom he had buried to solidify the earth of the marshes. Baiho copied the picture of Kiyomori and his wife at their residence in Fukuwara from a very ancient one lent to me by Kobayashi. The tomb is pretty but, like many other things of this kind in Japan, badly kept. It is a pity, some day the loss of these ancient historical landmarks will be bitterly regretted.

Kiyomori's tomb, Hyogo

FRIDAY SEPTEMBER 23RD   Dined last night with H.E. the Governor and awoke early with a splitting headache, the result of *sake*. Barring my head, I enjoyed myself very much at the Governor's excellent dinner and, according to etiquette, wrote early this morning to say so. 'Dear Mr Hattori, I was so delightfully drunk and enjoyed myself so much at Your Excellency's charming dinner last night that I was quite unable to say goodnight.' This is not exactly what I wrote for I was not drunk, but according to the strictest etiquette, as told me years ago by Sir Ernest Satow and confirmed since by Japanese, this is what should be written. I came away absolutely sober despite having swallowed over 100 cups of *sake*. What a beast, most people would say. All I can say is that it is unavoidable – the etiquette and forfeit games with *geishas* necessitate it.

This particular dinner was given to myself and Bonar[13], the Consul, and also present were Griffiths[14] the Vice-Consul, Groom, Reynell, and Mr Kodjira, the court's interpreter. As the dinner was to be an informal and a jolly one, we were told to make ourselves at home. The host sat on the extreme right, while his guests were assigned tables in the order he directed. At a formal dinner, the seat in front of the *tokonoma* [the alcove in which is hung a *kakemono*] is the seat of honour. We commenced with my favourite dish – *suppon* soup, and plenty of it too, but here I do not intend to go through the details of the food. Several dishes were served between 7 and 9.30 p.m., including three soups with what one might call three separate dinners between. All the dishes were excellently cooked.

The dinner was given in Marquis Ito's [Prime Minister] part of the Tokuwa Kadan teahouse – the best in all Hyogo. After some two or three courses had been eaten, the Governor came over and sat, first with one and then with another of his guests. When he arrives, your waitress fills your cup of *sake* and you drink to welcome your visitor. You then rinse the cup in a brass basin of water, the servant refills it and you hand it to the visitor. He, in turn, bows to you, hopes you are enjoying yourself and you have about ten minutes'

Dinner with the Governor – clockwise from top left: Bonar (Consul), Griffiths (Vice-Consul). Kodjira (court interpreter), geishas, Mr Hattori, Meynell, myself, Groom

general conversation, after which he moves on to someone else. When the host has finished his round of visits, you in turn go and call on him, when the same ceremony takes place. When all these visits have been fulfilled according to etiquette, the guests commence to call upon each other, returning to their own tables between each visit to snatch a few mouthfuls of food and be prepared to receive other callers. Now and then, the *geishas* either sing or dance and, when not doing this, come and sit amongst the diners, entering into conversations and, now and then, accepting a cup of *sake*.

The seven geishas present were all of the best and quietest kind in Hyogo – quiet even in their dress. Nevertheless, they were quite noisy when dinner was over and the forfeit games were commenced. *Ken*[15] is the name for many of these games, none of which I have entered seriously – a precaution, in a sense, for this saves many forfeits which, of course, mean the drinking of extra cups of *sake*. *Geishas* play *ken* with great rapidity and scarcely ever lose a point, while the European idiot, who fancies himself proficient, loses not only every time, but also half-a-dozen points in each game which generally leads to his hopeless intoxication. It is part of the *geisha's* business to see to this. The party broke up at about 11.30 p.m., much in the way that European parties do, all going more or less together. I think my *kurumayas* (rickshaw coolies) were both surprised and not over pleased to find their master sober. 'Surely,' they would think, 'he cannot have enjoyed himself.'

SUNDAY OCTOBER 2ND Fearful day. For some time it has been decided to shoot for the Port Arthur medal. The match was for twenty shooters, 100 birds each and no handicap. I only managed fourth place. No other Europeans shot, the rain and wind being too awful for anything. It seems rather funny to have won a medal given to celebrate the fall of Port Arthur but, nevertheless, I am having it set in a match box, and dated 1904.

154

CHAPTER 9

The Pearl Divers of Toshi

1904

Wounded soldiers at Osaka – train journey to Tsu – sojourn at Yamada – Geku shrines and pilgrims – rocks at Futami – introductions at Toba – the pearl divers and their equipment – voyage to Toshi – a special diving expedition – photographs, lunch and a gramophone concert – the giant crab – farewell presents

TUESDAY OCTOBER 4TH Left Kobe by the 7.30 a.m. train in beautiful weather, but the beriberi is troubling me sorely. Osaka station was full of wounded soldiers, some six or seven hundred lying and sitting all over the platform, waiting patiently for their turn to be carried to the enormous hospital which has been set up on the exhibition grounds.

We passed through Nara, and from there to Kameyama the scenery is splendid. Wild mountains like those seen in Chinese paintings rise tier after tier in pointed cones, some clad with pine and fir trees, others with only scrub and bamboo; dashing rivers and streams are everywhere. A splendid sporting country it looked but, alas for the Japanese laws, peasants have destroyed nearly all of it. At Kameyama we changed trains, and shortly after reached Tsu, the capital of the prefecture of Mie. There are two interesting temples here which I only had time to glimpse at in tourist fashion.

My real business at Tsu was to call on the Governor to whom I have letters from Mr Hattori. The Governor himself was in Tokyo, but his Excellency very kindly left a letter of introduction for me to the mayor and head man of the village of Toba. I was entertained to tea by Mr Naga (head of the Agricultural Department of Awa), and a most interesting man I found him. He showed me all the government books of fisheries, splendidly illustrated in watercolours by an excellent artist, now dead. He gave me a letter to the present best painter in Ise, Mr Saishu, and told me a good deal about the shooting in the province and offered to arrange some, so far as wild boar were concerned, whenever I liked. Mr Naga also told me much about the divers. 'If you go to the island of Toshi and those beyond it, you will have been, I believe, the only European who ever has; it will interest you, I think, though I myself have not been.' That was enough for me. Mikimoto's Island was visited by a German three years ago, and there may have been others, so Toshi was my choice.

We caught a train which brought us to Yamada at 8 p.m., where we put up at what is called the Gonikai Hotel, which to my mind is more of a teahouse

than an hotel. However, I was made very comfortable and given European food at a table with a chair to sit on. I sent off a telegraph to Egawa, to tell him to come at once, for I begin to dislike Fukai [temporary interpreter] so strongly that it may, with a little more provocation, lead me to break the law.

I also sent a letter to Mr Saishu, the artist to whom Mr Naga gave me the introduction, as I want him to paint for me a couple of pictures of the divers, something like those in the books at Tsu. There was considerable noise at night in the hotel – several parties with *geishas* were going on, and although by law they should stop at midnight they did not do so.

WEDNESDAY OCTOBER 5TH A most excellent night's sleep, which I little expected considering the early noise in the hotel.

Before I had time to dress, Saishu arrived from the country ready to paint my divers' pictures. He was a quiet-voiced, reserved man who set to work within twenty minutes of his arrival, saying that he had often seen the celebrated diving women. Though his paintings are excellent, he has painted them all wrong, red never being worn by any of the divers, unless in guide-book imagination; in fact, no one seems to know anything of the real divers, as my photos subsequently show.

After breakfast I set off to the Geku shrines[1]. It is interesting to know that these are exactly the same now, in every detail, as they were in 4 BC. Every shrine and wall is rebuilt every twenty years, the carpenters following exactly and in detail the previous shrine and its walls. Hundreds of carpenters are kept, their daily entry to the shrine's grounds is like men going to work in a government factory, only they are cleaner. Each has to wear short white drawers and a clean blue *kimono* – it is quite a livery. They are inspected by shrine guards before being allowed to enter the grounds of so holy a place.

The pilgrim farmers flock to the shrines more, perhaps, than anyone else. They are now here to thank the gods for their magnificent crop of rice, and to pray for another next year. They show not only thankfulness but also appreciation for good management, as it were, and pray for a continuance of the same.

As the mass of farmers with their families centred as much interest in myself as in anything else, I made friends with them, and made Fukai interpret. By this means I enjoyed myself considerably more and was enabled to watch the reverence with which the people approached the outer gate of the Holy of Holies, beyond which they are not allowed. In fact, over the gate, or entrance in the outer wall, are hung white cloths, and one cannot even look through unless the wind blows the cloth aside, though it is as well to give these curtains a wide berth if one considers what happened to Viscount Mori[2] in 1889.

All that the people carry away from these shrines is the comforting memory that they have been and prayed there. Besides this, they bring away charms, stamped and marked by the priest of Ise. The charms, as will be seen, are simply little wooden boxes made from old bits of the shrines, containing a little piece of wood from the inner or most holy shrine around which is wrapped a piece

*The shrine where the holy dances are held and, above,
charms from the outer and inner shrines*

of paper (*Go-Hai*). There are also four strips of white paper, evidently also holy, but not understood by myself. I suppose it is even sacrilegious to have broken them open as I have done, but my intentions are very much the reverse in doing so. It is to show what very little these people are contented with after their long journeys. Of course, many believe in the active virtue of these *mamori* or charms to protect them against illness or evil, just as the Roman Catholics do in a silver or golden medal, or, indeed, as we may do in a clergyman's blessing.

THURSDAY OCTOBER 6TH No sleep possible last night. Three Japanese guests keeping it up late with a dinner party and *geishas*. I got to sleep at 2.30 a.m. and was up again at 5 a.m. Just to annoy the others who had kept me awake, I made a great noise myself, by way of preparing my departure. Started at 7.30 a.m. by a *basha* (carriage) passing first through an open, ugly flat country of rice fields. Diminutive boats were everywhere, floating in this district which is so watered that the crops are harvested into the boats and then conveyed to higher and drier land. Futami is the commencement of the hill country here. It is pretty, but the rocks[3], which have such a reputation, are ridiculously disappointing. There are many stories of them and they are called the Union of Man and Woman in Matrimony. The principal Japanese story is that one of the gods begged the sun goddess, Amaterasu, to let him see what she was like. She bid him watch through the rocks at a certain time in the morning, and she arose exactly between them, just as the sun now does.

At 2 p.m., we reached the sleepy village of Toba, where I went first to call upon Mr Kitahara the mayor and present my letter from the Governor of Mieken. Mr Kitahara had never received a European before and, feeling considerably confused as to what to do with me, called his clerk, an old farmer, who appeared even more confused. I was thus enabled more easily to lay down just what help I wanted, and they gave it.

A messenger was sent to the headman of Toshi Island to appraise him of my arrival on the morrow. Twenty diving women were to be kept ready for me with five boats and two men in each. I was also to be given a fast boat with a strong rowing crew to take me to Toshishima. Having arranged all this, I retired to the Kinoura teahouse where my rooms were excellent, but where the noise

158

The wife and husband rocks at Futami

of songs and *geishas* prevented either sleep or rest.

Late in the evening, to my surprise and delight, Egawa arrived having come clean through in the same day. I know, now, that I will be able to get on with the people.

An excellent dinner was given me: seaweed soup with mushrooms in it; fried *tai*; *tokoroten*, an excellent jelly made from the seaweed for which the young girls dive, *awabi* (sea earshell) done in soy sauce; Ise crayfish, and some enormous prawns, beside two kinds of omelette. As I had my own bread I was happy.

We talked with the landlord and several others of stories about divers, ghosts and spirits; curiously enough, little was known of the divers. I bought photos in Yamada of them, but none like the ones I subsequently saw on Toshishima – those were the real ones to whom the following ancient story, as illustrated, is attached.

In the fourteenth year of the reign of Emperor Ingyo [412–53], a priest in a very holy shrine, a Kami shrine, told the Mikado that he knew for a fact that there was an *awabi* shell near the island of Akashi in Sumoto Bay, of such enormous size that no man could lift it; also, that it had been seen to throw out light by those who had been able to get deep enough in the water to see it.

The Mikado, hearing this, sent for the best divers who could be found in Toshishima who were, in those days, men and not women. A man called Osagi was the bravest and best diver amongst them. He gave orders that the best men of the island accompany him and then began to carry out the Mikado's wish that the shell should be brought to the surface. Several men tried, but none of them were able to detach the shell from the rock. 'It is a hopeless task,' they told Osagi, 'even you would be of no use here.' Osagi laughed, and said that what was undertaken at the Mikado's behest could never prove a failure. He

159

forthwith dived deep into the sea, with a large knife with which to detach the shell; Osagi remained at the bottom of the sea an extraordinary length of time, so long, in fact, that they all thought him drowned. Sad were all at such a thought for he was popular, brave, and much regarded amongst the Toshi Island people. Just before the sun began to set and when all were thinking of going ashore to report their misfortune, not only in not being able to carry out the Mikado's wishes but also in having lost their best man, wonderful rays of light came out of the sea followed by the end of an enormous shell. It was seen that Osagi had grasped it but looked ill with his efforts. Men sprang overboard with ropes to secure the shell and hauled it safely into a boat. Poor Osagi, however, sank, saying, 'Anything which the Emperor wishes us to do can be done.' In the shell was an enormous pearl from which the rays of light had come that had led to the shell's discovery. There are several songs to the memory of Osagi, but so far I have found no one who knows them – in fact, since hearing this story, I have told it to a number of Japanese, none of whom had heard it.

FRIDAY OCTOBER 7TH   At 7 a.m. I found a most dangerously unseaworthy-looking boat waiting for me, a three-oared sampan, flat bottomed and the narrowest I ever saw, being only about 3 feet wide at the gunwale and 2 feet across the bottom, while its length was about 33 feet. *Hiyai fune*, a fast boat, they called it. Indeed, I hoped so, for a seven or eight mile paddle in a choppy sea promised not to be the most pleasant part of the trip, let alone the chance of being upset some three miles from shore – nothing to these hardy Japanese fishermen, but not for either Egawa or myself. Besides, I had brought a good many of my toys which would be sure to be lost – a gramophone, two cameras and my best luncheon basket. Luckily, there was but little wind although the strong currents here and there caused an unpleasant sea and once or twice I thought we might have overturned, and we nearly did, but it brought nothing more to the boatmen's faces than the usual Japanese smile. Egawa, for a wonder, got sick; Fukai turned green, and the only passengers whose insides were not affected were the very solid old chief clerk, sent by the Mayor of Toba to escort me on the trip, and me. His name was J. Yuki and, in spite of his stolidness, he proved useful enough at hurrying up things when we got to Toshimura.

Toshi Island is a wild, rugged looking place about five miles long and one mile broad. There is a fishing village called Momotori on its western end, and the diving village at the northeastern end. Years ago the island used to contain many deer; pheasants are still there in fair numbers. The slopes of the uncultivated land – for it is nearly all so – are covered with stunted bamboo, which looked as if woodcock might be found there. Ducks are plentiful in winter, but very difficult to approach.

Kashima is another island much the same as Toshi. It has only one village, and that is of divers. In fact, this and the one on Toshishima are the principal diving stations in Japan. There are, of course, places everywhere where diving will be resorted to, to make profit from the bottom of the sea, but not like it is here, where it is carried on as it was a thousand years and more ago. What we call civilisation has not overtaken them, no missionary has been there to demoralise them by telling them that their lack of clothing shocks him; nor that there is wickedness and want of modesty in appearing thus. The people are quite notorious for their virtue.

At Toshi and Ka Islands only the small children dive for weeds, practising nearly all day in shallow water. They float tubs in front of themselves, going down as they please, but there is great rivalry amongst them in seeing who fills her tub first. When a girl is able to dive to about four fathoms for *awabi* or for large mussels she is allowed to accompany the boats, and is a proud girl indeed, for the object of all is to be of use to their parents by earning money for the family. All the divers wear tin and glass spectacles, while running from the corner of the eye to the ear is a rubber tube attached to a rubber ball covered by a copper box. This simple arrangement serves in some way as protection to the eye by preventing the water from touching it. I noticed no sore eyes amongst these people, such as one might have expected from their

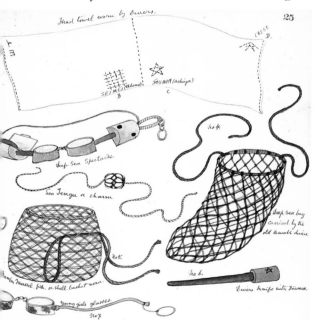

Diving gear – 1, head towel: A diver's name; B seimei [full name]; C doumon; D crest. 2, deep-sea goggles. 3, sea tengu or charm. 4, awabi bag. 5, bamboo basket for shells and fish. 6, diver's knife. 7, girl's goggles.

161

continual immersion. Besides spectacles, each diver wears a pair of rough gloves so as to enable her to tear away sharp shells from the rocks; they also enable her to hold onto anything slippery, such as an octopus. Of course, all wear a knife ready to draw under water, and they carry a sort of blunt instrument to knock *awabis* off the rocks. Sometimes the latter hold on so tight as to defy attack. In this case the diver puts in one or two wooden levers and returns for the shell next day when it is too tired to retain such a tight hold on the rock. If a good edible fish is swimming about in the diver's immediate neighbourhood she has a small thin lance attached to a line tied to the boat. Having speared the fish, a boatman hauls it up.

Each diver, as seen in my pictures, also carries a basket in which to put her shells. When ready to come up she pulls the rope hung over the side of the boat,

and is hauled up. They dive without being weighted, so far as one can see, but I think there is a stone attached to the rope which they seize after diving, for I never saw the rope pulled clear of the water.

To get back to our boat, which was conveying us to Toshi from Toba, we landed safely at a little cove close to the end of the island.

Even here the beach was strewn with earshells, giving it quite a pearly appearance. It seemed a pity to tread on and break such beautiful shells. We said farewell to our long narrow boat and crew with more thankfulness than sorrow that we had not to go back in it. Fishermen shouldered our things and we walked across the little peninsular through scenery that was truly romantic. A steep path led up to a little shrine of great age and a cemetery with moss-covered stones and figures of [the god] Jizo that must have been hundreds of years old. Some of the very oldest

gravestones had been freshly decorated with wild flowers in bamboo cups, showing that the people still venerated and respected their ancestors.

At the top of the hill is the boys' school, which overlooks a splendid panorama of bays and islands, fantastic rocks, and a blue sea whose heavy rollers broke on the rocks with a spray and surf as white as ivory. Alas, however, there were a few

The rocky road through the cemetery

A view from the eastern bay from the cemetery road

buckwheat fields, of diminutive size, and these were being watered and nourished with liquid manure, the stench of which made Egawa and myself sick on the spot. Never have I smelt anything so awful before – an emetic of invaluable quality. We almost ran the rest of the way to the village, arriving there out of breath, much to the astonishment of the people.

We were taken, at first, to call on the mayor in his office. Mr Yosuki, for such was his name, received us in true Japanese fashion and served us with green tea (which his clerk made in our presence). All this was done with great ceremony, and, I feared, delay. After more tea we were escorted through the narrow streets by the mayor and a crowd of fully 100 people, of whom seventy per cent were females. Though the streets were narrow and the houses poor, there was no smell. The streets were paved with broken mussels and earshells, giving the place quite a distinctive air.

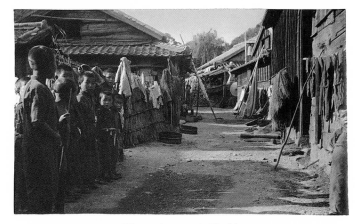

The main street in Toshi

At the beach we found fully 400 children and women assembled to see us off. The greatest good nature, sympathy, and kindness prevailed.

I had to go down a steep bank. The people felt sorry: 'Would the foreign gentleman be able to do this comfortably? What a pity we have made no steps!' Such, and many more kindly remarks they made. My boat, a six-oared one, had been strewn with red blankets and their best cushions to make me comfortable. Five boats were also allotted to me, with three women and a man in each, while five small divers were sent with me so that I might make them dive along the shallower water and pick up smaller shells. All the people on the shore wished they could have come along with the foreign gentleman.

The old mayor came down to the edge of the water to see that all was in order, and sent his head clerk, Mr Nishi Mawa, along to help and escort me the whole way back to Toba, after the diving and picnic was over.

Beyond Toshi are many rocks and some small uninhabited islands. One may dive anywhere here, in water from four to eight fathoms in depth (a Japanese fathom is five feet). They say that they can dive fifteen fathoms in the hot weather, but I don't believe it. They also talk of dives of three minutes when

*On the left, laughing, the best diver, aged 62,
and, right, the next best, aged 51*

the water is warm. The longest I timed today was 58 seconds, made by an old lady of 62. This old creature was by far the best diver, and on one occasion brought up an arm of an octopus she had pulled clean off by sheer strength. It came to the surface still clinging to her own. She then returned, fought him again and brought up the rest.

Having got well out between the islands, all the boats except my own anchored, and the work began in earnest. The women were up and down the whole time, very rarely empty handed; mussels, 10 inches in length, and another large and beautiful mother-of-pearl shell was found. Now and then there was great excitement when someone saw a very large fish and failed to spear it. Everyone dived at once to see if they could get it. Several black *tai* of about 3 or 4 lb were speared, and the old lady came up with a fine large Ise crayfish, which I promptly made up my mind to grill and eat for luncheon (it may be of interest to add that here the crayfish are noted for their excellence).

The fun went on without stopping for nearly two hours, the women only leaving the water now and then to warm their backs, which they did at a charcoal fire carried for the purpose in each of their boats. We had got quite as much as I wanted, so I called a halt so that we might try the younger divers nearer shore, and then land for lunch. The young girls chose some jagged rocks to dive around, where the sea swell came in, making them at one moment three feet out of water and at the next, three feet under. Most dangerous, I thought it. However, they wanted to show that, however deficient they might be, as yet, in being unable to dive *deep* or remain long under water, they made up for it in their fishlike ability to swim and to dive in such places without damaging themselves. Veritable mermaids, indeed, were they. They slid here, there and

The diving nymphs of Toshishima

everywhere, up and down, in and out, no matter whether the water was rising or falling. They scraped over jagged rocks and went with the water, bubbling down and out of sight, but coming up a few seconds later with a shell in their hands. It was a wonderful thing that none of them ever got even scratched. They seemed prepared to stop in the sea for the rest of the day, for when I told them to get back into the boats because we were off to the island, they quietly said they would follow and pick up what they could on the way. They swam quite as fast as three men could row the large boat and kept their faces down in the water, with spectacles on and eyes like hawks. If they saw anything worth having, up went their heels

The twenty diving ladies who formed my party for the day

and down they went in a second; the boat was slowed as they chucked in their shells before setting off again.

On arriving at the island we found that we had half a boat-load of things. Mostly, as I have said before, mussels and *awabis*.

The island was a perfect gem, so far as its rocks were concerned, the most remarkable feature being the colouring – grey, pink and light-green, with peculiar wavy lines resembling sea waves in them. The first thing was to photograph the divers – all twenty together, and next in age groups. The best divers are all old, and I have no young ones, except the five children. Judging from my 62-year-old friend, women dive apparently up to any age. They dive up to within a month of childbirth, and commence again a week after, for they are the main providers of food for their families.

The juvenile divers, from 12 to 14 years old, are wonderful swimmers

Having finished their photos I set about preparing the gramophone, while Egawa cooked luncheon, which consisted of baked crayfish, fried *tai*, mussels and *awabis* grilled and dipped in soy sauce as well as a bit of fried bacon, without which I never travel. I think it shocked them to see me eat so much of it.

Their delight at the gramophone was pleasing to see. They had never even heard of one; they could understand it in no way, but enjoyed it to the full. I was pleased to hear them say that it must have been brought by me to please them, and they made remarks entirely complimentary on that account, fully showing how quick-witted and kind they themselves were. In fact, I know of no Japanese people whom I took to so much as these islanders – it seemed to come naturally, at once. It was impossible not to like them, in spite of their looks. They are a fine, large lot of people, the men being, generally, as tall as myself which, for Japan, is huge. The women are large and strong too, but they are not good looking. Their hair turns light by continual immersion, while exposure discolours and tans their skins to a coarse roughness, almost like that of a tortoise's shell. Their characters stand very high amongst the Japanese gentry in all the surrounding departments of Mieken; so much is thought of their hardiness, their strength, kindness and bravery that they are often called upon to name children. If, for instance, a man lose, by death, his first child or two, and another is born, the first thing is to send over to Toshi or Ka Island for a diving woman. She arrives at the house, names the newborn child, and for ever after has an entrée to that house. She is a kind of foster mother; she also receives a handsome present, annually, on the child's birthday. This rather curious custom certainly shows the gentry recognise the goodness and the strength of the divers.

I was quite sorry when our island party was over, and dearly wished that I had known of this place before. What a place for my steam launch – all the fish from the Pacific must come here, and one might even find a gigantic crab.

The people told me that in the olden days they had often caught them here. As may well be imagined, they told extraordinary tales of their size. Baiho's painting is based on his ideas of comparative sizes, using the legs and body of a crab in my possession, which is 11 feet across. His picture is not much out, except in the forearm of the claw, but later I shall be able to show the man more accurately because I intend to take a photograph of one holding the claws. The

The result of Burt Shephard's 'Laughing Song'

The effect of a military band

divers, very naturally, spoke of crabs 300 feet across. It is the privilege of fisherfolk to see things through magnifying spectacles – why should they not? – they are the dwellers by the ocean, the contents of which no man knoweth, and it is pleasant to be allowed imagination in these infernal days of fact.

At 4 p.m. we had to leave, and say *sayonara* to our diving friends. We had a foul tide and lumpy sea for half the way, and it took us nearly two hours to reach Toba. During part of this time I opened mussels and was lucky enough to find a curiously formed pearl, the shape of a spiral shell, and very green. It will make a good pin and will call to memory one of the most enjoyable days I have ever spent, not only on account of the interest but also because of the charming manners and great kindness of these *wild, uncivilised, unchristian, yellow-skinned barbarians*, as some pale-faced hypocrite, or money-grasping, narrow-minded missionary would call them. I know to which I should prefer to be thrown if I wanted help of any kind.

At Toba I found Mr Kitahara, the mayor, at the teahouse waiting for my return and to hear if all had gone well. 'It has,' I said, 'and you are to be congratulated upon the men you, in particular, rule over. These islands alone are a backbone for your navy, the strength of which must double with sailors from them.' It is, in reality, a pity to take these men for soldiers, though nineteen had gone as such. Before leaving Toba each servant gave me a present.

If it were possible to keep out *geishas* and their gallants, I should have liked to stay here, but the noise is quite impossible. A long, dark drive brought us to Yamada late, where I dismissed Fukai, the ass of an interpreter.

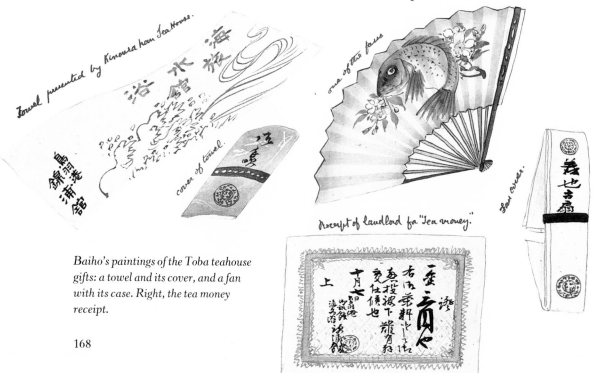

Baiho's paintings of the Toba teahouse gifts: a towel and its cover, and a fan with its case. Right, the tea money receipt.

CHAPTER 10

Lord of the Land

1904/1905

*The Governor's son loses an eye – Russian attack on Hull trawlers –
the disadvantages of monogamy – death and burial of Carlo –
firefighters in action – infantry manoeuvres near Osaka – 203-Metre
Hill – lakeside folktales – shooting a fox with Compie Pakenham –
donating British Museum nets – the Fall of Port Arthur – game-law
proposals – Ford Barclay interferes – the* samurai *spirit*

*Returning to Kobe from his pearl-diving interlude, Gordon Smith reflects on the Japanese
attitude to the war and on the reluctance of the British government to enter the conflict.*

SUNDAY OCTOBER 23RD   The Governor [of Hyogo Prefecture, Mr Hattori]
came to lunch. His son, I am sorry to hear, has lost an eye, which is very sad
for so young an officer. The Governor did not know which eye, and his son's
only request was, that they should not *talk or make any fuss about him.* True
heroes, all these Japanese, not only
in their bravery while fighting, but
in their modesty and even shyness
and dislike of notoriety.

MONDAY OCTOBER 24TH   Dull day and
cold. Thermometer 60°F. Russian
Baltic Fleet fire on our North Sea
trawlers, killing and wounding a good
many of these defenceless people[1].
Feel sorry for the sufferers, but hope
that this outrage will be the last that
even England will tolerate. In the
Club they talk of immediate action
and the necessity of either sinking or
capturing the Russian Fleet. However
desirous this action may be for the
maintenance of Britain's credit in the
East, let alone elsewhere, I fear that
England will do little more than protest and make a naval demonstration.

PUNCH, OR THE LONDON CHARIVARI.—JULY 6, 1904.

A LESSON IN PATRIOTISM.

*Japan lectures Britain on
the ultimate sacrifice*

FRIDAY OCTOBER 28TH Wrote letters. Japanese papers say England has given Russia until 12 o'clock tonight to answer a kind of ultimatum. I don't believe it, but hope it is true. The one person who has expressed to Russia the sentiments of emnity that *most* Englishmen feel in their hearts is the street boy in London who took it upon himself to try to smash the Russian Ambassador's carriage window. This boy might well be educated for the advantage of his country for he feels himself a patriot. I like this boy and should educate him myself were it possible.

SATURDAY OCTOBER 29TH With difficulty my large *suppon* was killed and made into soup. His Excellency the Governor, and Griffiths our Vice-Consul, came to eat it at luncheon. Talking of Russian prisoners, H.E. said they found the men had to be separated to prevent fighting amongst themselves. The Jews, the Poles, the Finns and so on all fall out and will not live or even speak together. Most are delighted to have become Japanese prisoners.

Two extraordinary letters in this morning's mail: one about what my Uncle Walter[2] said. I don't believe he could have made such a public statement. If he did, it shows that passing first in an examination for the Indian Civil Service and subsequently becoming Private Secretary to the Viceroy [of India], with all the knowledge coming therefrom, does not make a politician. I wrote to him to suggest the advisability of commencing the war a little earlier than the spring – at once in fact while our gallant allies are at them as well – and urged upon him the value of Japan if we were working actively together.

> London, October 2.
> A sensation has been created here by certain remarks concerning Anglo-Russian relations, attributed to Sir Walter Lawrence, private secretary to Lord Curzon. He was staying at a country house quite recently, when he electrified a dinner party by declaring that, without doubt, there would be a war between England and Russia next spring. It is not only his private opinion, but also that of Lord Kitchener and all of his officials in India, and he added that many big guns were being sent out quietly to India all the time, and every preparation was being made for a long campaign.

The other newspaper telegram is delightful. The Governor, Griffiths and myself drank heartily to the health of the Princess Charlotte of Russia. Oh happy Prince Bernhard of Saxe-Meiningen, fortune has truly favoured you with a good wife of great sense.

> Berlin, October 2.
> The Kaiser's sister, Princess Charlotte of Prussia, wife of Prince Bernard of Saxe-Meinengen, has written a pamphlet advocating polygamy, and the Kaiser is trying to suppress the pamphlet. Princess Charlotte urges polygamy as a remedy for social ills. She argues that divorce is the consequence of boredom, and if husbands were allowed to make several women happy a social millennium would ensue. Princess Charlotte is 44 and has one daughter, married to Prince Henry of Reuss. It is said the Kaiser has threatened to appoint an alienist commission to inquire into Princess Charlotte's state of mind.

MONDAY OCTOBER 31ST Shocked to read in the train that England has consented to arbitration over the North Sea affair. Went to Yamasaki, where quite a crowd came to meet me, amongst them a large number of children who seem to look upon me as one of their greatest friends. Visited Nanko and his boat and went up

Nanko on his boat

the river. Got four woodcocks only – all I saw. Snipe were about, but in the rice paddies where I would not go [out of respect for the crops].

TUESDAY NOVEMBER 1ST No news this morning which is not 'weak piffle', sickening to read, and depressing to one's mind. Lunched with Griffiths; an excellent meal, Bonar and Rentiers[3] also present. When I got home at 4.30 p.m. I found the house dumb with sorrow, for dear old Carlo had died. Egawa announced the fact solemnly, Yume, Kosa and the gardener seemed to feel it quite seriously. Carlo, who had been sleeping in his kennel as usual all day, came out at 4 p.m. and walked round to look for me. I being away, he found Egawa and put his paws up as usual for attention. Next he went and looked at Egawa's family, then the gardener and cook, after which he returned to his kennel. Half an hour later, just before I got in, he died. The old gardener, looking in to give him some milk, found him dead. Here I lose the best dog, with the most sense, I ever had. A dog whom I loved and who, I think, loved me. Poor old Carlo. In one way it is a relief, for it has saved his execution which I should have had to carry out myself as a duty.

My gardener and the men cremated him as soon as it was dark. Everyone believed so much in his wisdom that they say his *O-bake* (ghost) is sure to be seen. He was buried next morning at the bottom of the garden, his grave being basically Japanese – green bamboo and a bamboo [receptacle] for the flowers, a white *chochin* (lantern), and a post with his name on. In this case we wrote the Japanese for *Here lies Carlo, a faithful dog, who came with his master to Japan in 1900 and died in 1904.* If it had been myself I should have been given a new name. People's worldly names never appear on tombstones.

Carlo's Japanese grave

SATURDAY NOVEMBER 5TH Lovely weather. At the consulate, which was thrown into consternation when Prof. Pfoundes was announced. Everyone scurried away to get clear of that old lunatic.

SUNDAY NOVEMBER 6TH Sent Carlo's ashes off to the New Forest [in England].

FRIDAY NOVEMBER 11TH At Itami today I was much struck with an instance of Japanese superiority in organisation which showed not only commonsense, but the extraordinary rapidity with which the Japanese help each other in times of emergency. *They are always ready.*

An hour after I left Itami an enormous fire broke out. Two huge godowns, full of government hay, and a large woodyard caught fire, with a good few houses as well. The wind fanned the fire into one of the largest I have ever seen – I was three miles away. The first thing one heard were the fire gongs at Itami itself, next came the smoke, followed by the village *taiko* or drum. Every village was beating its drum within ten minutes of the Itami alarm, and within ten more, every village hand-pump brigade was on its way, the men running with

Village fire brigades on their way to Itami

all their might, and all in their curious blue and white fire uniforms. Considering that the men were all away working in their fields when the alarm sounded I call it a wonderful performance. There were perhaps thirty village brigades at the fire. The mere fact that every small village owns a hose reel and hand-pump is something to be proud of.

In the train from Kanzaki to Kobe were a number of priests of high order going to the front.

There follow five days filled with shooting and luncheons.

Military skirmishes along the way

THURSDAY NOVEMBER 17TH Up very early and by 8 a.m. I was beating up the bamboos and came across two companies of Osaka infantrymen who, so they said, had already done 8 ri (16 miles). They had piled arms where I met them, and were resting. Later, they were to get back to Osaka skirmishing the whole way and practising advancing through enemy country. The men, with few exceptions, looked tough and hardy. The order amongst them is wonderful. The officers have little to do in keeping this, and are in every way to be envied. Later in the day I found myself in an advance post engagement; luckily for me the fight continued towards Osaka and not where my best grounds are.

FRIDAY NOVEMBER 18TH Newspaper reports are extraordinary. They say that the Russian ships [the Baltic Fleet] are to pass through the Suez Canal with all due haste and that any merchantmen [sailing north] are to wait at Suez until the Russians are clear of the canal. Balfour[4] is confined to his room with weak veins and not allowed to attend to any business.

Were there ever two pieces of news more disheartening to the minds of Englishmen despatched in a day!! Surely merchantmen have the same rights in the Canal that men-of-war have. Especially in this case.

It is unpleasant reading also to see that 'a small vein in the leg' can so far incapacitate our premier as to necessitate his being kept absolutely quiet and prevented from attending to business. Is such a premier worthy of England's trust? Is a premier who refuses to attend to the nation's business, no matter *what his illness*, a patriot? We don't think so out here.

SATURDAY NOVEMBER 19TH The more one thinks and reads of the extraordinary directions said to have been given by the Governor of Suez, practically suspending the world's business, the more extraordinary does it seem that England's voice has not been heard. The Japanese will soon be entitled to consider the whole of Europe ranged against herself, for Denmark allowed the fleet to coal in her waters, France has been equally accommodating at Cherbourg, Tangier, and Dakar, while Spain showed the same benevolence at Vigo, and now the whole of the Suez Canal traffic is to be suspended in order that the Russian fleet may not be delayed in so much as an hour on its journey to the East!! If any sign of strict neutrality can be seen in this, my visionary and mental powers fail to grasp it.

SUNDAY NOVEMBER 20TH At home all day writing and thinking of the apparent hopelessness of England's foreign policies, of the madness that has seized some who see [only] Yellow Perils, believing such a real possibility, instead of blaming it on the jaundiced state of their livers. Give me a man who sees things in the light of Dr Rutherford Harris M.P.[5] His idea is strictly true and commonsense.

SUNDAY NOVEMBER 27TH In the morning a man brought me, *at last*, an ivory carving by Kouaiguiokou the celebrated carver who lived in the middle of the 18th century and under whom so many pupils studied. The peculiarity of his carving is its fineness. He used always white ivory – never stained it. He could carve coral in a way which no other man could attempt, and also ebony. Louis Gonse places him amongst Japan's very best. This particular carving, which it is my fortune to become the possessor of today, is one of Kouaiguiokou's finest. Outside, a fir cone; inside, a pine tree with all its branches open worked, and pine needles showing. Behind the tree and through its branches can be seen an old man and woman. The tortoises are seen with their long hairy tails, the lucky storks, and spring bamboo. Nothing is missing – the carving is marvellous, the whole under 1½ inch in height, and 1 inch in width. The reverse side shows the sun and the clouds.

THURSDAY DECEMBER 1ST A *banzai* day today, 203-Metre Hill[6] having fallen. No excitement. Everyone quietly pleased. Losses are hardly even thought of. The hill is most important – from it Russian ships can easily be sunk. Will they make a dash out or not? I say not.

FRIDAY DECEMBER 2ND Fine day with brilliant sunshine. Off to Nishinomiya early and commenced near the sea at the Saki [group of] villages where, with much difficulty, I killed my entire bag by 11.30 a.m. After this I went off west and north of the railway under, in fact, Bismarck Hill (as the Europeans call it, owing to its resemblance to Bismarck's head with four hairs on the top represented by pine trees). Go where I would, not a bird of any kind whatever could be found. So let the shooting be dismissed.

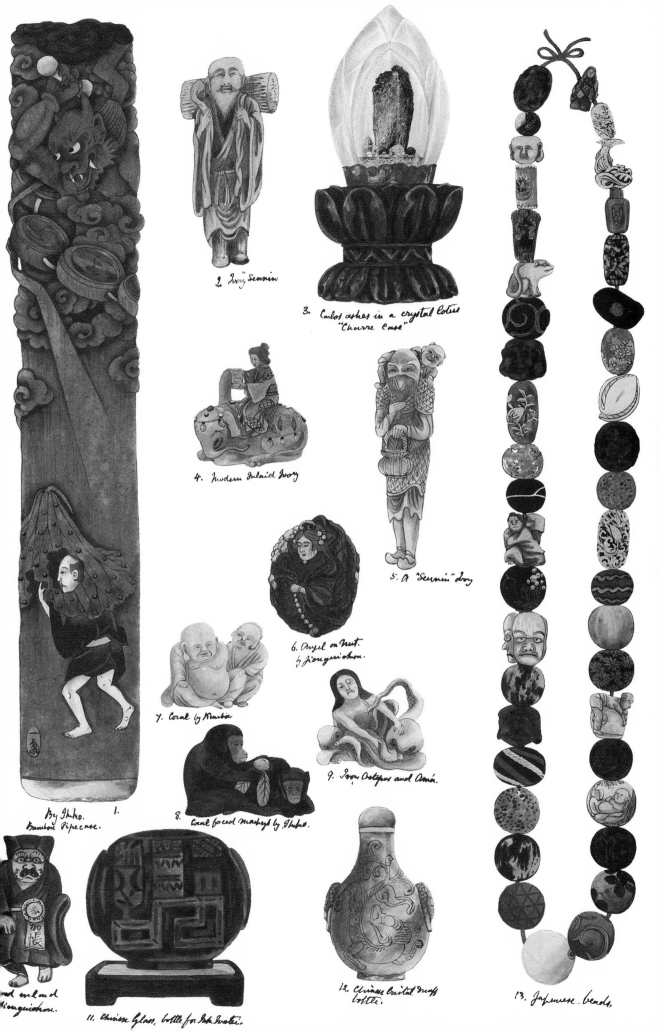

By Ikko.
Bamboo Pipecase. 1.

2. Ivory Sennin.

3. Carlos ashes in a crystal Lotus "Chasse Case."

4. Modern Inlaid Ivory.

5. A "Sennin" Ivory.

6. Angel on Nest. by Jiongui chou.

7. Coral by Rinba.

8. Coral faced Monkeys by Ikko.

9. Ivory Octopus and Ama.

...nd enk and Jiongui chou.

11. Chinese Glass, bottle for Ink Smoke.

12. Chinese Cristal Snuff bottle.

13. Japanese beads.

We lunched in a delightfully wild and characteristic mountain cemetery under the shadow of *roku Jizo* (six figures of the merciful [Buddhist] god who watches over travellers, [pregnant] women and children's [souls] known in Indian or Sanskrit as Kshitigarbha). O-Jizo-san has the sort of fascination for me that Lafcadio Hearn describes: if one gets accustomed to the vindictive and evil faces of some gods, even of the good God Fudo [of Justice], one must feel relieved in the presence of the kindly-faced Jizo who,

The six figures of Jizo

in Buddhist history, really replaces Christ. We lunched, as I say, under the shadow of his six figures.

I took photographs of my best Nishinomiya man, Kane, whom I have known for over six years and also his cap. He is not exactly handsome, but he is my best man in this district and really loves shooting. The photo of the new grave is also interesting because it shows so clearly all the details, including the two spirit lanterns and the stone attached to the straw rope to keep the spirit down or from going to Hell, the cups and saucers with

My best Nishinomiya men; Tada Matsu on the left

offerings, flowers in the bamboo vases, the rice bowl of the deceased, with water and a small green leaf in it, and various prayers. We left after luncheon to see if we could find a wood-cock along the pretty shores of a small lake, called Netetotekoi Iki, as we had done last year, but not a bird of any sort could we find – not even a pigeon.

Left, new graves; right, Kane

However, Tada Matsu told us stories about the lake that I had never heard before. It was one in which large numbers of lovers came to commit joint suicide, owing to their parents objecting to matrimonial alliances. A tall stone column was put up at the end of the lake sixteen years ago, to those who had committed *shinju* [joint suicide], though that in no way lessened the cases.

Besides lovers' suicides the lake contained an enormous *suppon*, weighing 60 or 70 lb, which was said to be an evil spirit with the power to decoy people into the lake for the purpose of eating them. Once, when the pond was empty, it was caught, and Matsu told me that he had himself seen it shown in Nishinomiya for 2 cents a head. After three or four days the gigantic tortoise became sick, and fearing its death and the revenge of its spirit, the farmer, who had captured it, had it returned to the pond. From that time on lovers' suicides became slightly less frequent, but the spirits of the lake were still able to cause many suicides, aided by the vicious *suppon*.

Another quite notable story was told. Some thirty years ago a pedlar from Toyama, selling patent medicines, happened to pass along the lake. He stood and looked into the clear blue water and after some minutes took off his *waraji* (straw shoes), threw them into the water, and he, himself, started to follow them. An old farmer, who happened to be carrying home a load of *daikon* (radishes), saw him, dropped the *daikon*, he caught him and said, 'What foolishness are you about to do; why do you throw your *waraji* into the lake?' The pedlar, who was sober and a healthy strong-minded man, turned on the farmer and said 'Good man, are you blind? Do you not see that beautiful house there? Look what beautiful green *tatami* (mats) they have on the floor. How can I go in and cross such mats with my *waraji* on? And can you not see they are calling to buy my medicine?' The farmer drew him away and explained the mysteries of the pond for which the medicine pedlar was truly grateful. Whether the large *suppon* is still in the lake, I know not, but there is no doubt that the stories attached to the place are mostly true. The reflections in the water might, by an imaginative person, easily be taken for anything.

The pedlar from Toyama

SATURDAY DECEMBER 3RD Morning papers give more details of the fighting. I should think the attack on 203-Metre Hill by the Japanese stands unparalleled in the world's history – *banzai* say I, and may the terrible loss of life be rapidly paid for by the advantages gained.

MONDAY DECEMBER 5TH A wire from Oto takes me to Itami by first train after daylight. [Gordon Smith's beaters would often telegraph him about game in their region.] I was met by my old lot [of beaters], but before we can start I have to go to the teahouse to inspect their new trousers, the money for which I had sent a fortnight ago. According to etiquette it was necessary that I should see that it had been correctly spent, and a sort of second thanks came to me.

Oto took me first up to the 'top place' near Ikeda, where we killed five out of the six woodcock found. My men lost me the sixth by vile eyesight, and thereby caused a full hour's delay. This was rather disheartening as it was entirely the fault of my own men Kosa and Yume, and nothing to do with the

The entrance to Torii village

Itami men. We lunched at what I call Torii village (Kozamura), where there is a very fine *torii* for such a small place, but the villagers tell me it is subscribed to by six other villages owing to the ancientness of its temple and grounds.

Curiously enough, this village is one of the few I had always held to be slightly hostile to myself, or less hospitable let us say, than other villages here-abouts, and I have always avoided its acquaintance but now I find they are as nice as the rest.

In these upriver Itami beats I have been made to feel by the villagers as if I were the Lord of the Land. The children have become so accustomed to me that when they see my rickshaw they run from their work, or from their houses, to bow as I pass. I candidly confess that is an extreme pleasure to me, because it shows that in spite of killing all the game on their land, trampling through their fences, and always doing more harm than good to them, we are, nevertheless, on excellent and most friendly terms.

FRIDAY DECEMBER 9TH Disagreeable row with the Kawasaki Dockyard over a bill sent in *twice*. I consider this company either grossly dishonest or grossly careless. The Secretary is Mr Yotsumoto, the Vice-President Mr Matsukata and the President Mr Kawasaki, and it is to the first I attribute the double

Hishi nut and leaf

charges, owing probably to carelessness. Drewell, my agent, was equally careless, in paying and not receiving a proper receipt for the account.

SATURDAY DECEMBER 10TH I went off to Yamasaki by the early train. We commenced beating at the place near the station where the lotus-lily beds are. As the leaves of the latter had considerably rotted down, the snipe were wild, and all I could get was seven long shots; about fifteen birds got away. Ruby emerged from these lotus ponds with about a hundred *hishi* nuts stuck into his hair. These water nuts are excellent eating when roasted or boiled; I like them raw. They have the taste of coconut and Brazil nut mixed. They grow just under the leaf of a water plant, the name of which I do not know in English [water chestnut]. Ruby's haul was so good I sent him in several times more, and he always came out covered as the nuts or seeds now lay at the bottom of the shallow water. In fact, Ruby was generally sensible and useful today. On one occasion I found him galloping on his back tracks as if the devil were after him. He had lost his collar and went back to find it, which he did, and brought it to me to put on him again.

TUESDAY DECEMBER 13TH Took my first turn at Kanzaki today, and took young Compie Pakenham [son of David Pakenham] with me. Went up the river in a boat, hunting right and left on both banks and getting woodcocks in the most unexpected places. At the railway bridge a policeman called to me, saying that a fox had just come out of the quail ground I was shooting and was in a patch of *daikon*. Drove him out, and he died, much to the delight of the policeman, several farmers and of Kosa and Yume, who eventually ate the whole of his flesh. The skin and skull went to the British Museum. No doubt shooting a fox rather astonished Compie because of his father's exclusively hunting background, but he has not yet been taught that foxes in Japan are a curse and hunting an impossibility – even beyond imagination.

Shooting with young Compie, up the Kanzaki river

SUNDAY DECEMBER 18TH A letter from Professor Ijima, who was delighted at the Governor of Hyogo calling on him and conveying my message about the British Museum nets etc., which I am now authorised to hand over to the scientific marine station at Misaki, belonging to the Imperial University of Tokyo. It seems rather hard that the gift should be given in the name of the Trustees of the British Museum for, had the things been sold, the proceeds would have gone to my credit. Moreover, the suggestion of presenting the nets was granted at my request after months of waiting and considerable expense. Had I been the presenter I should have received, Professor Ijima says, a silver cup from the Imperial Household.

MONDAY DECEMBER 19TH Warmer today. Baiho came and did some painting. He looks shockingly ill.

SUNDAY DECEMBER 25TH Christmas Day. Stayed in my paper house. Christmas is not a day on which either to go to the Kobe Club or to mix with the Kobe European, unless you are able to consume quantities of spirit, which do not agree with me. I gave a dinner party to my interpreter's children, Yoshi and O-Tama-san. Though only 8 and 10 years old their conduct was irreproachable – the manners, in fact, of adult people. We had English food: soup, fried fish with fried oysters, and two small roast chickens followed by the awful plum pudding (on fire, of course) from a Crosse & Blackwell tin. They enjoyed it immensely and simply

My interpreter's well-mannered
children, Tama and Yoshi Egawa

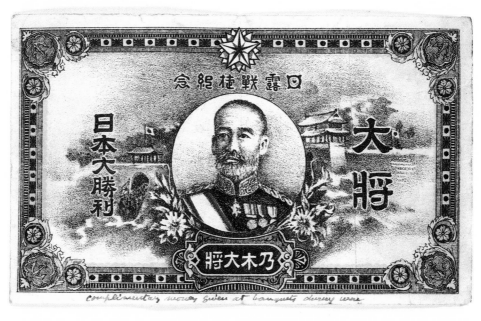

gorged themselves, eating fully twice as much of everything as I did, plus a large bowl of rice each in the middle of the meal. After this midday dinner, I gave them a gramophone concert and taught them how to beat time to the music.

SATURDAY DECEMBER 31ST The bank note is a 10 cent war note used by the troops in Manchuria. It was sent to Baiho by an artist friend who is serving near Mukden, and Baiho handed it to me.

My mind was filled this night with the idea that the Japanese at Port Arthur were making desperate efforts to capture the place for the New Year, as a present to the Emperor. Egawa is also of the same idea. I fear the night will be a bloody one over there.

MONDAY JANUARY 2ND, 1905 Rumours of the fall of Port Arthur were early about, but no confirmation is at hand. I believe there has been severe fighting and that Port Arthur has received another heavy blow.

There is a fair amount of *sake* imbibing going on today, as usual at this time of the year. Even the faithful Egawa was taken home incapable.

TUESDAY JANUARY 3RD This, thank goodness, is the last of the three-day holiday. Several visitors came to see me with very red faces, though still sober. It is true that Port Arthur has surrendered, though there are no particulars, except in Japanese telegrams which say that Gen. Stoessell has at last given in, only having 4,000 soldiers left unwounded, no provisions, no ammunition, and no clothing or covering for his 10,000 wounded.

It has been a magnificent fight on both sides. If one cheers the one, one must cheer the other, at least in these particular circumstances. I am delighted it is over and, moreover, the surrender has saved a deal of life.

THURSDAY JANUARY 5TH Excitement was a little more visible today, but quietly so – there are more flags out, more lanterns hung. There was a ceremony in Nanko temple to which I went. All day and in the evening fireworks were set off, and at the latter time the myriads of lanterns made the street truly pretty.

Decorations in my street to commemorate the fall of Port Arthur

SUNDAY JANUARY 8TH H.E. the Governor [of Hyogo Prefecture] came to luncheon, and brought me a present of two old sword handles, and the mountings[7] of two others by Joi and Kotem two of the oldest and best workers in metal (Kotem is mentioned in Louis Gonse's book on art). I am really very fond of this Governor; he has been especially kind to me and I enjoy his society immensely.

H.E. asked me to write out my ideas on game and fishing, for forwarding to the Government. I take this as a high compliment and will do my best, knowing that Japan really wants it.

MONDAY JANUARY 9TH Fireworks going off all day and until 10 p.m. Streets still gay with flags – tomorrow it is all to end.

I wrote nine pages about my proposed reform of game and fish laws for the Minister of Agriculture.

THURSDAY JANUARY 12TH Many of the difficulties of game preservation are obvious. Talking to Oto today, I explained the duties of game keepers, amongst which are, of course, the killing of vermin such as weasels. 'I could not kill an *itachi* (weasel),' he said, 'or ill luck would be sure to befall me.' This belief is so fixed in the minds of the Japanese country people that weasels are everywhere. Very little robbing of chicken is put down to them, but is attributed to the fox. Weasels come right into one's house, they go through poultry yards and do an infinity of harm, but get off scot-free, for fear of their supernatural powers.

FRIDAY JANUARY 13TH
Call on H.E. the Governor
and present him with my ideas on game-
law reforms which are to go on to the Government.

Watching troop trains and Russian prisoners, arranging his passage, and those of his dogs, to England, shooting, and making some last-minute curio hunts – these are Gordon Smith's concerns during the second part of January.

SATURDAY FEBRUARY 4TH   A letter from Ford Barclay which much annoyed me. It said he had heard from Rutherford Harris that Matsukata, Proprietor of Kawasaki Dockyard, had said that I had neither returned nor paid for three tons of lead ballast borrowed for *Snowflake*. As this was untrue I wrote for an apology at once. Matsukata replied by asking for an interview. I refused, as I wished to give Ford Barclay a pinch, if possible, for again meddling in my affairs. I insisted, in fact, and at 11 p.m. got the apology. It was extraordinary how Matsukata could have made the statement he did to Harris, and how the latter could have so exaggerated it in telling Ford Barclay, as to make the latter consult Captain Hutchison R.N. (the Naval Attaché) as to whether he should tell me or not, not having either opinion or initiative of his own.

I scored all around, but have come to the conclusion that Rutherford Harris is a dangerous man (much what poor dear old Charlie Breton told me of him in the early South African days).

TUESDAY FEBRUARY 7TH   Always a sad day for me leaving Japan, the more bitter now because I have liked the people better during their war than I have ever during their peace. Their conduct has been exemplary, their patriotism and quiet bravery fills one with admiration.

The day of going, having come, one must take it like the *samurai*, and with the spirit of the Yamato people – *Yamoto Damashii* they call it, which means high spirit, determined, blind, callous. I embarked early, at 10 in fact. It was very cold, but in spite of that, my dear friend Mr Hattori came all the way out to see me, and despite the fact that Admiral Togo was in Kobe and practically his guest as Governor of Hyogo.

H.E. told me that he was going to Tokyo on 12th and that he would then see H.E.s the Ministers of Agriculture and Finance, about the game and fish preservation scheme.

Gordon Smith spends March 1905 in Ceylon and arrives in England towards the end of April. Basing himself in London, he visits old friends in Southsea and his family who are now ensconced in Cheltenham. He has a good many social engagements with Japanese diplomats as well as political discussions with Arnold White and Princess Frederica of Hanover. He attends a variety of receptions including one given by the Royal Geographical Society in one of the great halls of the South Kensington Museum. His shooting at Hurlingham brings no success – at 47, he is, he thinks, 'too old'.

He decides to lobby for public subscriptions in England to help support the impoverished familes of Japanese soldiers and to this end writes many letters to The Times. Eventually the Director of the Foreign Department, Valentine Chirol, writes to him requesting a cessation in the correspondence. However, the publicity has encouraged public donations to the Japanese authorities. Determined to make his own contribution, Gordon Smith starts fundraising privately.

JAPANESE FAUNA.

Mr. R. Gordon Smith, of the South Kensington Museum, has during the past two years been occupied in investigating the fish fauna of the inland seas of Japan. He has just returned, bringing with him a mass of information not only on the immediate subject of his work in the Island Empire, but also on the natural history generally of the country. Several of his specimens of fishes are believed to be species new to science, and he has also obtained one or two new species of mammals. Mr. Gordon Smith proposes to return to Japan shortly to resume his labours in the inland seas.

The recurring illnesses of the East prompt him to consult Sir Patrick Manson, a specialist in malaria, whose only advice is to take the waters at Buxton Spa in Derbyshire. Four weeks in July and August are duly endured but Gordon Smith fears that he is worse, not better, for the treatment. After a further stay in London, he sails on the S.S. Sachsen and, pausing only briefly to see Sir Alan Perry in Colombo and Kronenberg in Shanghai, he arrives back in Japan in November. The shooting season is underway.

For practical purposes, the Russo-Japanese War ended in May 1905 but it was not until August that peace negotiations took place in Portsmouth, U.S.A. and not until mid-October that a treaty was signed. Russia accepted Japan's supremacy in Korea and ceded the lease on the Liaotung Peninsula. The terms were exceedingly disappointing to the Japanese people, who, having suffered such devastating casualties, expected to gain a great deal more. Unprecedented and violent rioting erupted in protest. Although both armies have been withdrawn from Manchuria, the Russian prisoners-of-war are a visible evidence of the bitter conflict.

CHAPTER 11

Winter Tales

1905/1906

*Prisoners of war – the January sales – arrival of the dogs – a false eye
– pruned daffodil – a sale of curios at the Japanese Club – New Year
1906 – winter shooting – General Sir Ian Hamilton's love-making –
the peony and the lion – Horridge defeats Balfour – three folktales –
Tokyo sideshows with Isao Ijima – wrestling with Lindley – the story
of a young otter*

THURSDAY NOVEMBER 9TH   Receive an official document from the Department of Agriculture requesting my assistance in all things 'connected with game and fish' [supplying specimens and advice on conservation].

The streets are curious just now – the town is full of soldiers returning from the war. Trainloads of Russian prisoners arrive during the day, generally in loads of from 500 to 700. They detrain at Kobe station and march through the streets to the Minatogawa where they embark. They do not realise as yet that they are cattle being driven to the slaughter house [i.e, returning to Russia] instead of to greener pasturages. The Japanese attitude towards them is one of quiet, respectful reserve. They look at them as they march through the streets and the Russians, as they pass, say *Sayonara, sayonara*.

Of the prisoners themselves little need be said. They are dirty and have twice as many

Russian prisoners marching through the streets of Kobe

clothes on as they appear to need. Some are fair, others are dark; there are Finns, Poles, Mongolians of many mixtures, and the fat clodhopping putty-faced Russian who resembles so much one type of German. They each carry bundles and one wonders, because of their size and number, what they have in them. I even saw dogs carried under the arms of some prisoners.

The sales – the time the ladies love

MONDAY NOVEMBER 13TH Received a large budget of Japanese letters today: from H.E. Mr Omori (Governor of Kyoto), the Mayor of Yamasaki, the Mayor of Toshishima and the Mayor of Itami. These were all letters of gratitude for the money I raised [for widows and orphans of Japanese soldiers].

TUESDAY–FRIDAY NOVEMBER 14–17TH Streets are gay with flags and decorations, the *seeru* or cheap sales having started on the 15th. This week is for women's happiness. Everything that is for sale is hung outside the shops where the women can revel, pulling the goods about without actually buying. It is a week for bargains, a week for street chatter. Children, girls, and old women all vie with each other as to how much they can pull about. They are *full* of business, and it is quite interesting to watch them – many pretty girls are seen.

The sales are extended during the following week but the fun is overshadowed by cases of plague. Deaths and subsequent fumigations of homes become regular occurrences. Meanwhile, Gordon Smith awaits the delayed arrival of his hunting dogs from England.

SATURDAY NOVEMBER 25TH At last the *Palermo* has arrived with my dogs. My dear old gardener, who has been busy for a week past making arrangements for their comfort, looked quite delighted in the morning when I announced that I could see the ship through my telescope. He set to at once with his brushes to clean away any fallen leaves which the foreign dogs might criticise as untidy.

Kosa, Egawa and I went down to the ship and found the dogs in capital condition. Both officers and men had been very kind to them and seemed quite sorry to part with them. The dogs themselves, of course, were delighted to get ashore, but little dreamed of the dangers awaiting them if they fell into the hands of the government dog killers [the *eta*, or untouchables], who are absolutely unscrupulous, according to all accounts, and who, moreover, love dogs' flesh to eat.

The first thing therefore, was to get them both photographed and send copies to the police stations with a polite request that if they were caught unmuzzled by the *eta* they should, being new to the ways of the country, 'have one more chance' and not be clubbed on the head while taking the air.

Ginger and Brush: 'Did you say we might be eaten?'

TUESDAY NOVEMBER 28TH Off to Yamasaki for my first shoot and we had quite a reception. The dogs were fairly delighted to get out with a gun having been, no doubt, afraid that they would never see one again. Shot the upper ground and got two fine cock pheasants, also two quail, which were all I saw. All my old men came to me and appeared very pleased.

As for civility, nothing was too much for the people to do. The inn was very clean, the bath was laid out for my use alone, and to make my bed all the *futons* in the house were offered to me.

Kosa and the first bag of the season

WEDNESDAY NOVEMBER 29TH Up at 5.30 a.m. having determined to make an early start and got down opposite my woodcock island just as the junks were setting sail after their night's 'camping'. My old boatman now being a soldier I had a new one – all hisses and smiles but very little sense. The concept that time lost meant less ground covered and consequently fewer birds seen, was unintelligible to him. We got across and I found six woodcocks on the island and killed the lot. On the mainland I got three more but saw nothing else. So far as killing goes, thirty woodcocks seen and twenty-one killed is a fair average for even the old Gun Clubber[1].

On returning to the inn I found the mayor, Mr Kawasaki, tall-hatted and frock-coated, his clerk, another gentleman and a farmer with a wounded soldier called Koyama who had had one of his eyes shot out, but had a new glass one from the Emperor of which he was immensely fond. Mr Kawasaki came to thank me for having had 15 yen sent from my 'widows' fund' to his village, and told me fully how it was being used. Already, an old woman whose son had left for the front had been kept in her house by the fund – without which she must have been turned into the street, for she was beyond wage earning.

Freight barges on their way to Kyoto

The eyeless soldier came to thank me on behalf of other soldiers' families and passed his eye over to me to see. I told him it was rather dangerous to take it in and out so often (for he had already had it out twice). 'No,' said he, 'it must come out to be shown, for it was a gift from our beloved Emperor, and I am very proud of it.'

'You should, in any case, wipe it,' said I. 'I also should be proud to have lost a limb for your Emperor, but your glass eye must be kept very clean or you may set up irritation in the socket.'

He was, of course, a farmer, this soldier, and I promised him some English seeds to plant – the biggest beans and peas I could find. I gave them some Scotch whisky to drink their Emperor's health, but they only just sipped enough to accept the toast and to drink to King Edward VII. It was quite a little entertainment, and very interesting, but as a result I only just caught my train.

THURSDAY NOVEMBER 30TH Baiho comes to paint; he is using rotten English colours and ruining his paintings.

THURSDAY DECEMBER 7TH Rain. Secured a fine and old coral carving representing the 10,000-year-old tortoise. I think it is the largest and most solid piece of coral I have ever seen. Another piece was of Hotei [God of Prosperity, one of the Seven Gods of Luck], also notable for its size but not so good in colour; both pieces came from a private collection. The red dragon is remarkable for its colour and is also an old piece.

I believe them to be the three best specimens of coral anywhere about, either here, in Osaka, Kyoto or, perhaps, even Tokyo – excluding the red dragon, which I picked up last year.

WEDNESDAY DECEMBER 13TH   Kobayashi brought me the skins of a Manchurian tiger and a leopard for inspection. The tiger measured only 10 feet and the leopard 7 feet 3 inches. The latter had fine fur, nearly 1 inch long, but the price of 50 yen I thought too high. The tiger skin was 150 yen if the claws were left in, but only 100 yen if they could be taken away for use as medicine. It was unusual to find a Chinese tiger with the claws left in. I fancy it might have paid me to buy both skins, but my bad luck combined with the villainy of London tradesmen is not an incentive or inducement for me to do so.

Kobayashi presented me with a curious daffodil. Cutting and pruning the bulb in a manner which is Chinese and requires a great deal of study and caution in operation, produces the result shown in the painting. Roughly speaking each bulb is cut in half and only the central core must be left uninjured. Slime will continue to flow daily from the several parts, and this must be carefully wiped off with a rag because it will rot the rest of the plant. When the roots begin to show it is advisable to cover them with wet cotton wool – they not only feel the cold but are also very delicate. The slime that comes away is said to be a wonderful cure and is used by women for sore breasts and chapped skin.

Several of these weird plants displayed in a large white shell are quite fascinating to see. The grotesque turnings and entanglements of the leaves or 'spears' fascinate the eye and make one try to unravel twistings of each.

THURSDAY DECEMBER 21ST   Visited the Kencho. Plague worse. While coming up the hill and passing the upper girls school I saw the young ladies cleaning the window glass and frames. What an excellent idea, and what a lot of good it would do both our boys and girls if they were made to work out and clean systematically the whole of their classrooms. It requires discipline of an almost military kind to get it done properly.

FRIDAY DECEMBER 22ND   Mr Takiji sent me his annual New Year card – pretty, very pretty, I call it, with his own two children 'Bansai-ing'.

Mr Takiji's New Year Card

SATURDAY DECEMBER 23RD The British Museum things arrive at last but one of the two drums of spirits is empty!

A fine cold day; thermometer about 40°F indoors, and there was ice in some places. Went to an interesting sale at the Japanese Club. The pace at which the things are sold is quite wonderful. There were a good many nice things there but mostly not in my line. I bid for a few Chinese things and got them cheaply. The blue glass plum is a really interesting piece, containing, as it does, what I take to be a black pearl. These lumps of thick heavy glass can no longer be made in China, I am told, with the lovely colours which used to be produced in the olden days. This art is quite lost. The lumps were used principally by priests as paperweights. No doubt this blue one is very old and has some [symbolic] reference to the growth of life.

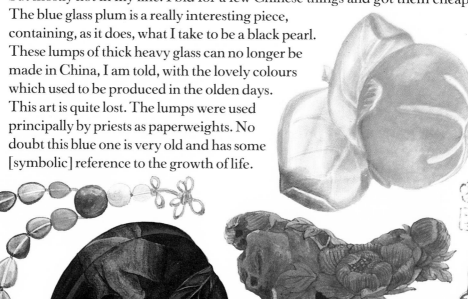

The plum and the pearl are both holy things. I do not know what the green object is, beyond the fact that it, too, is a plum and that the purple and green harmonise in a manner I never saw them do before. The old glass beads, also used by priests, were of colours that I never see in modern or Venetian beads and reminded me again more of Singhalese gems than anything else. During the day I added to my collection another piece of coral, which was brought by the man who goes about the country hunting for specialities on commission. This particular one comes from Tanba and is from an old gentleman's collection. It represents the flower (the tree peony) and two *shishis* (Holy Lions) as well as a rock, which probably means strength, long life and beauty. They are often represented together as the emblem of good luck. Baiho painted, too, the piece of amber which Jiro sent to me in England; it contained the green beetle which very much interested Dr Woodhouse and the professor who reigns over the Geological Department of the British Museum (Natural History). In its way it is rather wonderful being the only green beetle in amber which has retained its colour to perfection for over 2,000 years.

The white cabbage, so remarkably well copied for me by Baiho, is another of old Kobayashi's curiosities. The custom of using a cabbage as an ornament is actually Chinese. Kobayashi, always original in his ideas, has improved upon the ordinary round cabbage. To keep the cabbage perfect in appearance the Chinese daily take off two leaves from opposite sides but Kobayashi has improved upon this in originality by taking all the leaves from one side and watering the inside as well. The appearance reminds one of a grotto and evokes the one at Lourdes with the statue of the Virgin Mary in the background. Kobayashi himself, compared it to a cave with Buddha or to a cloud formation. However one may laugh at the idea of a cabbage being beautiful, it remains a fact that the cabbage probably contains more that is artistic than does any other vegetable or flower. Just look into the graceful curves of leaves, the way they meet on the top, the wave-like curls at the edges, and the delicate lights and shades.

Over the Christmas period Gordon Smith receives a visit from the British Vice-Consul in Formosa and he provides a special luncheon for his household servants. The mounting incidence of plague troubles the British and Japanese officials and Gordon Smith discusses with them its causes and cures. Meanwhile, the Japanese are getting ready for their big festival: New Year.

MONDAY JANUARY 1ST, 1906 The New Year is never a day of pleasure to me, especially in Japan. Everything and everybody is upside down and disagreeable, the only pleasing sights are the school children, especially the groups of girls who, with their new [clothes], give great colour to the scene.

Motomachi was full of people. The shops were shut and draped with blue and white calico. Instead, there were innumerable stalls of cheap-jack goods. Sweets in the shells of the *hamaguri* [clam] were many and pleased me for there were endless sorts, some of them being little works of art.

Proverbs from the fukare biscuit tin

*My photograph of O-Tama-San,
aged 11½, in her New Year clothes,
and her visiting card*

TUESDAY JANUARY 2ND   O-Tama-san came early to get her photo taken in her New Year clothes, bringing me at the same time a box of biscuits most diminutive in size, each being no larger than the kernel of a cobnut. They were called *fukuarare* and are made of pounded rice and seaweed, baked and almost burned a dark brown. They were quite excellent to eat and are an especial delicacy of Tokyo and Osaka. The usual proverbs conveying good wishes were enclosed in the tin.

O-Tama-san has the manners of a grown lady now and is quite different from the days when she used to go about on my shoulders as a 5-year-old.

SATURDAY JANUARY 6TH   Things are settling down again and people are sobering up, thank goodness.

SUNDAY JANUARY 7TH   A lovely day. A few more mammals caught. A curious thing is that only one out of ten I catch is a male beast. The cold still nights are those on which the females wander, while in the wet weather I find I catch more males, especially if it blows hard. I wonder why. Last night I caught a very large and particularly light-coloured vole. She had only the stump of a tail, the other half having been bitten off and healed long ago. It is evident from this that fair-haired and ginger-coloured ladies are as quarrelsome in animal life as they are in ordinary human life.

FRIDAY JANUARY 12TH   From a review I read today of General Sir Ian Hamilton's book on the [Russo-Japanese] War some very childish things appear to be published therein. By which I mean the story told of where the gallant general makes a most gallant speech to a fair *geisha* in Tokyo, telling her he would like to put her in a bird cage and take her home. The *geisha* sulked and went away. It was subsequently explained to the general that what he had said had been interpreted as 'I should like to shut you up in a box and take you away'!

When one is so extremely simple with one's love-making, it appears unnecessary to chronicle it in a book for the public to read, more especially by a writer who is highly paid and a much-to-be-envied public servant.

SATURDAY JANUARY 13TH I have as yet been unable to get hold of any idea why the peony flower and the shishi, or Buddhist Lion, should so often be seen together in art. Today, however, I did hear rather a pretty story about the peony flower itself. Here it is:

Many hundreds of years ago a high Buddhist priest took into his service a girl, who presented herself to him and asked for employment. The priest asked for her name and that of her parents; the girl, however, gave no answers beyond saying that she wished for no wages but merely a home to live in. Because of her extreme beauty the priest, fearing for her if he sent her away, took her into his house. The priest had a great love for flowers and the finest that he cultivated were his favourites, the peonies.

As time passed the priest fell a victim to the beauty of his maid and became desperately enamoured of her. He offered to leave the church – anything if she would marry him, but she withstood all his pleadings and advances. One day, he was trying to speak to her when she asked him to follow her into the garden to where the peonies grew in front of a high white wall.

There she told him that she was the spirit of the peony flower, that she had come to him because she knew he loved peonies, but she had never thought that he, as a priest, would have loved her as a girl. With that she flattened herself to the wall into which she disappeared – much to the disconsolation of the priest, who from that day on devoted more attention to his peonies than he did to his religion, hoping to bring her back to him. He died some years afterwards, and over his grave, in the bamboo *hanatate* [vase] some mysterious but invisible hand always places fresh peonies.

193

MONDAY JANUARY 15TH The newspapers today published the defeat of Balfour for East Manchester by my friend Horridge[2]. I am, consequently, delighted although differing entirely in politics. To my mind the Englishman who knocked out Balfour deserves the greatest credit for the latter's rottenness regarding the Baltic Squadron and our North Sea fishing fleet. *Banzai*, think I, for Horridge and, in spite of hard times, I could not resist spending 16 yen to cable congratulations to him.

There being no sign of game for the next few days, Gordon Smith makes an exploratory hike up Bismark Hill to admire the scenery. At home he records folktales – a hobby which is becoming more and more absorbing. He begins to fill not only his journals but also separate volumes with the ghostly stories which abound in this region.

WEDNESDAY JANUARY 24TH Three inches of snow on the ground this morning – more than I ever saw in Kobe before. I don't think either Brush or Ginger had seen any before for nothing would get them out of their kennels and Brush howled as if the most dire calamity had happened. My old gardener declared that Yuki Onna was the cause. That Brush should see Yuki Onna, the snow woman, seems to me a rather amusing idea. The old man thought the same, in a way, yet he did not appear to enjoy it as a joke or subject for chaff. [Yuki Onna was thought to lull men to sleep, and thus to their deaths in the snow].

'Have you ever seen the Yuki Onna?' I asked him. No, he had never seen it, but near Hida, his village, there were many people who had seen it between there and Mino [now Southern Gifu].

'Are people afraid of it?' I asked.

'No, she does no harm, but when you see her you will feel very cold for she is never seen unless there is wind. In the moonlight you may see her asleep on the snow – then her face is very large.'

Certainly Baiho has rather excelled himself in the faces which he represents as his idea of Yuki Onna. To my mind Yuki Onna is not believed in as a ghostly form, as Lafcadio Hearn seems to think, but more as a subject or fabrication of those with poetical minds. I myself have seen thousands and thousands of Yuki Onna's on the lakes of Northern Canada, in Korea and other places. The idea is pretty, for what closer resemblance to a ghostly female draped in white can there be than that caused by a whirlwind of snow? Alternatively one can often see the outlines of faces, flat on driven snow, when the weather is hard. That Brush did not like the snow was not curious, but why he should mournfully howl at it, I do not know.

Baiho's painting of my dogs seeing Yuki Onna

194

I sent off twenty-one pages of advice regarding game laws etc. to the Vice-Minister of Agriculture (Mr Wada). Its completion is a relief to me and I hope that some of it will bear fruit. If not, Japan, as a country for even ordinary sport, will be a place of the past; the better classes and the aristocracy, must become entirely commercial.

While looking at *kakemonos* today, I came across one that is frequently seen and represents the Gyoran Kwannon[3]. The story of the Gyoran Kwannon is as follows:

The Gyoran Kwannon appeared one day at a small Inland Sea fishing village called Kuishadan. She appeared as a young girl of 16 or 17 years of age, helped the fishermen in sorting their fish and in drying their nets and, in her basket, took away the fish which had been cast away by the fishermen as refuse. None knew from whence she came. She was extremely beautiful, and the fishermen deeply regretted her departure while marvelling at her sudden appearance and equally sudden disappearance.

The next evening as the fishermen were drying their nets and sorting their fish, the Gyoran Kwannon suddenly appeared again. She was asked from whence she came and answered:

'I come from Fudarahusen in Nankai (Southern India).'

The fishermen begged her to stay amongst them and become one of their wives, for she had completely captivated them all by her beauty and by her simplicity of manner.

Gyoran Kwannon took from her bosom a Kwannon-gyo or Buddhist bible [Sutras], and pointing out some prayer therein, said:

'He so ever who learneth this prayer by heart first, he will I marry.' All the fishermen vied with each other to learn the prayer and on the third day one, Baryo,

Gyoran Kwannon's first
appearance to the fishermen

accomplished the task and consequently took the goddess to his house and married her. After this she fainted and was put to bed and later as Baryo was about to retire for the night he found his bride was dead. After trying every means to restore her to life, he covered her with a *futon* and sought the help of a very good and clever priest. The priest came and prayed and lifted the bedding and disclosed a thousand Kwannon-gyos, saying to Baryo: 'The Kwannon of Fudarakusen of Nankai came amongst you here at Kushado to teach you the Kwannon-gyo

in order to reform your characters, for your habits have been evil.'

The fishing village reformed its morals and Baryo committed to memory the entire Kwannon-gyo, eventually becoming a very good priest who devoted his life to reforming the morals of fishermen.

This being a snowy and beastly day, one more story must be told. It was told to me by Baiho while he was retouching a *kakemono* and shows that there is comedy in tragedy.

In the village of Omori in Tokyo-fu, there lived a rich farmer who possessed a most beautiful daughter, who had been educated

mostly in Tokyo. Her name was O-Tabo-san and she was just 17 years of age when, contrary to all the reasonable hopes of her family, she fell desperately in love with a youth of 20, who peddled from place to place all those head decorations which help to make a Japanese maiden happy.

Shiroku was the name of this young gallant and, of course, he was equally in love with O-Tabo-san. Hairpins or no hairpins, Mr Shiroku was continually about the farm, until the two could think of nothing but each other.

One fine day, her father and mother told her that they had found a most desirable and charming husband and that she must marry him. Likewise the father of Shiroku had found for him a desirable wife and informed him of such fact.

The two lovers met – both broken hearted – but they decided that death was infinitely preferable to their separation and marriage with strangers. They decided accordingly to commit *shinju* (joint suicide) that same night in a lake at a place called Sushin-ga-Nori (the place where heads of criminals are stuck on posts). It was a wild rough spot on one side of the lake and, naturally, from its name a place of horrors, a place where things go wrong.

Well, Shiroku and O-Tabo-san started off after dark, when the moon arose, to commit *shinju*. They had reached the usual place for suicides to jump from when O-Tabo-san realised that, in her excitement, she had forgotten to bring her *mamori*. 'Wait here for me,' said Shiroku, 'and I will run back and fetch it for you.' While Shiroku was away, an old man, called Shobe, who peddled tobacco, was on his way with his old wife, O-Same-san, to a neighbouring village. Having got somewhere in the vicinity of the suicide place and there being every evidence of coming rain, the old man said to his wife, 'Wait here under this pine tree and I will go back and fetch an umbrella'. By this time Shiroku was on his way back with the charm and, taking the old lady for O-Tabo-san, he said, 'I have your *mamori*', and he flung her on his back and holding her hands around his chest jumped into the lake and they were, of course, drowned.

Old Shobe, returning later with the umbrella, mistook O-Tabo-san in the dark for this old wife. He told her to follow him and O-Tabo-san, taking him for her lover who had perhaps formed a new plan, did so.

At dawn O-Tabo-san saw the old man – with horror and surprise. The old man, on the other hand, was delighted – he thought some merciful and good god had transformed his old wife into the beautiful young girl he beheld; O-Tabo-san thought that her lover had been transformed by an evil god into the hideous old man, but, being as dutiful as a Japanese girl should be, she lived with him until the time of his death and then thinking him to be Shiroku she committed suicide in the lake near Sushin-ga-Nori or, the place of the heads of the pikes.

197

FRIDAY JANUARY 26TH Cold, raw day. Ginger leaves for Tokyo having been sold to Professor Isao Ijima. I am sorry to see him go, but there is no use in having two dogs as the end of the [shooting] season approaches.

SATURDAY FEBRUARY 3RD Called on Mrs Hattori and had a long talk about the wounded. She told me of one very sad case at Himeji, a man who had lost both his arms and both his eyes. His most devoted friend was with him at the time, also wounded and taken to Himeji hospital where he recovered and then made a vow that he would spend the rest of his life nursing his eyeless and armless friend. He hardly ever moved from the eyeless man's bed and now attends to his every want. This is in the hospital where I have sent illustrated papers because I thought they would have been much appreciated.

Hisako Nakamura

SATURDAY FEBRUARY 10TH Decide to go up to Tokyo by the *Zeiten*; embarked in the evening; ship too hot because of the steam pipes.

SUNDAY FEBRUARY 11TH Spent all day writing mail and the diary. At the end of it my legs swelled dreadfully from sitting in the heat on a bad chair.

The Lindleys[4] were on board; charming people, she, as a sister of Lord Lovat[5] must necessarily approach the ideal. Also on board was Captain Kaburaki, the Japanese Naval Attaché, whom I met through Lady Watts[6] at the Japanese Consul-General's party in London last summer.

MONDAY FEBRUARY 12TH Landed before the other passengers and got off to Tokyo by the 10 a.m. train. Arriving at the Imperial Hotel I found that they had reserved only a very indifferent room for me, thinking I was the newspaper correspondent, Gordon Smith, for whom very few seem to retain any liking. I fancy, after my experience of a year ago when his letters were being sent to me at Kobe (he evidently having given a false address), that he must have left considerable bills unpaid but not unforgotten.

I rectified matters, however, and the manager soon found another room. My old guide Kito, and Mr Hashimoto, came to meet me on the ship. The cold was great and in Tokyo there were nearly three inches of snow, with a freezing arctic wind.

I had a letter from Professor Ijima, who proposes spending a day sightseeing with me.

TUESDAY FEBRUARY 13TH   In the morning went to Ikeda's great curio place, where, as usual, the manager Mr Nakamura brought his little daughter Hisako to see me – and very smart she looked. This child is quite an interesting little thing to me. The first year I came to Japan, now some eight or nine years ago, I took a photograph of her with her father, mother and family. She was then a 6-month-old baby. Every time I have gone to Tokyo since then I am given a photograph of Hisako Nakamura.

WEDNESDAY FEBRUARY 14TH   Professor Ijima turned up in time for breakfast and did not look a day older than when I had seen him two years before. He and I set out on a round of cheap amusement such as is to be found at and around the great Kwannon Temple of Asakusa, or better said the Asakusa Temple dedicated to Kwannon, the Goddess of Mercy.

The professor pointed out a small praying wheel at the left-hand entrance to the arch in which are the two enormous Nio[7] figures. The wheel was a simple circular, saw-edged piece of wood. It was fixed between two parallel bits of wood and the whole placed close to a shrine dedicated to Jizo, the caretaker of little children, who go there daily by the thousands, turn the wheel, say their prayers and go away to play contentedly. The notches in this 'circular saw' of wood had been worn half-an-inch deep by their finger touches.

Leaving the more holy parts of the temple we struck out for the street of shows but went to few. There is a small museum for which a 10-cent entrance fee is charged, which is well worth a visit. Here I saw many strange things – the specimen of a Kappa amongst them. Of course, the figure is made up, but how I am unable to say: for, except where joints are visible, the thing is perfect and the skin, hair, etc. are real. There was also a mermaid arranged in the same way.

The Kappa

199

Amongst the really interesting genuine things was an enormous squid, which must have weighed half a ton, a two-headed viper, and another viper with two legs – the latter, I believe, was faked. There were two cats, each with six ears growing inside the other and two at the side. Also there was a grey cat with one amber-coloured eye and the other sky blue and which seemed to resent the light or being looked at to such an extent that I believe the ears had been sewn on, and the eyes doctored in some way. Kind as the Japanese are in their hearts and in their conduct to animals generally, they have no more idea of what constitutes cruelty than has the man in the moon. The small areas in which captive animals are allowed to move is everywhere a disgrace to the highly civilised ideas of the Japanese nation.

We then went to another kind of show which included a menagerie and, naturally, amongst the animals I saw nothing that I had not seen before except *renewed* and, I may say, *unintentional* cruelness in the short chains to which some monkeys were tied and, again, the small spaces in which the animals were kept. This must be seen to.

On returning to the hotel I found that Barclay had called, and that a letter from the Minister of Agriculture himself (H.E. Mr Matsuoka) had been left at the hotel.

THURSDAY FEBRUARY 15TH   In the morning I went off to a fur shop to enquire into the price of furs to get an idea of the traffic in fur-bearing animals. Of the Japanese furs I find otter the cheapest for its real value. Panthers were much cheaper than I expected, but they were mostly 'German' or Kianchan panthers.

After luncheon I went with Lindley, our new Second Secretary, to the Embassy to see the wrestling matches.

We got excellent seats and were well rewarded by a most remarkable spectacle. It was the seventh anniversary of the death of one of Japan's most celebrated wrestlers and consequently we came in for the whole religious ceremony.

At the present moment and for the past week there has been an immense gathering of wrestlers in Tokyo. They have a large tent, fully the entire size of an English circus, erected near the Imperial Hotel. The novices wrestle in the mornings, the modestly good men in the middle of the day, and the real cracks come on in the afternoon between 2.30 and 3.30 p.m.

Lindley and I saw the wrestlers between 3 and 4 p.m. on the last day, when the greatest excitement existed, but not once did we notice the slightest show of ill feeling. Ceremony and politeness was prominent both amongst the audience and between wrestlers themselves. I am not going to attempt a description of what Japanese wrestling is. To me it appears to be a combination of ceremony, etiquette, jujitsu and weight. The combination of the latter two is irresistible and hence the men with enormous paunches and a superabundance of fat invariably win.

In the evening Kaito told me another fable. It is about an otter and probably Baiho's picture will add to its importance amongst my collection.

The experiences of a young otter (or better, of a young ass)

In the province of Hida [present-day North Gifu] beside a river, there lived a young otter with the rest of his family – father, mother and all. One fine day the young dog otter was out trying to catch eels and, like all novices, failing in his first attempts. Sulking somewhat, but still being full of bumptiousness and much mischief, he came out of the water and sunned himself upon an island rock.

Along the river was a country path and the young otter had not long to wait before he saw something on which he thought he might fully revenge himself for his failure in catching eels. What he saw was a 'lobster-back' – a very old man who could hardly see or hear and, owing to his age, bent double.

Now, thought the otter, I will have some fun and show my importance. I am young and active and I will frighten that old man to death!

Being an otter – like the fox, the weasel, and the badger – he had supernatural powers of sorts, and transformed himself into a giant. When the old man had passed, he crept out of the river, and coming up slowly behind the poor old man he touched him on the sleeve. The old man, being nearly blind, wore an enormous pair of glasses, and, as he turned slowly to see who had pulled his sleeve, his bespectacled face so frightened the otter, who had never seen anything like that before, that in spite of his assumed giant form he fell dead on the spot.

There is always respect shown for the aged in Japan and the moral is that it is dangerous for young fools to scoff at them.

The transcribing of folktales and myths is taking up more and more of Gordon Smith's literary energies. As time goes on his entries in the journal become more sporadic and are limited to events of particular interest, rather than a daily record. He is also keen to illustrate as many stories as possible and experiments with a new painter, but finds him a slow worker. So, he asks Baiho to work for him every Sunday – both on the books of folktales and on his diaries.

As spring approaches, life in Kobe continues at an even pace punctuated by events of parochial interest: Lord Redesdale is to visit Kobe; Sir Herbert Jernyngham calls in on his way to Port Arthur; Ford Barclay returns with a motor car; Sir Ernest Satow stops on his way home from Peking for the last time; a man called Du Cros shoots himself on the hills behind Maiko – and so on.

When the shooting season ends, Gordon Smith turns his full attention to collecting mammals for the British Museum and, now, for the Japanese Ministry of Agriculture. In May he sends Oto to the Oki Islands – a small group to the west of Japan which are rarely visited. His man returns with an interesting assortment of fish, voles and moles.

At the beginning of July, Gordon Smith sets off for a three week trip to see his pearl divers at Toshi and Toba. He hires a boat to explore the Ise Bay area and to make a substantial collection of fish, small animals and also of local stories. He finds the villagers of Toshi more sympathetic than any others he has encountered and leaves them with a heavy heart.

202

CHAPTER 12

An Ordinary English Gentleman

1906/1907

Excursion to Lake Biwa: live carp for dinner; the great pine of Karasaki; shrine of the Goddess Benten – shells for sale in Kyoto – the Westley Richards shotgun is damaged – trouble with the farmers – jujitsu demonstration – an octopus from Toshi – a ghost in the dining room – the Order of the Rising Sun

WEDNESDAY SEPTEMBER 19TH Went up to Otsu by the early express and straight to the Sakamoto-ya, which is about a mile and a half beyond Otsu on the way to Ishiyama in the park known as Zeze. Its teahouse is quite celebrated: it is built on the foundations of an old castle, whose stones can still be seen in the lower part of the lake-wall. It is one of those delightful quiet places that only Japan produces, where you are well attended – even to the scrubbing of your back in the bathroom. The place is divided up into many small separate houses, so that one is entirely private.

The view from my window was continually interesting, though at this time of year the trout fishing is all at the northern, deeper end of the lake. This end producing only the *ayu*, which are now full of spawn and therefore, the

Casting a net on Lake Biwa

Japanese say, at their best. At this season they are cooked without cleaning, on account of a bitter green weed which the fish eat. When opened, the fish show an emerald green fluid, two or three drops of which contrast with the yellow spawn, no doubt appealing to the Japanese mind from an artistic point of view as well as from a gastronomical one. It is something like the bitter taste of a Scotch grouse, but stronger.

Lake Biwa could be a magnificent fishing area, affording sport to all the gentlemen in Japan. Its shores could be surrounded with summer villas, hotels and teahouses, affording employment for nearly the whole neighbourhood. As it is, the Japanese Government seems satisfied to allow the few ancient barbarous trap owners and netting fishermen monopolise the whole sheet of water, rendering its aspects hideous. The immense traps ruin its fisheries, thus utterly preventing possible future enterprise in either the hotel or teahouse line.

More and more evident does it become to me that Japan must sink from the highest standard of social ideals to those of the lowest. It will become a country of tradesmen, both high and low, with American morals and freedom, but there will hardly be a man or a gentleman in the land who could agreeably pass a day or two in the company of an ordinary English gentleman. Of guns, dogs, horses, farming, shooting, fishing and hunting they will know nothing. Japan will be an immense Chicago – socially and commercially. The more the pity.

Had a very good dinner at the Sakamoto-ya and, though every fish served was full of spawn, it was excellent eating. I had asked the cook if he was able to carve up a carp in the way it was done in ancient days for nobles' feasts. This is known as *koi-no-ikizukuri* (a carp cut up alive). The cook was quite delighted, and said so, and, alas, how few people ask for this ancient and honourable dish nowadays. 'Surely the Dana-san [master] was a *samurai?*[1] Not twice in the year do I now prepare the dish.'

'Bring it to me then, this evening,' said I, 'after you have given me some fried ayu fish, and keep my soup so that I may be able to wash the live carp down if I don't like it.'

I told my interpreter, Egawa, that he could dine with me and help me with the dish and interpreting.

The dinner was entirely of fish and quite excellent, so far as it went, but the sight of the carp was not an enjoyable one. It was brought in on a red lacquered

tray, just as in the painting. The fish opened and shut its mouth and gills, just as if swimming in water, and with the same regularity. Not a scale was missing or a drop of blood was visible. The dish was strewn with white sand and little black-brownish freshwater clams, which gave the fish the appearance of lying on the water's edge of the lake. Mountains of raw rice, which denotes luck and plenty, formed the background and there was a pine tree for old age and strength, a bamboo, also for strength and straightness, and a rice plant for prosperity. The dish was really pretty in spite of the gasping fish which, however, showed no pain and, as I said before, there was not a sign of blood or a cut.

'Now we are ready,' I said to the cook, and he proceeded to pour some soy sauce into the fish's eyes and mouth. The effect was not instantaneous: it took a full two minutes as the cook sat over him, chopsticks in hand. All of a sudden and to my unutterable astonishment, the fish gave a convulsive gasp, flicked its tail and flung the whole of its skin on one side of its body over, exposing the underneath of the stomach parts, skinned; the back was cut into pieces about an inch square and a quarter of an inch thick, ready for pulling out and eating. Never in my life have I seen a more barbarous or cruel thing – not even the scenes at Spanish bull fights. Egawa is a delicate-stomached person and as he could eat none, neither could I. It would be simply like taking bites out of a large live fish. I took the knife from my belt and immediately separated the fish's neck vertabrae, much to the cook's astonishment and perhaps disgust.

'Take it away and bring the soup,' I said, 'you have certainly operated beautifully but the sooner a law is brought in to prevent such cruelty the better.' No wonder the carp is taken as an example by all fighting classes and preached about to boys.

THURSDAY SEPTEMBER 20TH Up early to see a lovely sunrise but before 8 a.m. the sky had clouded over.

After an excellent breakfast of fresh eggs and *ayu*, I started off to see, for the first time, the great pine of Karasaki[1] or *Karasake-no-Matsu*. The road led more or less along the banks of the lake, through Otsu and on to the country beyond which now is a vast vegetable garden fertilised, apparently, by lake-weed manure, which the thousands of boats are daily collecting.

The tree of Japan is quite an impressive one, in fact, the most impressive pine tree I have ever seen. But, like Niagara Falls, it is a thing for study because, at first, it is difficult to imagine it being one tree owing to the vast number of [wooden] supports – 380. Its height is nothing; here are the particulars: height 72 feet; circumference of trunk 37 feet; widest extension of branches, east to west, 240 feet, and from north to south, 288 feet. It is the 'father' of all Japan's dwarf mushroom-shaped trees. Botanically *Pinus thunbergii*, it dates from the reign of Emperor Jomei (629–41), in which period Ushinaro Koto-no-natachi planted it in the courtyard of his residence at Karasaki, and called it the Nokiba-Mo-Matsu (the pine tree growing by the eaves of the house), so small was it when first planted.

Between 662 and 671, Emperor Tenji visited it on his way to Sakamoto. The little shrine at Karasaki, dedicated to the Goddess Wakemasa-Hime, was founded by the Empress Jito (690–97) and is attached to the great and ancient shrine of Hiyoshi at the foot of Mount Hiei, about a mile from Karasaki. It is our most popular Shinto shrine and attracts a great number of devotees during the festivals. Today, when I was here, there were but few, consisting of two family groups. A grandfather, his son, wife, and offspring each with packs on their backs came to say their prayers and go trudging wearily on until they came to the next shrine, which came into the programme of their fortnight's tramp.

For a full hour I sat talking to the few who came, but I found that they could tell me little and not even in the teahouses could I raise a story of the tree, though I know there were poems and legends by the dozen and the only one I knew I told, which gained me considerable respect. It was told to me by my painter about a month ago while talking of the Great Pine.

Many years ago, there lived at Karasaki an old man named Matahei. It is

said that in this time the pine showed signs of dying or, as we might less poetically call it, rotting. One evening as Matahei was looking at the pine and wondering gravely at its growth, an old old man, who was doubtless the spirit of the pine, appeared to him and spoke, complaining about his condition, or rather the condition of the pine.

'I beg for your help,' said the spirit. 'The old pine in which I dwell is withering and dying away. Do prevent such a calamity, which will drive me forth into the world again.'

The spirit suggested that glutinous rice should be poured into the rotting stem and branches so that it might revive the growth of the tree. Matahei returned home and for three nights dreamed of the interview he had had

with the old man, and then he spoke to the villagers.

'It is curious,' said one, 'that you should have seen this old spirit, for I also have seen him, not once but twice, but I have not dreamed at all.'

It was unanimously decided to follow the request of the spirit. Glutinous rice was spilled into every hole; it was strewn along the branches and was piled around the roots. They consumed four *koku* [a measure] of rice in doing so.

Afterwards, the tree began to resume its green appearance, and new sprouts and branches came. The tree was rejuvenated, but curious to relate, the pine needles, instead of growing in pairs as before, grew mostly singly, and to this day only one in every four grows as a pair of needles.

Today, great attention is paid to the tree: the central stem is roofed over and holes in its branches are carefully stopped with plaster. One man is employed exclusively to look after it and is in daily attendance. In every way the spirit of the old man should be satisfied.

Other than the tree there was nothing to see at Karasaki, but I saw two of the prettiest children I think I ever saw in Japan. On my way back to Zeze I stopped at Miidera Temple in Otsu and though I had often seen it before I had never been over it. Heavy clouds and a storm spoilt my photographs. Miidera Temple is the fourteenth of the thirty-three places[2] sacred to the Goddess Kwannon. The temple was founded in AD 675 and is consequently 1,231-years old and, as may be readily understood, all the buildings have been renewed. The trees and shady walks are lovely. The whole place impresses one with religion and solemnity.

What pleased me most was a small shrine erected to Goddess Benten [one of the seven Gods of Luck]. It was a sort of delightful, diminutive island against a background of huge cypress trees which met overhead, casting a mysterious gloom over the whole place.

To the left of this is a temple containing an immense iron bowl from which Benkei[3] is said to have taken his bean soup after stealing for fun the huge copper bell, which can be seen in another part. Benkei, who was notoriously powerful, is said to have carried the bell to the top of Hieisan, and there amused himself by ringing it all night, until the priest of Miidera in despair besought him to bring it back, which Benkei agreed to do if he was given as much bean soup as he could eat. Consequently the priest filled the immense 5-foot-diameter, 5-foot-deep copper cauldron and Benkei dragged the bell down. It is marked from that journey with grooves which are about half an inch wide and an eighth of an inch deep.

According to another story the bell was stolen in 1318 and taken to the top of Hieisan by unknown people and there, on being rung, produced but poor sounds which sounded only like 'take me back to Miidera, take me back to Miidera.' In a fit of rage the thieves threw the bell down the mountainside. Whatever may be the truth, there is no doubt that the extraordinary scratches show the bell has been dragged over very rough ground, for they are quite natural.

It is at Miidera that many Russian prisoners [-of-war] were kept in the churches and I notice many Russian words and drawings scribbled about on doors.

After leaving the temple I returned to Kyoto by the canal, which mode of subterranean travel I prefer infinitely to the everlasting rickshaw.

Arrived in Kyoto in time for dinner and stayed at the Kyoto Hotel. A large party of Americans arrived (seventy) from Los Angeles, California and put up four in a room.

The entrance to the canal's second tunnel

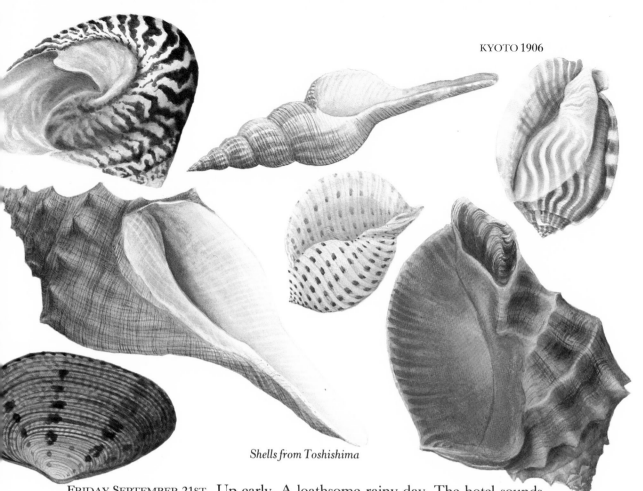

Shells from Toshishima

FRIDAY SEPTEMBER 21ST Up early. A loathsome rainy day. The hotel sounds like a farmyard, or rather a duck pond, with the cackling of over sixty American women of 35 years of age and over. Everything was a difficulty this morning, baths, breakfast, rickshaw, were all seen to give way before the *Los Angeles Times*, but I gave way to nothing and determined to make myself disagreeable by having everything I had paid for, just the same as if the hotel had been empty.

After breakfast I addressed a call on Mr Hirase to see his fine collection of shells, from Japan and the Linchu Islands, the latter evidently being prolific in their production of shells. Mr Hirase had two specimens of the shells wanted by the British Museum – each specimen different and consequently one of them must be new. Mr H. wanted £10 for one and £15 for the other.

The British Museum offered only £4 or £5 for a specimen. Surely they might afford to make a better offer – but there it is, they are beggars. The question is why? Is it high salaries to officials or waste? Both probably, while unfortunate idiots like myself, who spend their lives and their money for their country's benefit are laughed at.

SATURDAY SEPTEMBER 22ND Saw a Japanese playing lawn tennis today in only his shirt and shoes – a member of the club, no doubt, as he was playing on their grounds to the rear of my house. It looks very funny, but with the general screeching which came from the throats of the Japanese 18–25-year-olds as they tried to imitate Englishmen they are at their very worst.

Whereas they might just as easily be heard if they said 'Play', they roar with their weak cracked voices, 'Pll-ayy-ayer', as if they were drilling a brigade of troops, and when they net the ball one would think the Solomon Island cannibals were out enjoying a drunken spree. It is a pity, and has probably been copied from some insignificant European clerk. I hate it when I hear the same wild noises coming from the club at night when *jujitsu* is going on, and don't believe it is customary in Japan to make noises over games in this way. It may have come from American baseball.

Sent Kosa to Yamasaki to set 120 traps [for mammals].

During the first part of October, Gordon Smith succumbs to a bout of malaria and the entries in his journal are sparse. On October 15th the shooting season begins and he is once more in his element. Long days in the open air near Yamasaki and Itami restore his vigour – although some of the rickshaw boys are showing signs of impertinence.

On the home front a new servant is welcomed – she is one of the pearl divers from Toshi, and the Governor's interpreter helps Gordon Smith to translate some 'new' myths and fables.

SUNDAY NOVEMBER 25TH   Go to Osaka, and get a few *netsukes* and white pearls; the latter when bored are quite pretty and have the advantage of being entirely original as ornaments; [usually] they are sent to China where they are pulverised and used as medicine.

MONDAY NOVEMBER 26TH   Found a crack in the top lever of my old Westley Richards [shot]gun. This is most unpleasant because besides that one I have only a Paradox. I sent Egawa to the Osaka gunsmith who sent it back to say he could not do the repairs. Of course, this is absurd, he being able, practically, to make a gun. The serious part of it is that probably the gunsmith thought that if I were left gunless I should have to buy one from him – that would be quite up to his commercial instinct. Wrote to Professor Ijima [for his advice].

TUESDAY NOVEMBER 27TH   Seedy with bad chill and fever.

WEDNESDAY NOVEMBER 28TH   Went up to Kyoto and called on H.E. Mr Omori, the Governor, regarding the rickshaw men at Yamasaki; after which I went to Yamanaka's curio store to exchange a

The old ferryman

few *netsukes* which I find the only way economically to improve my collection. I photographed Yamanaka's model bronzes in his gardens, for they were well worth it, as will be seen. The storks particularly taking my fancy, though the Rakans (seven principal disciples of Buddha) are also very beautifully arranged. There is now a regular private temple in which Yamanaka places old Buddhas, to which, no doubt, he attaches stories of importance that enhance their value 500 per cent – should the proper kind of American tourist come along. The hotel was very dull and contained the most unattractive kind of people, excepting a young Australian, a friend of Dick Hawkers, whose name was, I think, Levien. There were several excessively vulgar men of my own nationality whose sole object seemed to be to ridicule everything Japanese, to chaff the servants, and generally render themselves objectionable.

THURSDAY NOVEMBER 29TH Got up in the dark, and caught the first train to Yamasaki. My men have not yet had the blowing up from police which I have determined they shall have for writing to me for an increase in wages. The policemen have been summoned to Mukomachi to report and receive instructions, so I suppose the storm will break over them soon. In the meantime I dismissed two – Kiku and the innkeeper and told that that I should make it hot for them. Yua (the rock) and Gomei were the most penitent, so I permitted them to come with me, and took three farmer's sons, who beat better than grown men and are more easily instructed because they have not the conceit of men. Shot with my Paradox and lost three pheasants in consequence – with No. 6 shot it will not stop an old green cock pheasant at over forty yards, or even less. On the island I killed a kind of spoonbill duck – new to me; it had a very broad bill in front, yellow feet and a grey-blue back. It will, of course, go to the British Museum though it is probably not new to them.

TUESDAY DECEMBER 4TH   Seem to have run into a bad streak of luck with a farmer today. At Nishinomiya a few shot fell from the skies on his bull and him as he ploughed. Never have I heard a greater noise or such screams of fear, since the shot were simply 'droppers', 150 yards away or more. Egawa and I went for him and his two men with words until we nearly got the farmer to come to blows, but this we did not quite do, unfortunately, for then I could have sailed in. Egawa was quite good and took up my tone of asking how such [a man] as he produced soldiers.

WEDNESDAY DECEMBER 5TH   Sent Egawa to the *kencho* to report the trouble with the farmer and his bull as I have determined to do all I can to suppress this state of affairs, which daily grows worse.

MONDAY DECEMBER 10TH   Sent a fourth collection of mammals to H.E. Mr Matsuoka, the Minister of Agriculture.

TUESDAY DECEMBER 11TH   Itami. Saw four cock [pheasants], got three – saw also one of the prettiest Japanese girls I ever saw in an Ikeda orange grove with her mother. She had an almost perfect 'Madonna' face.

WEDNESDAY DECEMBER 19TH   A letter from Oldfield Thomas at the British Museum tells me that my work with mammals has been so well done, that he finds no new ones in my recent collections.

SATURDAY JANUARY 5TH, 1907   Writing stories for the last three days, but today went to Nishinomiya — killed all I shot at but lost two pheasants, which I did not get a shot at owing to the stupidity of Kane.

SUNDAY JANUARY 6TH   Laid up with a bad chill. Mail arrives via Canada and a charmingly long letter from H.R.H. The Princess Frederica of Hanover who tells much news.

WEDNESDAY JANUARY 9TH   Ill ever since – still in much pain.

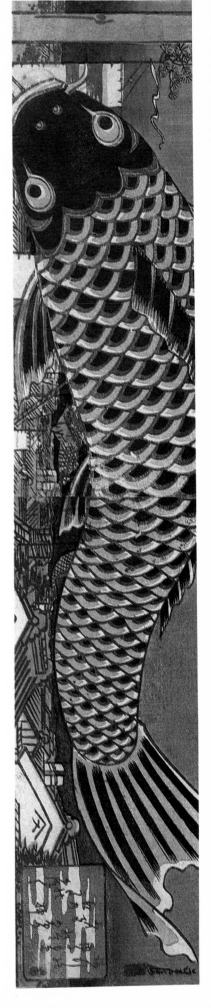

A New Year card from O-Tama-san

WEDNESDAY JANUARY 16TH Went up to Kanasaki and got ten quail of which I felt rather proud, meeting no less than four Japanese sportsmen with half a pack of hounds who had not got *one*. We were very polite to each other, both parties doing their best to put the other on the wrong road; needless to say they were not gentlemen but only Osaka bounders, who are doing much harm to the neighbourhood amongst the farmers.

FRIDAY JANUARY 18TH Saw an interesting assault of arms today given by Mr Uchimura, Chief of the Prefectural Police. (A Budo-kai, or Association for Military Exercises.) The *jujitsu* is so fast, in fact, that it is impossible to see what is done. A remarkable show of *throws* was given by Mr Sato of Kyoto and Mr Tanabe of Himeji, in which the latter was attacked allowing himself to be used as an example of what Mr Sato could do – and in consequence was thrown about anyhow. The same two gave examples of *choking* tricks which were rather ghastly and were kept more or less secret – they would not have been shown here had it not been a police exhibition. It appeared to me to be simpler

to kill a man by stopping the flow of blood than by the passage of air. Another interesting competition was girls versus men, the latter with double-headed swords made of bamboo and the former with the long spear-like weapon known as *nagmata*, which ladies and others used to carry. They simply cut the men's legs from under them with their side swipes.

Messrs Yano and Naito gave a most interesting exhibition of fighting with real swords and all the etiquette attached thereto.

Perhaps one of the most notable things of the whole entertainment was the extraordinary silence. Not a sound of applause came at any time except from an agent of the P.&O. who, with the exception of myself, was the only foreigner present. Also most creditable is the absence of jealousy, personal feeling, one might almost say, of rivalry, had the fights not been so real. Etiquette runs from the back of the heel to the tip of the sword, as it were. All personal feeling must be completely suppressed – not even a smile, for it might be a rude smile, hence it is better to have none. *Jujitsu* is hardly the thing for Englishmen – we are too much interested in finding the winner.

SUNDAY JANUARY 27TH   A man came all the way from Toshi Island to bring me an octopus which had no less than *twenty-three* arms, and I put it away for the British Museum, after paying the man's expenses and giving him 10 yen – as it will put him a full four days out of work or more. I wonder if the Museum will ever repay it.

MONDAY FEBRUARY 11TH Not been out shooting – not a bird is there in the market. There were 5½ inches of snow on the ground and Kobe looked quite pretty, even from my back window, as the photos will show. It is strange how many people went to the mountain to gaze at it. How utterly unsuitable their foot gear is for this weather – it never occurred to me before.

WEDNESDAY FEBRUARY 13TH   Today is the Chinese New Year, and it commenced with a horrible accident, a Chinese gentleman and a Japanese coolie being cut to bits at the railway crossing – a sorrier mess I never saw.

MONDAY FEBRUARY 18TH   Prince Leopold of Saxe-Coburg and Gotha[4] asked me to go up to Kyoto and dine with him, so I did. The Miyako Hotel dinner was indifferent and I would much rather have had a Japanese one. I think the Prince is less stout than he was two years ago. The next day was spent in shopping. Wherever we went a detective followed on a bicycle and telephone messages came to the [*netsuke*] shop to know if we had arrived safely and without mishap, though neither of us knew it at the time. Found quite

THE LATEST OCTOPUS.

June 18. 1907

NEW WONDER OF THE DEEP AT SOUTH KENSINGTON MUSEUM.

"Oh, yes, it is certainly a very wonderful thing," observed the polite gentleman who knows about all the big and little marvels of the vasty deep, as he gazed affectionately at the queer, doubled-up object in the bottle. It appeared to be nothing better than an amorphous brown blob—something like a jar of pickled fruit that had been standing too long in a grocer's cellar.

In point of fact, it was absolutely the latest thing in octopuses, and its claim to special preservation arose from its possession of twenty-seven arms. That seems absurd for an octopus, but is explained by the remarkable circumstance that seven of its eight limbs have each a series of branches. Every one of these branches is fully equipped with fearsome suckers; and there must have been considerable sensation among the community of small crustaceans whenever this weirdest octopus on record set out upon a hunting expedition. Those glories, however, have now departed, and henceforward the defunct octopus will dwell in the mitigated purgatory of a bottle of alcoholic liquid, ministering to such thirst for education as may possess the natural history students at South Kensington Museum, London.

Undoubled its length is about 35 inches, and the eight arms have an average of about eight inches each. It used to be cock-of-the-walk in a certain part of the Japanese seas, but an inquisitive fisherman come along one day and ultimately the unfortunate octopus was acquired by Mr. Gordon Smith. That gentleman has presented it, with other curiosities, to the Natural History Museum.

From the spectacular point of view Mr. Gordon Smith's octopus does not compare with the models of the umbrella-shaped giant octopus and the impossible looking giant squid that are suspended from one of the ceilings at the museum. They are not the genuine article, however, like this. Whether it will be displayed publicly is not settled; it is doubtful whether the ordinary visitor could appreciate its uniqueness

a few *netsukes*, and the Prince invested largely in damascene [inlaid metal] work at S. Komai's [the gold and silversmith].

TUESDAY FEBRUARY 19TH Busied myself most of the day with photographing some of the places which will forever remind me of Kyoto. Streets of delightful running water which in summer must be worth a great deal to the inhabitants who are fortunate enough to have the backs of their houses thereon. These streams are never dry. They even contain a few small *ayu* fish and it is not impossible that an eel may be lurking between or under the rocks which form the foundation of the houses.

Kyoto river street

The restaurants (of which there are far larger numbers than those shown) form my own favourite ones in hot summer months. Shall I ever see them again after taking these last photos? I hope so at all events.

I walked up to the Gion Temple [Gion-no-Yashiro, a Buddhist temple] and I was shocked to see the European 'improvements' all around the buildings. O happy Japan of the past, if you go on Europeanising yourself in this way, what will the tripper have left to write about?

In the evening I had dinner with Prince Leopold and we sat up and talked and smoked until far too late.

Good restaurants in Kyoto

WEDNESDAY FEBRUARY 20TH Left for Kobe, which I reached in time for my usual supper, and wrote to ask the Chief of Police to send me a detective while Prince Leopold comes to my house. The Japanese newspaper correspondents and interviewers are persons who are feared by everyone, and I cannot allow him to be bothered in my house.

FRIDAY FEBRUARY 22ND Lunch at the Consulate with Mr and Mrs Rentier. Bonar ill.

*Kakemono to the
Goddess of Beauty*

SATURDAY FEBRUARY 23RD Prince Leopold came to lunch, then we went shopping and he bought a *kakemono*, returning to my shanty and remained there until dinner time. I think H.R.H. enjoyed himself.

THURSDAY FEBRUARY 28TH Still no shooting. H.E. the Governor came to lunch. We discussed the Government and the stupidities of English trade, so far as I, who understand but little, was able. I do understand, however, that we English 'carry German goods to Hong Kong in "English bottoms"'. Thus they appear on our trade-returns as English goods, cheating everyone at home! Why do our trade reporters not see this?

The Japanese see our clerks in Treaty Ports as useless compared with the Germans. Our Consuls, Ambassadors and others – none of them lend an ear so friendly as that of the German Consul or German Ambassador, who give parties, spend money, make introductions and in every way assist their trade. Our people are all *above* this. What the devil are they for is what I want to know!

SUNDAY MARCH 3RD My servants and I saw a ghost in the dining room! It made me laugh – for it really frightened them and was, of course, probably only a shadow, though there was no means by which a shadow could appear in my little dining room. As I sat down to my egg and tea (with an electric light in the centre of the room) I saw a black shadow appear at one corner and pass to another and disappear right through the inch-wide opening in the shutter or *shoji*. I said nothing, but looked up, thinking that the shadow might have been cast by one of the servants – but both my servants called at once, '*Nanda? Nan desu ka?*' (What? What is that?). I asked them if they had seen anything and their answers were most positive and emphatic: they had just seen what I had. It left an unpleasant and uncertain cold feeling with me. At the same time Brush, my dog, came in from the other room looking miserable, shivering all over, and positively refused to go back and lie down in his proper place, and would not leave me until I went to bed two and a half hours later. I am not a believer in ghosts, but what we three saw was very curious and unnatural.

SUNDAY MARCH 10TH Presents are beginning to pour in before my departure [for England].

MONDAY MARCH 11TH Lunch with the Rentiers, Madame Hattori comes to assist me and spends an hour over my books. I hear whisperings that I am to be decorated. So much the better. I shall be very proud indeed.

SATURDAY MARCH 16TH I am decorated, and most magnificently with the Order of the Rising Sun (4th Class). The Governor came himself, straight from Tokyo to give it to me. Never have I been thus honoured in my life and I feel that had I been given a *6th* or *7th* it would have been more than enough, but the *4th* is altogether too much. I mean, actually, I am delighted, and I must do more than ever and in some way pay it back.

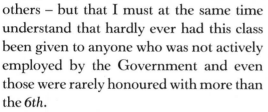

Whitehall, May 13, 1907.

The KING has been pleased to give and grant unto Richard Gordon Smith, Esq., His Majesty's Royal licence and authority that he may accept and wear the Insignia of the Fourth Class of the Order of the Rising Sun, conferred upon him by His Majesty the Emperor of Japan, in recognition of valuable services rendered by him.

SUNDAY MARCH 17TH Call to pay a farewell visit on Madame Hattori and the Governor. H.E. tells me that giving me the 4th class is entirely due to a collection of things [mammals and/or fishes], and that Viscount Hayashi and he, especially, wished it, and also H.E. the Minister of Agriculture and several others – but that I must at the same time understand that hardly ever had this class been given to anyone who was not actively employed by the Government and even those were rarely honoured with more than the *6th*.

Really I felt highly complimented.

Postscript

Richard Gordon Smith continued to spend a large part of his life in Japan, punctuated by regular trips back to England. His income began to show signs of strain and the financial demands of his family were not decreasing. His wife resorted to running up bills which resulted in numerous letters from solicitors which he found very aggravating. In 1910, she asked for a formal separation but there is no indication that he ever gave it her. Eventually he was forced to sell the last of his family land in Poulton-cum-Seacombe and the significance of this step weighed heavily upon him.

Amidst his tribulations there were still triumphs. In 1908, A.&C. Black published his Ancient Tales and Folklore of Japan *– the collection and writing of which had taken years of effort and application. It was not, unfortunately, a commercial success and a second manuscript he was preparing (on what subject is not known) never saw print.*

For his contribution to German museums of natural history, the Kaiser awarded him the Order of the Red Eagle (4th Class). In 1912, he undertook to train two hunting dogs for Crown Prince Yoshihito who, rather charmingly, named them Gordon and Smith and presented their namesake with a pair of silver bowls.

At the start of World War I, Gordon Smith tried to join up, but at 56 he was too old and unfit. Indeed, each year sees a decline in his health, which had been undermined by beriberi and malaria. He collected copious cuttings about the war in Europe and jotted down some comments, but wrote very little. The last entry in his Diary is on 10 September 1915. For the three years until his death we must assume that he was too ill or tired to continue.

This selection from his journals, full as it is of his experiences and observations on Japan, is only a small part of Gordon Smith's story and of the many journeys he made. Let the last words be his:

THURSDAY OCTOBER 31ST, 1901   In looking through a Japanese book today I came across a translated verse that interested me. Called 'The Smallness of the Earth', it was as follows:

> How small the world has grown!
> Methinks that now
> It cannot measure more than four foot six
> For I, a humble man, scarce five-feet tall,
> Find it impossible to fit myself
> Into its small dimensions.

Notes

CHAPTER 1

1 *Geisha*: a professional entertainer hired to enliven all-male teahouse dinners. It was usual for upper-class *geishas* to have a patron, and not unusual for lower-class ones to be little more than prostitutes.

2 *Musume*: a word for a girl from birth up to the age that she married.

3 While still a Spanish colony, the Philippines had been trying to gain independence. In 1898, as a side-effect of the Spanish-American War, the U.S.A. embarked on a four-year war with the Philippino revolutionaries.

4 Mitsui was a great merchant-banking family; powerful since the 17th century it continued to flourish in the Meiji period.

5 The Sino-Japanese War (1894–5) was fought in Korea. The Japanese victory revealed the military weakness of China to the Western powers.

6 Sir Ernest Satow, K.C.M.G. (1843–1929): Minister Plenipotentiary in Tokyo from 1895 until 1900 when he was transferred to Peking. He had an extensive and academic knowledge of Japan which was widely respected. Gordon Smith dedicated his book, *Ancient Tales and Folklore of Japan* (London 1908) to him: 'in remembrance of his kindness'.

CHAPTER 2

1 Lt.-Col. Arthur Gillespie Churchill: Military Attaché in Tokyo, 1898–1903.

2 Ralph Paget: Second Secretary to the Legation in Tokyo, 1895–9.

3 Ronins: *samurai* warriors who, having lost their feudal lord, had become leaderless. They often performed valiant deeds which gave rise to dramatic stories. In 1871, A.B. Mitford (Lord Redesdale) published his translation of 'The Story of the Forty-Seven Ronin' in his *Tales of Old Japan*. In 1898, RGS had evidently not read this although there is good reason to believe he did so later.

4 Hurlingham: a fashionable sporting club in London for pigeon shooting. RGS shot there regularly and won a number of trophies, including the Goodwood Cup in 1893. The Hurlingham Club still flourishes but with an emphasis on cricket, tennis and croquet.

5 Gordon Smith had three daughters: Edith May (1886–1971); Lillian Valentine (1888–1953); Constance Augusta (1892–1960).

CHAPTER 3

1 James Beetham Whitehead was posted to Tokyo in 1898 and stayed until 1901.

2 In both Japan and Burma, RGS mentions that he is to be tattooed – or to have them renewed. The only design he describes, on one of his arms, is of an eagle with a snake in its talons.

3 Alexander Cameron Sim (1840–1900): a pharmacist dispenser who arrived in Kobe via the Naval Hospital in Hong Kong. He set up as a chemist and, being a keen sportsman, founded the Kobe Regatta and Athletic Club.

4 Kentaro Kaneko (1853–1942): Secretary to the House of Peers in 1890.

5 Kokichi Mikimoto (1858–1955) expanded his father's pearl business, making it the world's largest. He was the first to cultivate pearl oysters.

6 Arasuke Sone (1849–1910): Minister of Agriculture, Commerce and Finance. Created Baron and later, in recognition of his services in the financial field during the Russo-Japanese War, a Viscount.

7 Miyanoshita was a popular spa in the Hakone region, southeast of Mount Fuji. The Fujiya Hotel had been built in Western style in 1878.

8 Yoshiwara, originally a district particular to Tokyo, became the generic term for the licensed red-light quarters in many cities. In the Yokohama Yoshiwara in the evening, the prostitutes waiting for custom sat in long narrow rooms with wooden bars that opened on to the street. It was this cage-like effect which Europeans found so remarkable.

9 So that they could support their families, the occupations of shampooer and masseur were reserved for blind people. According to A.B. Mitford, they were also often moneylenders.

10 Brigade-Surgeon Lieutenant-Colonel Henry R. Smith of the Hampshire Regiment, 3rd Volunteer Battalion.

11 In the 1880s and 1890s, RGS and his family often took leases on houses in Southsea and Portsea – notably for a number of years on 2 South Parade, Southsea.

12 It seems possible that Kuniko was a daughter of the Ushi (or Uchi) family in Yokohama.

CHAPTER 4

1 Hyogo, a large town adjoining Kobe on the southwest, had been the port for native trade before Kobe was opened to foreign trade in 1868.

2 *Torii*: the arch or gateway in front of a Shinto shrine, formed of two uprights and two horizontals.

3 The Paradox: A shotgun patented by Col. Fosberry in 1885. Double-barrelled, with rifled chokes, it could shoot either cartridges containing shot, or special cartridges with bullets or balls. As its name suggests, it was intended for both big game and birds.

4 The shooting season was mid-October to mid-April. Foreign sportsmen were restricted to a 10-ri (24 -mile) radius of the Treaty Ports (Yokohama, Kobe, Osaka, Nagasaki, Hakodate and Niigata). Later RGS applies to various officials to shoot in 'Japanese' areas.

5 A reference to the review of the British Fleet in the channel between the mainland and the Isle of Wight.

6 One of the local photographers in Kobe where RGS liked to develop his photographs, or oversee this task.

7 To travel beyond the restricted 10-ri radius of the Treaty Ports (see note 4) it was necessary for foreigners to obtain permits and letters.

8 Inari: the Goddess of Rice. Perhaps as a tribute, images of foxes were traditionally placed in her shrines, and in popular imagination, she became a fox deity.

9 *Netsukes*: carved toggles intended to attach a purse to a belt. Made from any number of materials, from ivory to bamboo to semi-previous stones, they became collector's items.

10 The Kobe Club and the Recreation Ground for cricket, baseball and lawn tennis, were at the eastern end of the European Settlement. Designed particularly for an English membership, they did not exclude Japanese.

11 Theodore John Warrender Prendergast (1858–1926): entered Cheltenham College in 1872; attended the Royal Military Academy in Woolwich in 1876 and by 1907 was a colonel in the Royal Engineers.

12 Cheltenham College: a boy's public school in Gloucestershire, where many of the pupils are destined for army careers.

13 Probably Gustavus Conolly Pakenham (1856–1925), who attended Cheltenham College and was known to have been in business in Kobe. Perhaps he preferred to be called David. He married Ella Compton Bayne, daughter of William George Bayne of Japan, and their first son, born in 1893, was named Compton. There was also a naval attaché, Capt. W.C. Pakenham, based on Tokyo between 1904 and 1906.

14 The Inland Sea is divided into five areas: the Harima, Bingo, Mishima, Iyo and Suo Nadas. The Japanese did not conceive these to be a single sea: the 'Inland' Sea was a European invention.

15 He surely means a species of pufferfish (Tetraodontidae). They are capable of inflating themselves to twice their own size, and because many of them have spines they look like floating pin-cushions. Poisonous as they are, the Japanese prepare them as a delicacy – one which is often fatal.

16 The Relief of Mafeking, 17 May 1900. Mafeking, in the Transvaal, had been held by Col. Baden-Powell against the Boers.

17 Fish which produce their young alive – viviparous fish – were not unknown at the time. RGS writes to *The Field* and *The Naturalist* about his 'discovery' and is informed that he has caught a specimen of *Ditrema argentea*.

18 The Boy's Festival (Tango-no-Sekku) was one of the most visually exciting holidays because whole towns and villages were decorated with paper or cotton carp floating from poles. The carp was a symbol of strength and determination – swimming up-stream against the flow.

19 Ethel: his wife; Mr and Mrs Ximiney Mabsen: friends whom RGS met on board ship in 1898; children: Edith, Lillian and Constance; mother: Annie née Lawrence; *Field: The Field, The Farm, The Garden – The Country Gentleman's Newspaper*; H. Cox: Major Harding Cox, author of *A Sportsman at Large* 1923, and founder of the Fox Terrier and Cocker Spaniel Clubs, Master of the Old Berkeley Foxhounds.

CHAPTER 5

1 *Samurai*: the warrior, or military class in the pre-Meiji era, also, by definition, the gentry.

2 The Foreign Legations in Peking were beseiged by the 'Boxers' for eight weeks in the summer of 1900 and relieved by an international force (see note 6).

3 Halma: is a board-game, popular in the late 19th century. The object is to leap-frog your pieces from one corner of the board to the other – hence the game's other name: hoppity.

4 Lafcadio Hearn (1850–1904) wrote about the 'Insect Musicians' in *Exotics and Retrospectives* (1898). He wrote extensively about Japan, was for some time editor of the *Kobe Chronicle*, married a Japanese woman and took the Japanese name of Yakumo Koizumi. From 1896 to 1903 he was Lecturer on English Literature at the Imperial University of Tokyo.

5 Probably Lt.-Col. Walter Ernest Lawrence of the Royal Scots Greys. Born in 1871, he was a second cousin to RGS on his maternal side.

6 A reference to the Boxer Rebellion, whose aim had been to oust all foreigners from China – particularly Christian missionaries. Of the 50,000 men in the international force sent to restore order, 18,000 were British – hence RGS's astonishment at the Japanese representation. It was not until September 1901 that a treaty for the resumption of diplomatic relations was signed.

7 A Chinese title for emperor: Son of Heaven. The traditional Japanese word is *mikado*.

8 Arnold White (1848–1925) met Gordon Smith on a trip to Spitzbergen. A writer with strong social and political views – particularly on immigration, colonization and the navy, he travelled widely, wrote for a paper called *The Referee*, and stood, unsuccessfully, for Parliament on several occasions.

9 The museum often commissioned people to send back specimens of fish and mammals from their travels. In RGS's case, the museum provided some of his equipment but he found it unwilling or tardy in paying expenses.

CHAPTER 6

1 Either the London *Globe and Traveller*, or perhaps the Canadian *Globe and Mail*.

2 Sir Claude Macdonald K.C.B. (1852–1915): British Minister in Peking, 1896 to 1900; organized the defence of the legations in the Boxer Rebellion. In October 1900 he was transferred to Tokyo where he served as Minister Plenipotentiary until his retirement in 1912.

3 Sir George Head Barclay (1862–1921): First
Secretary to Tokyo Legation from 1902–5
when he became Councillor of the Embassy.

4 Probably Henry Ford Barclay, brother of the
above. Born in 1860, he travelled widely and
eventually married a Japanese girl.

5 Alphons von Pawel-Rammingen, 6th Baron,
was born in Coburg in 1843. As Honorary
Colonel of the 6th Battalion, Essex Regiment,
he spent time in Biarritz and the Pyrénnées,
where he met young Gordon Smith in the
1870s. He became a naturalized British subject
in 1880 prior to his marriage at Windsor to
H.R.H. Princess Frederica of Hanover.

6 Major Alfred Rene Heneage, D.S.O. (1858–?):
son of Edward Heneage M.P.; educated at
Cheltenham College; entered army in 1876;
served in the Egyptian Expedition and fought
at the Batle of Tel-el-Kebir, and in the South
African Campaign, 1899–1902, including the
defence of Ladysmith; decorated twice before
receiving D.S.O., 1901.

7 Port Arthur, now known as Lu-Shun, was the
Russian base in Manchuria and of crucial
strategic importance. The Russian defences
were formidable and the Japanese made
repeated and concerted attempts to capture it.
In one major onslaught between 19 and 24
August 1904, there were 15,000 Japanese
casualties – after which General Nogi sent for
heavier guns. Port Arthur was not taken until
January 1905.

8 The *Retvizan* and the *Tsarevich* were not sunk,
but damaged and towed away. The cruiser
Pallada was run aground while the battleship
Poltava, and the *Diana, Askold* and *Novik* were
damaged on the waterline. Reports of Japanese
successes were often wildly exaggerated to
boost morale.

CHAPTER 7

1 The mouth of a beam trawl net is kept open
with a beam, that of an otter trawl by otter
boards on each side which flare apart with the
pressure of flowing water.

2 William George Aston (1841–1911): acting
Consul in Hyogo between 1880 and 1883;
Japanese Secretary at the Legation in Tokyo in
1886; translated the 'Nihongi' – the Chronicles
of Japan – in 1896, and wrote *A History of
Japanese Literature* (London 1899).

3 The Rev. James Legge, D.D. (1815–97): the
first professor of Chinese at Oxford University;
missionary in the East, 1839–73; best known for
his translations of Chinese classics.

4 Japanese suicide crews sailed five old merchant
ships towards Port Arthur with the intention of
blowing them up to block the harbour, thus
preventing the withdrawal of the Russian
squadron. Detected before they could reach
their positions, the ships were destroyed by the
Russians without affecting the navigation
channels. The crews were saved by Japanese
torpedo boats.

5 General Sir Ian Hamilton (1853–1947): senior
British observer of Russo-Japanese War; wrote
his account in *A Staff Officer's Scrapbook* (2
vols, London 1905; 1907).

6 Marquis Hirobumi Ito (1814–1909): a leader of
the Restoration of the Emperor, and first
Prime Minister of Japan, 1881–8. The
Russo-Japanese War occurred in his second
term of office; he was assassinated by a Korean
nationalist in 1909.

7 Sir Sidney Colvin's *Guide to the Exhibition of
Chinese and Japanese Painting in the Print and
Drawing Gallery of the British Museum* (1888) or
his *Descriptive and Historical Catalogue of a
Collection of Japanese and Chinese Paintings*
(1886).

8 Keigo Kiyoura (1850–1942): three times
Minister of Justice; once Minister of
Agriculture. He became Privy Councillor and,
later Prime Minister.

9 As RGS indicates, his notes are taken from
Louis Gonse's *L'Art Japonais* (Paris 1886), so
the names of the *netsuke* carvers are in French
translation.

10 The anniversary of the death of the first
Mikado, Jimmu Tenno.

11 Vice-Admiral Sir George Warrender
(1860–1913): from 1907 to 1909, C.-in-C. of the
East India Station.

12 Three Japanese divisions under Gen. Kuroki
crossed the Yalu upstream from the Russian
defences and made an unexpected attack.

CHAPTER 8

1 General Alexei Nikolayevich Kuropatkin:
Minister of War; from February 1904,
appointed to command the Russian landforces
in Manchuria.

2 J. Gordon Smith: a war correspondent for the
London newspaper *The Morning Post* – but no
relation to RGS.

3 The *Hitachi and Sado Maru*: Japanese transport
ships torpedoed by the Vladivostok squadron
in the Tushima Strait, 14 June 1904.

4 Rear-Admiral Hikonojo Kamimura
(1849–1906): C.-in-C. of the Second Squadron
during the Russo-Japanese War.

5 Vyacheslav Konstantinovich Plehve: Russian
Minister of the Interior; assassinated 28 July
1904.

6 Vice-Admiral Alexander Bezobrazoff
commanded the First Squadron of the Russian
Pacific Ocean Fleet between May and October
1904.

7 Major-General Anatole Mokhailovich
Stoessel: commander of the Russian defences at
Port Arthur.

8 The Battle of the Yellow Sea began 10 August
1904. Japanese land victories threatened the
safety of the Russian Baltic Fleet's First
Squadron at Port Arthur so it was ordered to
Vladivostok. Admiral Togo gave chase and the
Russians might well have escaped had not
Admiral Vitgeft been killed and communi-

cations become confused. Some Russian ships were forced to seek assylum in neutral ports and the rest retreated to Port Arthur.

9   The Vladivostok fleet had been sailing to assist Admiral Vitgeft – unaware that he had already lost the battle.

10 Beriberi, known in Japan as *kakke*: a disease of malnutrition which affects the nervous system and weakens the heart. Lack of meat and vegetables, and a diet of white, polished rice is thought to be the cause of a severe deficiency in Vitamin B1.

11 Professor C.J.W. Pfoundes: a licensed guide for the Kobe Welcome Society. His letters in the *Kobe Chronicle* indicate he considered himself a senior member of the English community. Also wrote about Japan and collected folk tales ('Folk-lore of Old Japan', published by the Birmingham Philosophical Institute in 1881).

12 The Rev. J.G. Wood's *The Illustrated Natural History* (London 1853).

13 Henry A.C. Bonar, C.M.G. (1861–1935): entered Japanese consular service in 1880. Consul in Hakodate, 1896, and, from 1903 to 1909, Consul in Kobe before becoming Consul-General in Korea.

14 Ernest Alfred Griffiths (born 1863): Vice-Consul for Hyogo and Osaka, residing in Kobe.

15 *Ken*: a game of forfeits in which players make hand signs for different elements. In Fox Ken, the elements were a fox, a man and a gun – one will always dominate.

CHAPTER 9

1   The Great Shinto Shrines of Ise consist of some sixty-five buildings divided between two shrines, Geku and Naiku, about three miles apart. Because they had no trace of Buddhist architectural style, they became very important when Shintoism was declared the state religion at the Restoration of the Emperor.

2   According to Murray's *A Traveller's Guide to Japan*, Viscount Mori was assassinated not long after he drew aside the curtain.

3   The two rocks at Futami are connected with the myths about the legendary creators of Japan, Izanagi and Izanami. Known as the Wedded Rocks, every year the straw rope (*shimenawa*) which links them is replaced at a special ceremony.

CHAPTER 10

1   The Russian Second Squadron, on its way from Libau (now Liepaja, in Latvia) to Japan, sighted Hull trawlers signalling to each other with rockets – a usual practice. Fearing a British attack, the battleships opened fire, sank one trawler and damaged others, causing considerable injury and loss of life.

2   Walter Roper Lawrence (1886–1940): brother of RGS's mother. He had been Private Secretary to Lord Curzon, the Viceroy of India, and was appointed Chief-of-Staff to the

Prince of Wales for his Indian Tour of 1905.

3   John Baptist Rentiers: First-Class Assistant to the Consul in Kobe, 1898–1904; became Vice-Consul in 1906.

4   Arthur James Balfour (1848–1930): Conservative M.P. for Manchester East, 1885 to 1906; Prime Minister 1902–1905.

5   Frederick Rutherford Harris (1856–1920): M.P. for Dulwich. Before his tour of China and Japan, he made a speech in support of a continued and extended alliance between Britain and Japan. He had once been Cecil Rhodes' confidential agent in South Africa.

6   203-Metre Hill, northwest of Port Arthur, was the key to its defeat. On 25 November, General Nogi led a determined assault which, although victorious, resulted in the death of 12,000 Japanese and 3,000 Russians.

7   RGS may be referring to the highly decorated circular guards through which the sword blades passed; they were collector's items.

CHAPTER 11

1   RGS had been a member of the Gun Club in London.

2   The Rt. Hon. Sir Thomas Gardner Horridge (1857–1938): Liberal M.P. for Manchester East, 1906 to 1910. RGS met him on one of his voyages and became a great friend.

3   Kwannon, the Boddhisatva God of Mercy was represented in feminine form because of some confusion in China. Kwannon is usually depicted as standing on a carp but this particular representation of the deity, in which she has carp in her basket, is called the Gyoran Kwannon – *gyoran* means 'fish basket'.

4   Rt. Hon. Sir Francis Lindley (1872–1950): married the third daughter of the 13th Lord Lovat. A Second Secretary to the Legation in Tokyo 1906–08; crowned his impressive diplomatic career by becoming Minister-Plenipotentiary in 1931.

5   Major-General Simon Joseph Fraser, 14th Baron Lovat (1871–1933), had a most distinguished career in the army.

6   Possibly the wife of Colonel Sir Philip Watts, K.C.B., whose father lived at Southsea.

7   Nio are two martial figures, deva kings, which guard the left and right sides of the entrance to a Buddhist temple.

CHAPTER 12

1   The great pine of Karasaki is dead, but a new pine is growing from its seeds.

2   Once, pilgrims believed that a visit to the thirty-three places would preserve them from hell.

3   Benkei-no-Shiruhabe was a popular folk hero. T. Philip Terry in his *Japanese Empire* (London 1914) remarks that 'The priests in charge of the two doubtful relics will recount a lot of balderdash to whosoever will pause to listen.'

4   Probably Prince Leopold Clemens Philipp August Maria (1878–1918); nephews of King Ferdinand of Bulgaria.

Index